# Conflict Management
# and
# Counseling

RESOURCES FOR
CHRISTIAN COUNSELING

RESOURCES FOR CHRISTIAN COUNSELING

VOLUME TWENTY-NINE

# Conflict Management and Counseling

## L. RANDOLPH LOWRY, J.D.
## RICHARD W. MEYERS

RESOURCES FOR
CHRISTIAN COUNSELING

General Editor

Gary R. Collins, Ph.D.

Unless otherwise indicated, all Scripture quotations in this volume are from the New International Version, copyright © 1983 International Bible Society, used by permission of Zondervan Bible Publishers. Scriptures indicated NASB are from the New American Standard Bible © 1960, 1962, 1963, 1968, 1971, 1972, 1973, 1975, 1977 by The Lockman Foundation. Used by permission.

**Library of Congress Cataloging-in-Publication Data**

Lowry, L. Randolph, 1951–
   Conflict management and counseling / by L. Randolph Lowry, Richard W. Meyers.
      p.   cm. — (Resources for Christian counseling ; v. 29)
   Includes bibliographical references and index.
   ISBN 0-8499-0602-4
   1. Pastoral counseling.  2. Conflict resolution.  3. Interpersonal conflict.  4. Reconciliation—Religious aspects—Christianity.
I. Meyers, Richard W., 1942–  .  II. Series.
BV4012.2.L69  1990
253.5—dc20                        90-22222
                                       CIP

12349  AGF  987654321

*Printed in the United States of America*

# ACKNOWLEDGMENTS

This book has just the names of two authors on the cover, but many people made it possible. Without their contributions, whatever good may come of it would not have been achieved.

Consistent support for our work has come from Willamette University President Jerry Hudson, and from Dean Leroy Tornquist and Professor Carlton Snow, both of the Willamette University College of Law, and Dean Ronald Phillips of Pepperdine University School of Law. From their vantage points in education, law, and ministry, they saw the potential for new thinking, innovative education, and needed services in conflict management.

Tremendous assistance came from those associated with Word Publishing. We extend thanks to Gary Collins for his vision of a book in the newly developing field of conflict management and his careful guidance as it was written. Carey Moore and David Pigg pushed us to finish the book, but showed patience with all of the work and travel interferences we experienced. And most significantly, we thank our editor, Sue Ann Jones, whose knowledge and tenacious work massaged a book into existence.

At the Institute for Dispute Resolution, several research assistants and staff members provided tremendous help to us, especially Alan Collier, Jack Harding, and LeeAnne Goldsmith.

Finally, we owe a great deal to our immediate families: Rhonda, John, Janet, and Melinda Lowry, and Dianne, Jonathan, and Daniel Meyers. They allowed us to focus on this effort when they deserved our time and attention, themselves. We are grateful for their love and support.

# CONTENTS

# EDITOR'S PREFACE

WHEN I FINISHED MY GRADUATE WORK and got my degree in clinical psychology, I went to work in a university counseling center on the West Coast. Later I shifted into teaching and for the past twenty-five years I have subjected students to my classroom presentations. I have no plans to quit, not yet, but already I can look back on rich years of interaction with students, many of whom have become friends and have taught me as much or more than I have taught them.

One of my first graduate students was Rich Meyers. His home was a long way from the school where he was enrolled and I was a professor, so he and his wife often visited our family and sometimes they spent holidays with us. After his graduation, many years passed before we met again at a conference in Oregon. It was there that I learned both about his interest in conflict resolution and about his periodic work with Randy Lowry. Shortly thereafter, Rich and I met with Randy and the plans for this book were launched.

Some time has elapsed since that initial meeting and the writing has been complicated by a job change that has put these two writers in different geographical locations. In this age of telephones, express mail, and fax machines, however, the book has been completed—the first in the series to be co-authored by one of my former students and the first to have a lawyer as one of the writers.

This lawyer-counselor combination may be new and many of the ideas are innovative and potentially helpful, but in some respects this book is like the ones that have gone before. As many readers now know, Word's Resources for Christian Counseling books all attempt to address issues that are encountered often in our counseling work. We have sought authors who have a strong Christian commitment, impeccable professional credentials, and extensive counseling experience. We have attempted to produce books that are useful and helpful examples of accurate psychology, books that utilize sound scriptural principles. Each book is intended to have a clear evangelical perspective, careful documentation, a strong practical orientation, and freedom from sweeping statements or unsubstantiated conclusions. Our goal has been to provide books that would be clearly written, up-to-date overviews of the issues faced by contemporary Christian counselors—including pastoral counselors. The books are all bound in similar covers and together they comprise what we hope is a helpful library of Christian counseling.

Many years ago, a pastor in Ohio called and asked if I would speak at a conference dealing with "the most common and difficult issue facing Christians today." That issue, according to the caller, was the inability of people to resolve conflicts and to get along with one another.

People still have trouble getting along. Perhaps they always will. But I hope this book will better enable you to help others cope with conflict. Professors Lowry and Meyers have made a useful contribution to this series and to the Christian counseling and Christian mediation literature with this volume.

*Gary R. Collins, Ph.D., Kildeer, Illinois*

# CHAPTER ONE

---

# DISCOVERING THE
# MINISTRY OF RECONCILIATION

MORE THAN A DECADE AGO, Derek Bok, former president of Harvard University, observed a transition in the way interpersonal conflict is handled in America. Recognizing a growing trend away from highly adversarial approaches to managing conflict and toward more cooperataive methods, Bok called alternative dispute resolution "the most exciting social movement of our time."[1] The trend continued as the 1980s brought forth a wave of new processes, institutions, and values which promote a more cooperative, less competitive approach to dealing with conflict.

A decade ago, the assumption could have been made that acute conflict between people would be handled ultimately through violence or a highly adversarial legal system. From the historical image of gunfighters facing off for a shootout on Main Street to the television popularity of "People's Court," our cultural values have encouraged competition, even when attempting to resolve a difference.

No longer is that always the case. Today, courts in most states require that divorcing couples caught in conflict over property division or child custody be sent to counselors skilled in mediation.[2] Institutions, including churches, involved in business conflicts often resolve them through third-party arbitration.[3] Labor-management agreements are increasingly achieved through collaborative negotiation.[4] A growing number of employees' problems with employers are handled through grievance mediation.[5] And the guidelines of many state and federal agencies now require that disputes over public policy regarding complex environmental issues be resolved through facilitated problem-solving.[6]

Organizations focused on providing alternative dispute-resolution assistance emerged during the 1980s. For example, the Christian Conciliation Service is a nondenominational ministry of independent organizations loosely affiliated as a national association which now provides mediation and arbitration in twenty-five cities as an alternative to secular courts.[7] In addition, more than four hundred community dispute-resolution mediation programs now assist in the reconciliation of tens of thousands of disputes each month—a reality that once was only a dream in the minds of visionary community leaders.[8]

A decade ago, the courthouse had only one door—the door to litigation. Now alternative dispute-resolution courthouses throughout the country provide diverse options.[9] The idea of the victim of criminal action and the alleged criminal resolving their conflict through negotiation materialized in the 1980s into the nationwide Victim Offender Reconciliation Program.[10] Although it is still overshadowed by the adversarial and competitive approaches to conflict so representative of Western culture, this embryo of social movement is steadily growing, transforming our neighborhoods, churches, and judicial system.

This book attempts to connect the dispute-resolution movement that is impacting society as a whole to those in the

Christian community who deal with conflict on a daily basis through professional practice, ministry, or volunteer assistance. Information is presented here in the context of the Christian faith, with substantial reference to social science. The described skills and techniques are easily applied to conflicts between individuals in homes, churches, the workplace, and communities. The book is based on the premise that knowledge developed in a variety of contexts may be a rich resource for those seeking to help others.

The values of the dispute-resolution movement reflect an increasing national desire for processes and institutions that are productive, humane, and respectful of the relationships between people and organizations. Such values come from a variety of sources, but certainly are found in the Christian faith.

## THE MINISTRY OF RECONCILIATION

Throughout this book, when we refer to the *ministry* of reconciliation, we are describing a ministry *all Christians* are called to perform, regardless of their choice of profession or avocation. This directive comes from Paul's second letter to the Corinthians, in which he reminds all of us that we are to carry the "message of reconciliation" to the world. Depending on our choice of work as counselors, mediators, ministers, or lay leaders, we may follow this calling along different paths, and walk it out in different ways. But the ministry is the same. In Paul's words:

> Therefore, if anyone is in Christ, he is a new creation; the old has gone, the new has come! All this is from God, who reconciled us to himself through Christ and gave us the ministry of reconciliation: that God was reconciling the world to himself in Christ, not counting men's sins against them. And he has committed to us the message of reconciliation. We are, therefore, Christ's ambassadors, as though God were making his appeal through us. (2 Cor. 5:17–20)

Consider what might have been on Paul's mind as he wrote those words. He was thinking about a church where he had invested considerable time—a church he had founded, and

3

later visited at least twice, perhaps three times. But his first letter to the Corinthians reveals that this church was not what Paul had envisioned when he started it. In the first letter, Paul expressed concerns about the lack of Christian values and relationships, divisions in the church, conflict as to whom the Corinthian Christians should be following, sexual immorality, lawsuits among believers, conflict in marriage and over divorce, the worshiping of idols, and people's lack of love for each other.

Paul was also concerned about the conflicts between those who believed Christians have liberty in the Lord, and those who wanted to bind their fellow Christians to tradition or specific practices. The Corinthians were at odds about how people came together to participate in the Lord's supper, and the role of women in worship. Their conflict also related to spiritual gifts, and to the lack of unity among believers.

Paul was writing to a church that really was in trouble—a church that had enough conflict to keep counselors, ministers, and dispute resolvers busy for years. He wasted few words in describing his dismay.

These same concerns must have been on Paul's mind as he wrote his second letter to the believers in Corinth. He began tactfully by expressing his joy and confidence in the Corinthians. Then Paul reminded them that they had been reconciled, that they were still being reconciled, and that they were to continue to engage in a ministry of reconciliation. While it is obvious that Paul's primary concern was reconciliation between all people and God, he was also vitally concerned about humans' relationships with each other. In addition, he was distressed to learn of the Corinthians' conflict over those things we listed previously, and he sought to encourage their reconciliation and unity.

Reconciliation is the overriding theme of this book, just as it was the focus of Paul's ministry two thousand years ago. Christians are still called to be reconciled with God—and to each other. We also are called to a *ministry* of reconciliation to bring about this unity with God—and also with each other.

In the pages ahead, we will look at some of this ministry's characteristics and challenges.

## Responding to a World in Conflict

People, institutions, and communities around us are filled with conflict that ranges from subtle to extreme. It may be as seemingly trivial as a parent and child disagreeing about the school clothes to be worn that day, as divisive as church members arguing about a change in worship style, or as destructive as an industrial labor dispute that erupts in violence. The evidence of conflict is everywhere.

*Families.* Statistics tell us that conflict causes new marriages to have less than a fifty-fifty chance of success.[11] Furthermore, when there are children from a first marriage in a parent's second marriage, there is a greater likelihood that the second marriage will also end in divorce. In fact, we can expect more than 60 percent of those second marriages to end in divorce.[12] No marriage, not even the most successful, is immune from conflict. All marriages can benefit from the ministry of reconciliation.

Just as conflict occurs between happily married spouses, it also exists in happy, healthy families. For many parents and children, conflict occurs on a daily basis—it is a part of life. Many times, it is healthy conflict that enables parents to help children sort out values and priorities. Sometimes, though, when not handled well, the conflict becomes a force that destroys the fabric of those sensitive relationships. The ministry of reconciliation can help hurting families before they are broken.

*The Workplace.* For most people, work is the greatest consumer of time; but the workplace is often filled with the seeds and reality of conflict. Most managers spend at least a quarter of their time responding to conflict,[13] and employees feel such stress from workplace conflict that stress is often considered a legitimate reason for paid leave. In the last decade, extensive legislation has been enacted to prevent workplace conflict related to discrimination and sexual harassment.[14] Still, some kind of conflict is too often a part of the job, negatively impacting the workers, whether they are owners, managers, salaried employees, or hourly wage earners. Thus, the ministry of reconciliation is applicable to the workplace and the multitude of relationships involved in it.

*The Church.* Conflict is evident in the church, as well. Someone once declared, "The strife is over; the battle is done. The church is split. Which side won?"[15] Those involved in the church recognize, perhaps reluctantly, the truth in that statement. While Christians are expected to reflect a special unity, unresolved conflict fractures many congregations, and at times divides our fellowships. Here perhaps is the most important opportunity for the ministry of reconciliation.

## Reconciling a World Separated from God

When a magazine cover story focused on survivors of the 1989 United Airlines plane crash in Iowa, the banner headline read, "People Who Found God."[16] It was this headline that caught my* attention; but as I read the testimonials, it was amazing to me how few of the survivors actually talked about God. Some did describe how their relationships with the Lord solidified during their forty-nine-minute ordeal as the plane, damaged by an explosion at thirty-seven thousand feet, descended to its destiny. But other survivors revealed their lack of belief in God, and stated that the spiritual realm had had no influence on them during that critical time. Headlines can claim a dependence on God; but reality sometimes reflects the need for reconciliation between God and his children.

## Derived from Personal Experience

We can help others move toward reconciliation by sharing our own experiences. Once again, we think about the personal experience of Paul as the writer of 2 Corinthians, and as one who understood reconciliation far better than most of us ever will. Paul, or Saul, had been the chief prosecutor of Christians. Yet after his personal reconciliation with the Lord, he moved to the other side. Looking back on the change in his own life, Paul knew that if God could bring about such change in him, then God could do the same for us. This is true in all ministries. People are most effective when their enthusiasm

---

* Even though this book has two authors, first-person singular pronouns will be used when a co-author recalls personal anecdotes or expresses personal opinions.

6

and advice come from the credibility of their own personal experiences.

I know a woman who sells a food supplement. I have heard her sales pitch and do not remember any of it, but I remember her enthusiasm for the product. This enthusiasm did not result from her reading about the supplement in some book, but rather because she takes two teaspoons of it per day and believes her life is different. The ministry of reconciliation must be the same. It must spring from personal experience. We need to take two teaspoons per day, then with new understanding and skillful approaches be able to say, "Now, my life is different."

## Reflecting a Vision

When we see people who are hurting and in the midst of conflict, we must have a sense of vision that things can be different for them. If we do not have that kind of vision, there is no way we will be able to minister.

Think again about the apostle Paul and his relationship to the members of the church in Corinth. As he prepared his second letter to those Christians, they appeared to be no better off than when he had first met them. But he still had a vision about how the Corinthians could be reconciled to God, and to each other.

We need to imagine harmony, even at the point of greatest conflict. When people walk into my office and want me to mediate their dispute, if I cannot visualize them achieving harmony, there is no use starting. Even I wonder at times if such vision is possible. Here they are in my office. They have been fighting for years. They have invested emotionally in the conflict. They may have spent thousands of dollars going through highly adversarial legal processes. Now I have to imagine a circumstance where they can come together, where they move from opposite sides of the table—fighting—to the same side of the table to try to solve their problem together. That has to be a matter of vision.

Those who are most successful at bringing a spirit of reconciliation to hurting people are those who have a vision of something that is much different than reality. God has a vision for his relationship with his people, even though we may regularly disrupt it. Similarly, Paul had a vision for the church at Corinth, even though it regularly let him down.

7

CONFLICT MANAGEMENT AND COUNSELING

When my wife was recently in the hospital, my daughter drew a picture for her. It is amazing how a three-year-old child can draw a picture full of creativity and color. When I asked, "What is it?" her verbal description was far different from the scribbles I saw on the piece of paper. But she had a vision of her picture that I simply did not see.

The same is true in conflict; we must have the vision of something different. When Paul stood before King Agrippa, defending his faith, he proclaimed, "I was not disobedient to the vision from heaven" (Acts 26:19). Even while on trial, Paul still maintained his faithfulness to the vision he had been given. He was committed to the belief that people could be different.

I think of the words of George Bernard Shaw, paraphrased by Senator Ted Kennedy as he eulogized his brother, the late Robert Kennedy: "Some men see things as they are and say, Why? I dream of things that never were and say, Why not?"[17] We would not be where we are today if others had not had visions that were greater than the existing reality. Our circumstances would be remarkably different if those who went before us, including Paul, had looked at the reality of their day, shaken their heads, and lamented, "Why?" Thankfully, some responded to the vision of reconciliation from heaven and said, "Why not?" We can capture a similar vision for people experiencing conflict.

## Motivated by Great Love and Irrational Confidence

There is no question that Paul loved the people of Corinth. He was distraught to learn that some had interpreted his first letter as reflecting his dislike for them, when the real motivation for the letter had been his tremendous love. Unless we really love people, we will not be effective in the ministry of reconciliation. We need to love them as they are, and use that love as the foundation of our ministry.

In addition, we must have "irrational" confidence—irrational because that might be the way this work appears to those who are not sensitive to the ministry of reconciliation. They might consider it irrational to believe that people can reach the fulfillment of vision, even when every circumstance around them says that will not happen. But that is what we do, remembering

Paul's words in 2 Corinthians 7:4, ". . . I take great pride in you, I am greatly encouraged; in all our troubles my joy knows no bounds." He was not writing to people who had it together. He was writing to people who had tremendous problems. And yet he was saying, "I have great confidence in you. My joy is in you. There is no end to my joy." He was able to have irrational confidence that they would move to the point of fulfilling the essence of his vision.

Several months ago, I was mediating at a major aerospace company. On one side of the table was the captain of the security force. On the other side of the table was a security officer. The issue was insubordination. If there is one issue that is next to impossible to resolve in a paramilitary organization, it is insubordination. From the standpoint of management, insubordination is a lot like pregnancy; you can't be just a little bit insubordinate. You either are or you are not.

As the captain sat down in all of his military glory, and the security officer sat down with his .38 strapped to his side, I thought to myself, *This is completely irrational. How in the world can I believe that these individuals, who have been in serious conflict for six to eight months, are ever going to be affected by what I do?*

In some cases, including this one, individuals will not be affected by the ministry of reconciliation. Success is not guaranteed. Even so, there must be the kind of irrational confidence that says, "I see the vision of resolution and I am irrational enough to believe that I can help these people make progress toward it." Sometimes that is all we have to go on; but often it is exactly what we need.

Is it not that way with our children? Sometimes we have to have extreme confidence. When they let everything we have set up for them fall apart, all we can do is be like Paul, and say our love is unconditional and our confidence is irrational. Many times this kind of belief in the mediator will be the primary basis for progress.

**Requiring Personal Involvement**

Think about the nature of all ministry, not just the ministry of reconciliation. It is impossible to imagine a circumstance

9

where people are engaged in meaningful ministry but have removed themselves from that circumstance. What would happen if a nurse decided he was tired of personal involvement with his patients? "Tell me over the intercom what you need and I will get it for you; but I do not want to be involved with you," he might say. What if a counselor one day said to the client, "Write down what is wrong and I will give you a written reply; but I don't want to spend time with you"? Or consider whether a missionary could work effectively for residents of a foreign nation if she stayed in her home country and communicated with the people she served only by telephone or letters. The ministry of reconciliation is no different from these ministries; it requires personal involvement. We are able to be instruments of reconciliation, helping people come into harmony with themselves, with God, and with each other, only because we roll up our sleeves and get personally involved.

A number of years ago, a colleague and I were mediating a dispute between a peace group and the local sheriff. It was one of those disputes where we worked for three days straight and never even got the two sides to sit down at the same table. In private conversations, we found several bases for agreement. But we could not get the two sides to sit down and talk in the same room at the same time. So we met with them in their homes. We met under the trees in a park. We drank coffee at a dingy little coffee shop on the edge of town. We met them in an Episcopal pastor's office, in the sheriff's station, and in the Attorney General's office. For our ministry to work, we could not wait for them to come to us. We had to go to them and become personally involved with them where they lived and worked.

The ministry of reconciliation must become very personal. Again, our example is Paul, who did not just write a letter and then remove himself from the Corinthians. Yes, he did write to them. But he also sent personal representatives, and he visited them, himself. His was a true ministry of reconciliation. He worked with them, suffered with them, prayed with them, and cried with them. A ministry of reconciliation is exemplified by personal involvement, and personal encouragement. That is rarely comfortable for the mediator; but it is always important.

## Succeeding Because of Faith

Consider the incident regarding the paralytic in the second chapter of Mark. The passage describes a person who needed the healing power of Jesus. Yet, there were so many people surrounding the Lord in Peter's house that the paralytic's four friends could not get in through the door. They had to take him up on the roof and literally cut a hole in it, then lower him down so he could be healed.

Did you ever consider what motivated Christ to heal the paralytic? Scripture says the man was healed because of the faith of those who brought him there! We have no indication that the paralytic, himself, was a believer; but his stretcher bearers surely were. Their actions touched Jesus, who must have thought, *Here are four people who are carrying this stretcher, providing the opportunity for me to minister. I will heal this man because of the faith that I see in his four friends.*

In the broadest terms, those who accept the ministry of reconciliation sign up to be stretcher bearers, to be part of other people's conflict. We could walk away; but we choose not to. We sign up to be involved in their lives, to bear the stretchers of those who are troubled so the Lord will see our faith and respond to them in a loving, healing way.

For some, the ministry of reconciliation is a natural adjunct to their professional work as counselors, lawyers, ministers, teachers, managers, or physicians. For others, it is a focus of their voluntary efforts in communities, families, and churches. In whatever context, the ministry of reconciliation responds to a world in conflict. It springs from our personal experience in being reconciled. It reflects vision. It is motivated by great love and irrational confidence. It requires personal involvement. The ministry of reconciliation combines biblical principles and personal skills to help resolve conflict and achieve reconciliation in a cooperative rather than a competitive way.

It is consistent with the sweeping changes transforming society's structures for dispute resolution, and complements society's search for what former Chief Justice Warren Burger described as "a better way."[18]

Before getting to specific techniques of the ministry of reconciliation, however, some background on conflict is important. Such is the focus of the next chapter.

# CHAPTER TWO

# CONFLICT:
# DANGER AND OPPORTUNITY

IN DEFINING CONFLICT, WRITERS OFTEN refer to a character in the Chinese language that is made up of two different symbols. One symbol indicates danger, while the other signifies opportunity.[1] The character, which is usually translated as crisis, or conflict, aptly describes the focus of a ministry of reconciliation. Counselors and others who work with people in conflict often encounter both *danger* and *opportunity* as they lead individuals through the dispute-resolution process.

## CONFLICT IS DANGER

To say there is a dimension of danger in conflict is an understatement. Whether it is represented by a senseless shooting between gang members, the physical abuse of a spouse during an uncontrolled family dispute, or a visible disagreement between leaders of a church, the danger of conflict between people, relationships, and institutions is great. Instinctively, we avoid places where disagreement is common or potential for conflict is high, because we sense danger in those places. We fear the conflict might escalate into actions we cannot control.

While the Chinese character for conflict offers a two-sided definition, the Latin translation is less optimistic. The Latin word for conflict, *confligere,* means to strike together.[2] This gives us a mental picture of physical conflict escalating to the point where one person angrily strikes out at another. The circumstance presents danger to the people involved in the conflict—and to those around them.

Other definitions also suggest the potential for danger. Conflict has been described as a situation in which the concerns of two people appear to be incompatible.[3] Conflict also exists when two people try to occupy the same place at the same time.[4] When two people vie for the same parking space, two athletes collide on the playing field, or two children want the same toy, conflict exists. More sophisticated illustrations could be provided, but the point remains the same—conflict occurs when competing interests clash. And that clash produces danger.

This danger looms especially large for those who have experienced acute and damaging conflict in the past. An example, familiar to all marriage and family counselors, is that of someone who has struggled through the turbulent end of one relationship and is now contemplating commitment to another one. At that point, even while celebrating a new relationship, the person feels great fear that the hurt and disappointment caused by the earlier conflict will be repeated if the new relationship does not work out. The experiences of the past underscore the danger in conflict.

Danger is also present in modern circumstances. The gang member who joins his comrades in activities on the street recognizes the potential for conflict and the life-threatening danger that accompanies it. The teacher who sends a young student home to abusive parents reflects uncomfortably on the child's dangerous situation. The young soldier on watchful patrol is confronted with the imminent danger of conflict. The committed Christian struggling with the conflict between Christian and worldly values confronts the danger of that conflict—and the various responses to it. Wherever there is conflict, there is the possibility that how it is handled (or not handled) will result in danger to those involved.

## A Clash of Different Perspectives

As people who live, work, and play together, we cannot escape the reality of our differences, especially differences in our perspectives on the events and activities of our lives. Clashes are most apparent in our differences over facts, methods, values, and goals.

*Conflict over Facts.* Often conflict results from differences over what we believe to be facts. We read the same words in a book, but argue over different meanings. We witness the same event, but disagree as to what transpired. We analyze the same research findings, but contend the implications are quite different. In essence, our experiences are the same— reading, witnessing, and analyzing—but our understanding is different.

This kind of conflict is demonstrated daily in courtrooms across the country as lawyers bring in experts who analyze the same facts—and arrive at different conclusions. In the case of someone who injures a knee on the ski slope, for instance, one side may produce an expert witness who sees the injury as the direct fault of the setting of the ski bindings. The other side may call an equally credible expert who attributes the injury not to the setting of the bindings, but to the performance of the skier. Credible people can observe the same facts and develop dramatically different perspectives.

Historically, Christians have clashed over differences in perspective, and such clashes have caused great divisions. Catholics believe, based on their interpretation of the facts, that the pope is infallible, and therefore his word is the word of God. Protestants believe, again based upon facts, that the pope is not infallible and thus his words represent only the hierarchy of the Catholic church.

Another clash occurred in the 1980s with the emerging issue of women's roles in the church. To some, the facts of Scripture allow women to be ordained and hold offices in the church. To others, factual reading of Scripture suggests that women are not to be placed in such roles.

Still another conflict over facts involves the nation's largest denomination. The Southern Baptists endure great conflict over the meaning and application of the inerrancy of Scripture. The factual differences, even among the church's seminaries, come to a head each year as the president of the Southern Baptist Convention is elected. For several years, the election has been a referendum on that factual difference.[5]

When perspectives about facts differ, there is the potential for conflict and all of its ramifications.

*Conflict over Methods.* Not only do we differ on *what* should be done, but we experience great disagreement over *how* it should be carried out. The methods of carrying out any task, when viewed by a number of people, provide fertile ground for difference and conflict.

The Institute for Dispute Resolution, a nationally recognized program affiliated with Pepperdine University School of Law, is involved in both dispute-resolution education and practice. Its staff members intervened in a conflict between a city and a group of Hispanic day-laborers. The background of the dispute involved the day-laborers arriving in the suburban city each day by bus and congregating on a particular street corner. There they waited for employers who might come by to offer them a job that day. As it became known that work was available, the number of laborers grew substantially, with sometimes more than a hundred of them congregating on the corner. As can be imagined, this caused several problems for the community, and particularly for an adjacent shopping area. One problem was the lack of public restrooms or scheduled trash pick-up near the street corner. Thus, concern increased for the sanitary conditions.

The reaction of the city council in this affluent community was to propose legislation simply banning people from standing on public street corners waiting to be picked up for work. A public-interest law organization, however, objected to that approach. In fact, it informed the city that it would challenge the constitutionality of the ordinance by filing suit if it were passed. In addition, the local law-enforcement agency, while carefully staying out of the politics of the dispute, quietly indicated that it simply would not enforce such an ordinance, because it did not have the staff or resources.

Anger developed as people took sides in the conflict. Some believed a law banning day-laborers was appropriate and necessary. Others suggested that alternative methods could be found, such as the designation of a waiting area which would include sanitary facilities, or the creation of a telephone job-referral system.

In essence, there was no disagreement that the current circumstance was a problem. But there was substantial disagreement on how that problem might be addressed. As the proposal for arrest and prosecution became more pronounced, emotions increased and the conflict generated angry feelings in a usually quiet community. The conflict in this case was not over the facts of the matter but over the methods proposed for addressing and resolving it.

*Conflict over Values.* Just as conflict can result from a clash of different perspectives on facts and methods, it also can result over different values. In his outstanding work, *Conflict Resolution and Prevention,* John Burton suggests that values are those ideas, habits, customs, and beliefs that are characteristic of particular social communities. They are the linguistic, religious, class, ethnic, or other features that lead to separate cultures and groups.[6]

This is demonstrated in the current conflict over values related to abortion. Our society is dividing over the values of "life" and "choice." These issues have become a litmus test for politicians and appointees to the U.S. Supreme Court as people seek to have their values reflected in the legislative and judicial branches of government. As the introduction to Harvard law professor Lawrence Tribe's book *Abortion: The Clash of Absolutes* suggests, "a bitterly divided America now stands at a cross-roads of decision on abortion, in which no one—from the President, Supreme Court and Congress to a perplexed public—will be spared the burden of tragic choices."[7] Tribe's book

17

is about a clash of absolutes, of life against liberty. When values differ, the clash of conflict becomes a reality.

*Conflict over Goals.* Finally, conflict is a clash of perspectives as people express different goals. In his book, *Preaching Through a Storm,* H. Beecher Hicks describes being caught in a storm of conflict over goals:

> I was caught in a storm for three years as pastor of one of the largest black Baptist congregations in America. At first the turbulence centered around the church's decision to replace a century old structure with a new edifice for our Christ but it spread until it encompassed the whole congregation. It left in its wake the unavoidable debris of accusation, misunderstood motives, threats, violations of Christian principles, the abandonment of traditional discipline, and a people, although not irretrievably split—confused, uncertain and groping for light in a sea of doubting blackness.[8]

He goes on to describe not only the nature of that conflict over the goal of a new physical facility, but his role in preaching the congregation through it. One cannot read his words without having a vivid sense of the tension and danger generated by that conflict. It moved to the point where the pastor was told in an anonymous telephone call that he should not go to the pulpit again, that if he tore down the old church to build a new one, he would be dead. Then Hicks described with a sense of real emotion how he did return to the pulpit for the last sermon in the church—wearing a bulletproof vest, and escorted by an armed bodyguard.[9]

The clash of different perspectives related to the goals of individuals or groups can indeed result in serious conflicts.

## An Expression of Different Attitudes and Emotions

While stemming from the clash of different perspectives on facts, methods, values, and goals, conflict also reflects people's different attitudes and emotions. Speed Leas, one of the nationally recognized authorities on conflict in churches, suggests that conflict can be placed in one of three categories: it is substantive, stemming from the differences noted above that may be generated by a particular issue; it is interpersonal; or it is intrapersonal.[10] In essence, conflict is closely connected with who we are as people and how we as people interact with each other. It is in the last two categories that the expression of attitudes and demonstration of emotions are most prominent.

One of the first questions I ask as I intervene in conflict between people is this: "Do you want the conflict, or do you want the resolution?" The answer to that question provides great insight into the emotional state and attitudes of those involved.

At times, the people's attitudes and emotions strongly suggest that they not only want the conflict, but in fact are thriving on it. Perhaps it is because of unresolved conflict within themselves that they so vividly and dramatically become involved in conflict with other people or within their organization. It may provide an emotional outlet for the satisfaction of needs that otherwise are going unmet. Such involvement may reflect lifelong attitudes toward people and problems. Or it may simply be a distraction from other realities which are more difficult to deal with or accept.

Recently I sat in a restaurant with a very experienced mediator after we had completed an emotionally charged meeting with representatives from twenty neighborhood organizations fighting an environmental project. "I wish they all had better marriages," she said, referring to the people involved in the dispute. I wondered what that had to do with the emotions expressed during the vocal meeting. With a certain sense of sarcasm—as well as a grain of truth—she said that in her experience, many of those who get involved in highly charged community and public policy conflicts are people whose lives are not peaceful in other areas. Her sense was that if they had great marriages and had their lives "together" in other respects, they might be more constructively involved when it came to handling conflict.

A wide variety of attitudes and emotions can be expressed in a conflict. These attitudes and emotions are not inherently bad, but conflict *is* capable of bringing them to the surface in a way that is not constructive. If not controlled, they can even escalate into a situation that is dangerous for those involved in the conflict, and others around them.

## CONFLICT IS OPPORTUNITY

Conflict also has an element of opportunity, however. It presents the opportunity to change, to struggle, to grow, and to reflect God's power in relationships and in our world.

If it were not for the challenge of conflict, few changes would take place. For example, the 1990s have been designated by many observers as the decade of the environment, with the press of a growing population and rapidly changing political climates causing prominent concern about natural resources. But this decade does not promise to be one in which we all work in harmony on environmental issues. In fact, the legal conflict expected over pollution, land development, and government regulation is projected by the American Bar Association as one of the seven fastest growing areas of law practice in the 1990s![11]

While the conflict may be stressful for many, change will take place because of it. New decisions will be made regarding the cutting of old-growth timber, the protection of animal species, the use of water, and the methods of transportation, as well as the extraction of earth's fuel resources. As those decisions are made in response to conflict, changes will occur in how we live, where we live, and the nature of our stewardship of this earth.

Conflict also presents the opportunity for people to struggle and grow. Dr. James Mallory, in his book *The Kink and I,* comments: "People seem to assume that conflict is inherently bad or that the ideal life would be conflict free. Anybody that is conflict free is not experiencing growth. . . . the important changes in us take place within the framework of struggle."[12]

We may not look forward to the struggle that results in growth, but we must recognize it. The admonition of a high-school football coach rings in my mind: "There's no gain without pain!" And certainly the lives of many who provide inspiring testimonies of success despite hardship reflect the struggle which leads to growth.

During my early-elementary school days, one of my best friends was a boy stricken with muscular dystrophy, a degenerative disease that attacked his youthful body and restricted him to a wheelchair in the third grade. Daily, I observed Bruce and his family struggling in conflict with that crippling disease.

He was as normal as any boy my age in all ways, except for his physical limitations; and he did his best to overcome those. Day in and day out, his parents would surround him with the normal activities—school, scouts, swimming, professional baseball games, birthday parties, and church. Day in and day out, Bruce would struggle with the conflict of his physical limitations.

But the legacy he left after his death in his twenties was not a legacy of conflict; it was one of growth and success. He grew in maturity as he encountered his physical struggle, and each of us who knew him grew by observing it. I do not clearly remember all of his conflicts, but I was touched by the spirit he demonstrated, and I cherish the opportunity I had to push his wheelchair.

Similar opportunities for growth exist in interpersonal conflicts. Although it's easy to forget this when we're shouting our way through a heated argument or struggling to survive an angry confrontation, we should try to remember that the same conflict that divides people can also cause them to work harder at building a durable relationship.

Like most Christians, I am captivated by what is described in the New Testament; but I am equally intrigued by what is not revealed. Take for instance the relationship of the apostle Paul and John Mark. We know that they were co-workers on Paul's first missionary journey, and that the decision not to take John Mark on the second journey was the result of a "sharp disagreement" reported in Acts 15:39. We can only imagine the substance and circumstance of that disagreement; every indication suggests the conflict was significant enough to dramatically impact their relationship.

Can you imagine the tension as Paul told John Mark that he was not invited on the journey? Can you sense the tension the next time the two men were together? Were the two of them able to resolve the conflict by themselves? Or were others involved in mediating it? I am intrigued by the reconciliation that obviously must have taken place. It was a resolution to their conflict that was so enduring that years later, as Paul wrote his last letters to the churches, he asked to see John Mark. Can you sense the celebration that was there as they sat, together,

*21*

toward the end of Paul's life? It will be awhile before we know the answers to these questions about how they resolved their conflict. But one suspects that both Paul and John Mark grew through it.

Finally, conflict presents the opportunity to show the power of God intervening in the lives of his people. Norman Vincent Peale's popular magazine *Guideposts* regularly records the stories of people caught in conflict, and God's intervention in their lives. We are inspired as people face seemingly insurmountable conflicts—and then see God's hand in their resolution. Over and over again in the ministry of reconciliation it is God who intervenes to dissipate anger, soften hearts, and bring people's spirits together in resolution.

Many situations involve the potential for both danger *and* opportunity, not just one or the other. How would you evaluate the following situation? Sitting in a restaurant with my sons, we heard a conversation among five women. The women were so excited and verbose that their conversation dominated our area of the restaurant, even eclipsing that of my three- and nine-year-old boys.

The women were so excited because only hours before they had discovered that someone had moved the church dishes from a cupboard in the kitchen to another cupboard across the room. For almost an hour they discussed all the people in the congregation who might have moved the dishes—and why. One woman exclaimed, "Whoever they were, they will hear about this violation of authority!"

Unfortunately, my guys wanted to leave before I could hear the women's final plan. My best guess is it was going to the top, beyond departmental coordinators or church committees. Somebody big was going to get the full blast of their anger if the dishes were not restored to their original position. There seemed to be much about the women's description that signaled danger. Yet there may well have been opportunity, too—opportunity to resolve a difference in such a way that their needs would be addressed, their relationships strengthened, and their future ministry enhanced. Conflict presents both danger and opportunity. The next chapter suggests some initial responses to it.

# CHAPTER 3

# RESPONDING TO CONFLICT

IN A RECENT TELEVISION INTERVIEW, a former professional football player compared his present role as a minister of the gospel with playing football. He insisted repeatedly that his successful ministry was far more difficult than his strenuous athletic career had been. Foremost in his mind were the ministerial challenges of dealing with conflict.

Most of us can only imagine the thousands of hours of practice, the mental intensity, and the denial of physical pain that is required of a professional athlete. When that becomes the basis of comparison for ministry, and the conflict involved in ministry exceeds the emotional and mental demands of a sport like football, such is worthy of examination.

Much of the conflict encountered by Christian counselors, church leaders, and other helpers goes far beyond the normal intensity of conflict that occurs in most believers' lives. It is compounded even more by the responsibility they accept to assist and lead others who seek help in untangling the conflicts which enmesh them. Acknowledging these helping individuals' added responsibilities, one can understand the comment of the athlete-turned-minister.

Because this book is written for Christian counselors and others who engage either professionally or as volunteers in the ministry of reconciliation, it is appropriate to acknowledge a sense of the demands brought on by conflict and the impact of such work. While we realize that generalization is dangerous, we offer the example of a church ministry to illustrate the point.

## CONFLICT SETS THE AGENDA

In a study conducted for the Christian Conciliation Service of Orange County, California, ministers from a variety of churches were asked to report what they thought was the actual amount of time in their ministry they spent dealing with conflict. Of the 135 individuals who responded, almost 10 percent of the group reported that they spent more than 40 percent of their time managing conflict. Another 26 percent indicated that they spent 20 to 40 percent of their work time dealing with conflict. The remaining respondents said they spent less than 20 percent of their ministry time in settling disputes. In essence, more than one-third of the responding ministers spent more than 20 percent of their time actually involved in attempting to resolve acute conflict.[1] That figure is roughly equivalent to spending an entire day each week, or more than two months out of each year, managing conflict.

The results of this somewhat informal study are consistent with the observations of others. Lyle Schaller reports in his book *The Pastor and the People* that on any given day of the week in three-quarters of all churches, the ministry of the congregation is reduced significantly as the result of nonproductive and even destructive conflict. Conflict is so severe that in one-fourth of those churches it must be reduced before the church can redirect its energies and resources in accordance with its goals.[2]

What might it mean for even 20 percent of a minister's time to be spent on conflict? A sense of conflict's impact on church organizations can be formulated by looking at studies of secular institutions. For example, it is reported that business managers spend about 25 percent of their time dealing with conflict, ranking it of equal or higher importance than planning, communication, motivation, and decision-making.[3] This attention is necessary because conflict within an organization can result in lost work time, lowered job motivation, or even sabotage. But dealing with it can also result in losses, such as wasted management time, reduced quality of decisions, and loss of skilled employees who may leave in frustration, sometimes causing the restructuring of the organization. One could extend similar costs of conflict to other organizations, including churches.

We could also consider the *types* of conflict ministers spend their time dealing with and compare that information to the business setting. Participants in the Christian Conciliation Service survey were asked to provide examples of the three most challenging instances of conflict in their congregations in the last twelve months. Almost three hundred separate, identifiable conflicts were reported. They included:

- Staff conflict due to different expectations
- Doctrinal disagreements among church leadership
- Differing priorities about financial expenditures on facilities
- Sexual abuse of congregational members
- Marriage conflict and divorce
- Scheduling problems with church school and worship
- Disagreements over use of the church facilities for weddings
- Attempts to fire the minister
- Feuds among church leaders
- Development of a budget
- Clashes over church music and style of worship
- Conflict related to new employees
- Arguments about redecorating the sanctuary
- Love triangles within the congregation[4]

Notable on this list are the extremely emotional conflicts such as sexual abuse, marriage dissolution, or personally held religious differences. Such issues go to the core of personal lives. While not wanting to denigrate the business manager's challenge in handling conflict with boards or with differing opinions about corporate goals and methods, the minister has the more difficult, painful, and potentially destructive issues to face.

Ironically, though, even with these emotionally ridden issues of conflict evident in churches, there seems to be a hesitancy on the part of churches to address it. Loren Vickery, a church consultant and repeated observer of church congregations, stated in a telephone interview, "Churches which are [supposed] to be characterized by unity are instead characterized by conflict, and seem not to recognize it or do anything about it."[5] Dr. Rodger Bufford, chairman of the graduate psychology program at George Fox College, provided a reason for such avoidance when he stated in an interview, "Ministers don't report that they are having much conflict in their ministries because they are not supposed to have conflict."[6] Peter Robinson, former director of the Christian Conciliation Service of Los Angeles, another ministry which focuses on dispute resolution and reconciliation within churches and between individuals, has concluded after working with hundreds of ministers that their preferred mode for dealing with conflict is avoidance.[7]

It is unclear whether conflict is avoided because it goes unrecognized or because of other, more deliberate choices. What *is* clear is that most ministers have never received any training in conflict management. A study completed by the Institute for Dispute Resolution focusing on nineteen randomly selected churches in a Southern California county revealed that while the ministers of those churches had a total of 168 years of post-high-school education, none had any education or training in managing conflict.[8] While they perhaps have the biblical knowledge for the ministry of reconciliation, by their own admission most ministers are ill-equipped to handle it.

## TERMS AND GOALS USED IN MANAGING AND RESOLVING CONFLICT

With conflict so prevalent, the terms used to describe this work need to be considered as we study these processes.

Such frequently used terms as "dispute resolution," "conflict management," and "reconciliation" all suggest a variety of responses.

## Dispute Resolution

In the legal world, "dispute resolution" seems to be the term most readily used. This stems, perhaps, from the tendency of the legal system to quantify an injury or wrong into an identifiable "dispute." The system seeks to resolve such disputes, usually through an adversarial process that adjudicates the correctness of positions in a circumstance where there is a winner and a loser.[9]

To address conflict exclusively from the perspective of dispute resolution, however, limits assistance to only the most acute and concrete conflict. Studies suggest that "disputes" in our society represent only about 45 percent of the conflicts.[10] One categorization contends that events or circumstances which are believed to be unwarranted or inappropriate are "grievances." Some of these grievances then turn into "claims" when communication about them includes an assertion of entitlement or desired resolution. Finally, claims become "disputes" when the claim based on the grievance is rejected. As shown by the dispute pyramid illustrated in Figure 3–1, for each one thousand grievances, it is estimated that fewer than half could be classified as disputes. Only 10 percent of the original one thousand grievances will evolve into the need for lawyers, and only 5 percent will eventually utilize the court system.

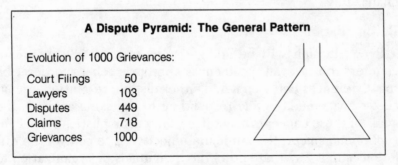

**A Dispute Pyramid: The General Pattern**

Evolution of 1000 Grievances:

| | |
|---|---|
| Court Filings | 50 |
| Lawyers | 103 |
| Disputes | 449 |
| Claims | 718 |
| Grievances | 1000 |

**Figure 3–1**

## Conflict Management

There is a sense in which the term "conflict management" is more useful than dispute resolution. Placing an emphasis on *resolution*, as used in the legal world, implies that all conflicts can, in fact, be resolved, which common sense tells us is impossible. The sense of conflict *management* gives one greater freedom to address a wider range of problems. It also implies assistance but not necessarily complete resolution.[11]

Perhaps the word "manage" can be used here in the same way it was used by a skier who, while having his broken leg set, was asked how he was going to get to the office on Monday. He replied, "I haven't figured that out yet; but I'll manage somehow." In this case, to manage means to "get along" or "to make out" or to "muddle through." Churches or individuals manage conflict when they do their best under the circumstances to oversee, direct, and control differences.

Conflict management and dispute resolution find common ground when they are used as descriptions of problem-solving. They connote a number of communication and facilitation skills that are directed toward the needs of the people involved. They are processes that deliberately attempt to manage and resolve differences in a way that preserves or enhances relationships. Both processes are guided not by competition, but by cooperation.

While such definitions are helpful, in reality they are almost impossible to use systematically. In this book, the terms conflict management and dispute resolution will be used almost interchangeably.

## Reconciliation

Reconciliation will be addressed more fully in subsequent chapters, but a brief comment is appropriate here to describe the differences between it and either dispute resolution or conflict management. While responding to the same conflict, the goals of these concepts may differ. Stated simplistically, in *conflict management*, the minimum objective is to control the differences in a way that allows the individuals or organization to function. In *dispute resolution*, the objective is to conclude the conflict through some process. In *reconciliation,* the objective is not only to resolve the conflict, but also to restore the relationship of the people involved.

Sometimes conflict management and dispute resolution are accomplished, but reconciliation is not. In helping others involved in conflict, we must acknowledge that reconciliation cannot always be achieved, but that this assistance to people nevertheless can be quite valuable and even set the stage for later reconciliation.

## FIVE APPROACHES TO CONFLICT

The approaches to conflict are as diverse and complex as the people involved. They dramatically affect how conflict is handled and the outcomes that are possible.

Either deliberately or passively, people have preferred ways of dealing with conflict. Behind these styles are certain attitudes that shape behavior. Our responses reflect who we are, our experiences, and our perceived values. For example, a person who assumes conflict is basically evil will tend to avoid it. Others who see conflict as a part of life will take a more active role when they experience disputes.

The approaches to conflict will be seen in the figures accompanying this discussion. These diagrams illustrate how various

**Values Shaping Approaches to Conflict**

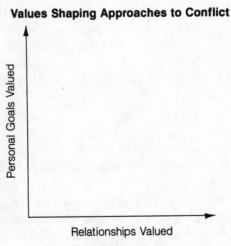

Relationships Valued

**Figure 3-2**

**Approaches to Conflict: Avoidance**

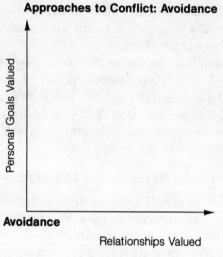

Figure 3-3

approaches to conflict—avoidance, accommodation, competition, compromise, and collaboration—depend on whether the individual places a higher value on maintaining good relationships, or on achieving his or her personal goals. While approaches to conflict are capable of change and combination, the five categories discussed here accurately portray the most predictable responses.[12] Figure 3–2 portrays the two sources from which styles of conflict emerge. The horizontal line reflects the extent to which relationships are valued. The vertical line reflects the extent to which personal goals or objectives are valued. Each is directly related to the approaches to conflict.

### Avoidance

Avoidance, the most commonly used style of conflict management, reflects the belief that it is impossible to both accomplish our personal goals and maintain relationships while in conflict. It is illustrated in Figure 3–3, where avoidance has been placed on the diagram that will eventually show five approaches to conflict. The basic strategy of avoidance is to withdraw, avoid, suppress, and deny the existence of conflict. A person using this style is unassertive, neither pursuing his or her own interests in the situation, nor supporting others in achieving theirs. This person will not cooperate in defining the conflict, seeking a solution, or in carrying it out.

Church leaders use the style of avoidance frequently for the sake of appearances—they want themselves or their congregation to look good. Over and over in my work I have heard such leaders reflect the approach of avoidance when discussing conflict. Many times it is with a statement such as, "Ours is a loving church. We just don't discuss those matters on which we disagree."

Avoided conflict will typically resurface at some point, most likely with more intensity and a greater potential for destruction than when first identified. As an indirect method of resolution, avoidance takes the least effort in the short run, has the longest life expectancy, and has the most costs which cannot be charged back to the original conflict. It can increase the stress level, result in hostile interactions, and foster low morale.

As with all approaches to conflict, avoidance can be appropriate in some instances and inappropriate in others. When returning to an office and finding a pink telephone message from someone with whom you do not want to talk, avoidance may be appropriate. Some problems simply go away or are resolved by themselves. If, however, the call is from a boss or a spouse, avoidance could have serious consequences. Like with all approaches, the approach of avoidance is not inherently good or bad. Wisdom is reflected in choosing it at the appropriate time.

### Accommodation

The accommodating response to conflict is characterized by a high concern for preserving relationship, even if it means conceding one's own goals. It is illustrated by its addition to the diagram in Figure 3–4 on the horizontal line reflecting the valuing of relationships. The assumption underlying this approach is that a relationship is preserved without conflict. The accommodator may feel guilty if he or she causes conflict. In many cases, life experiences may have taught the accommodator that it is not safe to have conflict. Other reasons for choosing this approach might include a high need for acceptance by

**Approaches to Conflict: Avoidance and Accommodation**

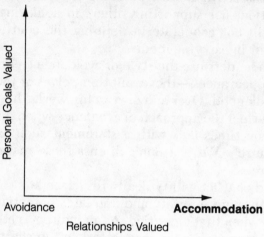

Figure 3–4

others, and the belief that accommodation will allow those needs to be met.

The person who uses the approach of accommodation accepts the burden of responsibility for maintaining the relationship. The choice to be accommodating can be advantageous, especially if a person is capable of choosing a more direct, competitive style when it is merited. Without the capability of choosing another style, however, the message is sent that what the accommodator wants or needs is unimportant, thereby making that person subject to exploitation.

Accommodation, too, can be appropriate or inappropriate. When walking through a dark alley you feel the cold steel of a revolver pressed up against your neck and the raspy voice of a hoodlum demanding your wallet and car keys, that is a pretty good time for accommodation. You want the best relationship possible with the assailant, even if it means giving in to all of his demands!

On the other hand, however, there are times when accommodation is inappropriate. A teen-ager may demand the use of the car, an extremely late curfew, and use of the family credit cards for a night out on the town. While a parent hopes for a valuable relationship with the teen-ager, accommodation of every demand will not result in either a responsible young person nor, ultimately, a genuine respectful relationship between the parent and child. Accommodation can be both effective and ineffective in approaching conflict.

## Competition

The competitive, win-or-lose style of conflict management is characterized by a very high concern for the achievement of personal goals, even at the risk of damaging or destroying relationships. In Figure 3–5, competition has been added to the diagram, appearing on the vertical line reflecting the valuing of personal goals. The person who uses this style may not desire harm to come to the others, but he or she is willing to sacrifice almost anything to achieve personal objectives. People who employ the competing style do not always go head to head with the opposition. Sometimes they work subversively. At other times they use the power of words to humiliate and weaken their opponents, until they finally bring them under control.

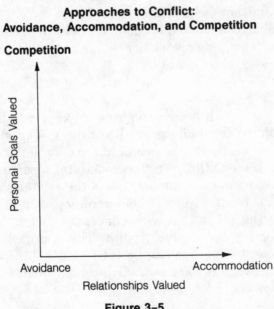

**Approaches to Conflict:
Avoidance, Accommodation, and Competition**

**Competition**

Personal Goals Valued

Avoidance　　　　　　　　　　　　Accommodation

Relationships Valued

**Figure 3–5**

There are times when competing is the best style to use in a conflict. When quick, important decisions must be made because of an emergency, competition is appropriate. The same assailant who was accommodated in his demand for your wallet in the alley may be the recipient of great competition if he enters your home and attempts harm to your child. When a conflict concerns the protection of those we love, rights that are fundamental to our existence, or beliefs that are held dear, competition may be appropriate.

Quite frequently in counseling, clients may need to be taught how to "compete" in conflict with an abusive mate or a rebellious child. In this situation the counselor helps the client develop strategies to do so in a safe way. In a Christian context, this is done in a way that respects the person, but may be confrontive to his or her behavior.

On the other hand, competition is often inappropriately used. In his excellent book *No Contest,* Alfie Kohn contends that our competitive approach to education and business does not result in the most productive learning environment or the most efficient business operation. Competition used in other settings, such as the justice system, does not always result in the best outcome for those who have differences.[13]

As with avoidance and accommodation, the challenge is not to decide whether competition is good or bad but rather to wisely choose when to use it.

**Compromise**

The person with a compromising style of conflict management proposes a middle ground to others. This style is illustrated in its location at the center of the diagram in Figure 3–6. It reflects some willingness to compete for a particular resolution but also some accommodation of the relationship between the parties. Inherent in the compromising style is the idea of providing the other side with concessions while at the same time expecting concessions from it. This approach is based on the premise that no one can be fully satisfied, so all those involved must submit some of their personal desires to serve the common good of both parties.

**Approaches to Conflict:**
**Avoidance, Accommodation, Competition, and Compromise**

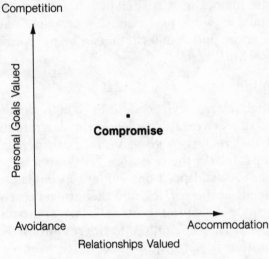

Figure 3-6

The sense of compromise can have a negative connotation. Compromising integrity for personal gain or compromising long-held beliefs for short-term advantages may be perceived as inappropriate to some in conflict. Many times the idea of moving from an enthusiastically taken position to a point where agreement can be reached, feels unacceptable. Compromise can lead to half-hearted commitments and recurring conflicts under the guise of new issues. It rarely sets the stage for high satisfaction, and many times it leaves behind feelings of frustration and disenchantment.

Compromise does have some very appropriate applications. It allows parties to achieve some of their goals without jeopardizing relationships. Labor-management negotiations assume that there will be compromise from the extreme positions initially taken by the opposing parties. Legislators elevate compromise to an art-form as they give and take in order to pass legislation. Churches utilize compromise when designing facilities, formulating budgets, and agreeing upon the ministry agenda. In each

35

of those instances compromise is perceived as an effective way to handle differences by providing some of what each party needs while maintaining sufficient relationships so the parties can continue to work together. Compromise, like avoidance, accommodation, and competition, can be appropriately and inappropriately utilized.

## Collaboration

The collaborative style combines a high concern for both people and objectives. It is added to the diagram in Figure 3–7 at a point that reflects high value for both personal goals and relationships. It asks the question, "Is there a way to move beyond the adversarial positions evident in conflict, understand the true needs of the parties, and then use a creative process to find a mutually-satisfying solution?" This approach works best when all parties are committed to the resolution of conflict.

Collaboration is not always possible or even desired. Some parties simply do not care about or expect to have a future

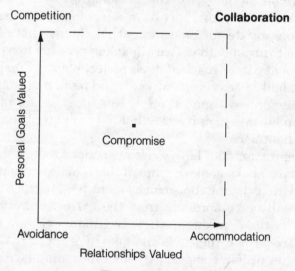

**Approaches to Conflict:
Avoidance, Accommodation, Competition,
Compromise, and Collaboration**

Competition        **Collaboration**

Personal Goals Valued

Compromise

Avoidance        Accommodation

Relationships Valued

**Figure 3–7**

relationship as illustrated by those on two sides of a personal injury dispute. An injured passenger involved in an automobile accident wants the appropriate payment from the insurance company after which neither anticipates dealing with each other again. There is little reason to expect collaboration.

But alternatively, collaboration holds great potential for those in conflict. The couple going through a divorce in their marital relationship may pretend that they have no reason to work toward a collaborative resolution, even concerning the children, but those who serve as resources for the family know how much they will relate to each other—even if the relationship is defined outside of the previous marriage. A collaborative resolution of the family issues can maximize the resolution of conflict and establish the possibility of an acceptable relationship in the future.

The effects of the collaborative style are positive when it is consistently applied. Increased trust, stronger relationships, enthusiastic implementation of goals, and a higher resolution of conflicts are often achieved. Individuals who are able to concentrate on the issues without getting caught up in negative emotions will find this style produces more satisfactory outcomes. The challenge with this approach is that it takes a great deal of time because it necessitates exploring the needs of all parties and crafting solutions that meet those needs. It also requires communication skills and a genuine commitment to resolve the conflict.

As described, none of the approaches is inherently good or bad. Even in the ministry of Jesus he utilized a number of approaches to conflict. Jesus competed when his objective was cleansing the temple. He avoided conflict with the crowds when he retreated from them. He accommodated others in washing Mary's feet—and in the ultimate sacrifice of his life. The critical point to recognize is that people may choose from a variety of approaches to deal with conflict, and the choice will have an impact on both the way the conflict is resolved and the people involved.

As conflict is recognized, it becomes obvious that it sets the agenda for counselors and those with whom they work. Conflict presents both dangers and opportunities. It may be managed or resolved. In some cases, it sets the stage for reconciliation. When confronted with conflict, people respond in a variety of ways: avoidance, accommodation, competition, compromise, and collaboration. With that basis, the next chapter suggests biblical principles for addressing conflict in the Christian community.

# CHAPTER 4

# BIBLICAL PRINCIPLES
# FOR RECONCILIATION

"HE SHOULD BE DISCIPLINED!" exclaimed the man as he pounded the table and glared at his business partner. The intensity of his anger quickly caught my attention as he and his partner described their acute conflict to me. Both Christian businessmen, they were in the midst of a year-old battle over marketing rights, contract terms, and responsibilities to each other; now their conflict was so severe their businesses were at the point of bankruptcy and their relationship was in shambles. One man had come to the conclusion that the only solution was to "discipline" his adversary. Based on his interpretation of a passage from Matthew 18, he sincerely believed that through harsh discipline and accountability, his partner's behavior would change and the conflict would be resolved.

As the third-party facilitator, I could see the clear need for resolution as I daily witnessed the destruction of two valued businesses and an important relationship. And I could not disagree that accountability and responsibility were necessary ingredients for a productive business relationship. But the fervent and angry insistence on "discipline" startled me. It caused me to think seriously about the passage referred to and the role of discipline in reconciliation. What did the angry man mean by "discipline"? Was he suggesting it as a path to reconciliation? How could discipline be imposed? Under what conditions might it be accepted? Most importantly, what role might the relationship of the individuals have in the acceptance of discipline and the ultimate hope for reconciliation?

Such questions lead us to a brief examination of the concept of reconciliation as used in Scripture and to a more detailed description of three scriptural teachings about conflict resolution.

### THE BIBLICAL DEFINITION OF RECONCILIATION

Four Greek words help us understand the New Testament concept of reconciliation.[1] The first word, *katallasso* (1 Cor. 7:10), means to change from enmity to friendship. Thus, one dimension of reconciliation would suggest a change in a relationship from one of hostility to one of friendship.

The second Greek word, *apokatallasso* (Col. 1:20), means to reconcile completely. Going further than *katallasso*, it suggests that all enmity and impediment to peace is removed.

The third Greek word that translates as reconcile is the word *diallassomai* (Matt. 5:24). It means to bring about an alteration—to exchange, to reconcile in cases of mutual hostility, yielding to mutual concession.

The fourth Greek word, a noun, is *katallage*, meaning a change on the part of one person, induced by an action on the part of another. It is most often used to describe the reconciliation of human beings to God through God's love expressed by Christ. See Romans 5:11, for example.

Taken as a whole, the definitional collage from the Greek text suggests that reconciliation means more than just coming to an agreement; it also means restoring the original understanding and relationship that existed before the hostility. It is a process that does not occur instantly, but rather evolves over time. In terms of one's reconciliation to God, it is a lifelong maturation.

Ron Kraybill, former director of the Mennonite Conciliation Service, describes biblical reconciliation as a process, not an event. He sees this process working as a cycle: "The key to enabling . . . reconciliation is the knowledge that it is a process that follows a predictable cycle. . . . Only when an individual passes through the cycle does his heart catch up with his head."[2]

The cycle of reconciliation is graphically illustrated in Figure 4–1. Kraybill describes the cycle this way:

> The cycle of reconciliation begins with an open relationship. Individuals share, trust, and risk themselves with others in an open relationship. The second stage is injury. At some point in all relationships, expectations are not met. A risk is taken and instead of a good outcome, injury results. The next stage is called withdrawal. People tend to pull back after injury to assess the situation. Withdrawal may take a second or a decade. At this stage people attempt head reconciliation. They try to will themselves into a restored relationship. People think they are reconciled but still feel distance, coldness, and caution with the other party.

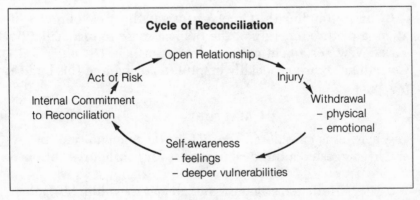

**Cycle of Reconciliation**

**Figure 4–1**

The pivotal stage in the cycle is called self-awareness. This is beyond withdrawal and comes when a person becomes aware of his emotions. He can admit he is angry, hurt, and confused, not just concerned. Part of this stage includes tapping wounds from earlier battles that relate to the present conflict. Often the present incident evicts an emotion from a trauma that occurred a long time ago. Becoming conscious of past traumas causes the emotions to lose power.[3]

Kraybill encourages people at the self-awareness stage to find a supportive friend who can listen nonjudgmentally to the story as details of the grief, anger, fear, or embarrassment are described. After doing so, his advice is to start at the beginning and tell the story again, and then to continue retelling the story until it becomes boring. He suggests that when an individual begins to yawn at his or her own account, the trauma of the conflict has lost its power to rule the present. Kraybill continues:

The fifth stage is called internal commitment to reconciliation. This is an act of the will where a person makes a conscious choice to put forth the effort to be reconciled. The last step is called act of risk. This is an act of choosing to take a risk in re-establishing communication with the offending party. Rejection by the other party is a distinct possibility.[4]

By understanding the Greek words and the cycle of reconciliation, a picture emerges of the biblical sense of reconciliation. Three New Testament passages from Matthew 18 and 5, and 1 Corinthians 6 are especially helpful in completing this biblical perspective.

## MATTHEW 18

When Jesus considered conflict in the community of believers, he suggested a three-step process for conflict resolution:

If your brother sins against you, go and show him his fault, just between the two of you. If he listens to you, you have won your brother over. But if he will not listen, take one or two others along, so that "every matter may be established by the testimony of two or three witnesses." If he refuses to listen to them, tell it to the church; and if he refuses to listen even to the church, treat him as you would a pagan or a tax collector. (Matt. 18:15–17)

This passage suggests the dispute-resolution process begins with an attempt to achieve reconciliation through individual contact and dialogue. However, when the initial step is not successful, one or two additional people are to assist and witness the effort. While the group is now larger, the value of the relationship, simplicity of communication, and environment of confidentiality are still maintained. Finally, if that process is not successful, the individuals are instructed to "tell it to the church," bringing the unresolved conflict into the open so the power of the church body can be utilized to achieve reconciliation.[5] The final step of this process is defined by many Christians as church discipline.

Several observations from this model of dispute resolution can be applied to the ministry of reconciliation. First, we see that the initial objective is reconciliation. Next, we realize that time must be invested in the first two stages of the process if this method is to work. Finally, we investigate the limited conditions in which individuals might accept discipline by the church.

## The Objective of the Biblical Process

At first, the objective of the biblical process of conflict management may seem obvious—until the application of church discipline is considered. In many cases, the initial objective of a dispute-resolution process may have been restoration of the former relationship;[6] but when the idea of discipline is brought into the conflict, the purpose may very quickly change to vindication.

For example, in one instance of church conflict, the church leadership sought to bring back into fellowship a member who was engaged in unacceptable personal behavior. At the outset, the intentions of the leaders were good and their motives were sincere. They truly wanted to bring the member back into a right relationship with the congregation and God.

Initially, the leadership faithfully followed the biblical process from Matthew 18. As leaders, they went to the individual in love, expressing concern for her behavior and its implication for her reputation and that of the church. But later, when there was disagreement as to the actual behavior and the person renounced membership in that church body, the leaders could not stop. Having taken a stand that was made very public in the small community, their reputation was "on the line," and the only way for them to save face was to pursue publicly a matter which no longer directly concerned them, since the individual had withdrawn from the community.

In short, what should have been a process of reconciliation became a process of proving who was right and who was wrong. The focus changed to winning, and the hope of reconciliation was lost.[7] When that occurs, relationships are damaged, if not destroyed.

### The Need for Time

All too often the first meetings in a conflict situation are perceived as opportunities to "set out the charges" and "give the person an opportunity to repent." If that result does not quickly materialize, momentum is gathered to "tell it to the church."

Professionals, whether they are counselors, church consultants, attorneys, or ministers who work in church conflict resolution recognize that change and reconciliation usually take place over a much longer period of time. One church body has wisely concluded that at least seven attempts at personal reconciliation must be made in each of the two preliminary stages before "telling it to the church" is appropriate.

Most of our professional work as mediators demonstrates to us that conflict is not resolved and relationships are not healed overnight. Many times it takes weeks of intensive work just to get the two sides to come to the table. It is not unusual to invest hours just agreeing on the process to be followed.[8] All of this preliminary work should be done at the outset of the conflict, when it involves only two people or one or two outsiders. Time invested then will maximize the likelihood of restored relationships, while hurrying this stage may lead to public humiliation and destroyed relationships.

### Conditions for Enacting "Discipline"

Many may feel that the other person in a conflict should be disciplined. They sometimes make such statements as, "He should be made to pay for that act," or "I've been hurt and she has an obligation to make it right with me," or "Somebody needs to get him in line." But discipline is usually bitter medicine, and often people agree to accept it only if there is no other choice.

Not long ago, I had the opportunity to talk with one of my city's law-enforcement officers about the speed limit I was exceeding in a residential area. He was an instrument of discipline, and I was the recipient of it. Discipline in this case involved the humiliation and frustration of being singled out, as well as the pain of paying a fine. I accepted it because I really had no other choice; I could only swallow hard and accept it. While the forced acceptance of discipline is a reality of life, it often leaves one embarrassed, depressed, and angry.

But discipline may also be accepted voluntarily. This occurs when the consequences of accepting the discipline are perceived to be better than the consequences of not accepting it; often this decision is based on the perceived value of the relationship.

For example, if our children are ultimately going to accept our discipline as parents, part of that acceptance is going to be related to their relationship with us in many other areas. We cannot have the desired impact—some degree of acceptance, as opposed to rebellion—through discipline if we have not demonstrated love, compassion, and friendship at other times.

This is true in the church as well. If someone is going to accept church discipline as an approach to reconciliation, it is because he or she values the relationship with that body more than the alternative of having that relationship taken away. Consequently, if Matthew 18 is read outside the context of a thriving, nurturing New Testament fellowship, the chances of its successful application are remote. People generally will not be persuaded to submit to discipline unless the relationship is sufficiently important. If Matthew 18 is considered within the context of dynamic and strong Christian fellowship, then the power of that process in resolving conflict is dramatic.

## MATTHEW 5

The difficulty of the Matthew 18 approach described above is probably reflected in the church's unwillingness to use it, because, when taken to its extreme, the process demands a willingness to withdraw fellowship. Few churches are willing or able to follow that teaching.

Dramatically more challenging, however, is Jesus' instruction about reconciliation recorded in Matthew 5:23–24. This lesson occurs within the larger context of some of his most prominent ethical teachings, which address such problems as murder, anger, adultery, lust, divorce, swearing, and responses to evil. He includes conflict between people in that list, and instructs:

Therefore, if you are offering your gift to the altar and there remember that your brother has something against you, leave your gift there in front of the altar. First go and be reconciled to your brother; then come and offer your gift.

The Jewish listeners understood the importance of sacrifice as the avenue to God's forgiveness, and they also recognized that penitence included an attempt to rectify wrong. So these listeners were profoundly impressed when Jesus proclaimed that reconciliation was so important they should leave the place of worship and sacrifice so they could achieve the reconciliation of human conflict. As William Barclay described it, "Jesus is quite clear about this basic fact—we cannot be right with God until we are right with man. . . ."[9]

As we interpret this teaching in today's world, the Christian community must equate the centrality of sacrifice in the Jewish tradition to the centrality of worship in the Christian community. In doing so, our responsibility is clear: We are to make reconciliation a priority. As stated in an insightful book on church conflict, *When the Saints Come Storming In*, the issue is not a choice *between* reconciliation and worship; reconciliation is needed *in order* to worship![10] One might ask why Jesus placed such importance on reconciliation. In answering that question, we perceive some of the results of accepting such responsibility, and see how it benefits the worshiper, the opponent, and the church community.

## Benefits to the Worshiper

Jesus recognized the distraction from worship that results from interpersonal conflict—even conflict that is not the fault of the worshiper. One of the impediments of contemplating the forgiveness of the Father is the haunting feeling that we might need to forgive someone, ourselves. Forgiveness is an act that may or may not lead to reconciliation. But keeping reconciliation as a priority, accepting it and acting upon it, can allow worship to take place with true freedom from the burdens of conflict.

## Benefits to the Opponent

Human nature resists the initiation of a reconciliation process. That resistance may be the reason that the passage in Matthew 5 is directed as it is, stating, "if . . . your brother has something against you. . . ." In other words, if you are the "defendant," the responsibility is yours to provide the opportunity for reconciliation.

Myron Augsburger, in his commentary on Matthew, describes an instance during a communion service at a church in the South Pacific when a man, kneeling at the altar to partake in a communion service, suddenly left, obviously agitated. He had seen another person at the altar with whom he had great conflict, and had vividly remembered his need to achieve reconciliation prior to continuing in that sacrament.[11] That man demonstrated the willingness to seek reconciliation that we all should incorporate into our worship, because it provides the opposing party with the possibility for freedom from conflict, even as it creates that same possibility for us.

## Benefits to the Christian Community

This passage about reconciliation is a corollary to Jesus' statement in Matthew 5:14–16 concerning the example of Christians to the world. As those who occupy "a city on a hill,"[12] Christ reminded his followers that it is imperative that they be consistent in the message they preach and the relationships they portray. When Christians worship God while they are in conflict with each other, they destroy the church's credibility.

Recently I visited with pastors at a very large church which had dynamic ministries, more than five thousand members, and tremendous impact in its community. I was involved with the church, however, because it was embroiled in highly charged conflict with a nearby community where it intended to build its new facility. Conflict had occurred for months over issues related to the size of the building, hours of use, increased traffic, and its impact on the character of the neighborhood. When I became involved, the disagreements had escalated to the point that the church and community were engaged in litigation. The fight had taken on almost spiritual tones, with the church leadership wanting to "defeat the forces of Satan and win for the Lord!"

I asked the pastors to describe the people on the other side— what they were like, why they were concerned, and how they felt. To my dismay, the pastors admitted that they did not even know them! That church continues to worship a God who brought reconciliation to the world, but it does not even engage in the most basic communication with those on the other side of its own conflict.

As I left the meeting, I wondered to whom Matthew 5 was written, and how a spirit of reconciliation might influence that conflict. But more importantly, I wondered about the church's long-term ministry to that community. Sure, the church might define as good stewardship its spending millions of dollars to win the battle to be able to build. It might prevail on the use of the property, the size of the building, or the height of the steeple. But what about its ability to do those things that would be eternally significant? What about ministering to the community, reaching out with the healing power of the Lord, and influencing lives for Christ? Sadly, that church is attempting to carry out its ministry through victories in court.

The instruction Jesus gave in Matthew 5 was an instruction that prioritized reconciliation above church buildings, and even worship. In giving this instruction, Jesus shared with the world a different and more important image of his community.

## 1 CORINTHIANS 6

The third passage that provides a biblical perspective for reconciliation is found in Paul's first letter to the Corinthian church. In the sixth chapter, he instructs those Christians regarding lawsuits among them.

> If any of you has a dispute with another, dare he take it before the ungodly for judgment instead of before the saints? Do you not know that the saints will judge the world? And if you are to judge the world, are you not competent to judge trivial cases? Do you not know that we will judge angels? How much more the things of this life! Therefore, if you have disputes about such matters, appoint as judges even men of little account in the church! I say this to shame you. Is it possible that there is nobody among you wise enough to judge a dispute between believers? But instead, one brother goes to law against another—and this in front of unbelievers!
>
> The very fact that you have lawsuits among you means you have been completely defeated already. Why not rather be wronged? Why not rather be cheated? Instead, you yourselves cheat and do wrong, and you do this to your brothers.
>
> (vv. 1–8)

It is not surprising that Paul suggested Christians ought not sue each other. Observers of human culture from Paul's time to the present have recognized the dramatic and often destructive impact of adversarial litigation. Abraham Lincoln once said, "Discourage litigation. Persuade your neighbors to compromise whenever you can. Point out to them how the nominal winner is often the real loser in fees, expenses, and waste of time."[13]

In the same vein, Judge Learned Hand once commented, "I must say that, as a litigant, I should dread a lawsuit beyond almost anything else short of sickness and death."[14]

Of great interest is Paul's contention that those who resort to the legal process have already "lost." In a judicial resolution, there will always be a winner and a loser when the verdict is read. But Paul contends that the Christian loses in this kind of dispute resolution, regardless of the verdict. This loss may be economic or emotional; it may also be the loss of one's reputation or ministry.

### Economic Loss

The first loss of those who turn to the litigation process is financial. Studies of the justice system now estimate that legal fees for an average civil trial in a major metropolitan area to resolve a dispute over a contract or an injury will be fifteen to twenty thousand dollars.[15] To cope with these high costs, many corporations are rapidly increasing the size of their internal legal departments, while they look for alternatives to litigation. These costs have precipitated such a crisis in corporate America that the general counsel for a Fortune 500 company recently complained, "Every year I give my legal department an unlimited budget, and every year it is exceeded!"

Taxpayers also are called upon to financially support the public judicial system that provides this option for dispute resolution. We pay close to four billion dollars each year for the courtrooms, the judges, and in some cases, the lawyers.[16] There may be instances where such investment is warranted because of the importance of a particular principle, or because of the need to defend oneself against legal action taken by another. But many of the disputes that evolve into litigation could be settled in other ways. Unfortunately, Christians are oftentimes involved in this burgeoning amount of litigation that is pushing the costly legal system into ever-increasing expansion. Surely we could find other places to invest resources provided by God. Good stewardship alone may suggest using a more enlightened and collaborative dispute-resolution process.

### Emotional Loss

Those engaged in litigation also have lost emotionally. Several months ago, I sat with a young woman who had completed four years of litigation against her former employer, a major American corporation. She described the anger she had felt at having been run through the mill of lawyers, physicians, psychiatrists, and other experts as her employment-related claim was handled in the court system. When all was said and done, she looked back on the process and evaluated the emotional cost she had paid, regardless of who "won"; it included the loss of her relationships with two of her closest friends, as well as her physician, and even her lawyer. Tired and spiritually drained, her final, tragic comment was in the form of a question: "I have given four years of my life to this case, and for what?"

## Loss of Reputation

The most serious loss incurred when conflict among Christians results in litigation may be the church's loss of reputation as a community of believers. Scandals in the church have always provided ammunition for its detractors and set it up for outside criticism. Recent headlines dramatizing the fall of popular television evangelists illustrate this fact. But sex scandals and financial scams, while spectacular, are perhaps not the most serious injuries to the church's reputation. If the ability to attract the world to Christ is in any way related to the reputation of his church, that reputation is tarnished as soon as Christians prove themselves unable to resolve conflict and turn to the secular system to do so.

Recently I was visiting with a colleague whose denomination is the dominant one in the city where he lives. We were discussing the process used in his church to deal with conflict and agreed that it could deal quite effectively with doctrinal matters and other internal disagreements. Recognizing that a majority of the people in the community belong to that denomination, I asked about lawsuits among believers. He quickly and matter-of-factly informed me that "the church's process was designed to take care of church problems," and that there was no process to take care of conflicts between members of the church not related to religion, itself.

On my flight back home, I pondered what that says about that church and that community. I remembered a study, reported in the book *Tell It to the Church*, which revealed that in one medium-sized metropolitan area, approximately eight thousand cases were filed each year involving people on both sides who identified themselves as Christians. Legal fees for such cases reached perhaps twelve million dollars a year.[17] Such statistics make us wonder if the principles of our faith translate—*really* translate—into our relationships with each other. Do those principles affect not only the minor parts of our relationships, but how we handle major difficulties, as well? As one commentator asked, "How can we call the world to Christ until the church is the reconciled community Christ intended it to be?"[18]

## Loss of Ministry

Finally, those among us who engage in litigation have lost the ability to minister to others. While the reputation of the church sets the stage for ministering, it is the ministry of individual Christians that affects people personally. How are we to minister to a world filled with conflict if we are unable to resolve conflicts among the Christian community in a constructive way? How are we to respond to a family in conflict while battling our own church family conflict through an adversarial process? How are we to reach out with the healing power of the Lord to those struggling with internal conflict and at the same time litigate against each other? How will we offer hope for the health of organizations if we as a church organization are sick? Litigation takes away the opportunity for effective ministry.

It may be easy to quickly accept Paul's admonition not to sue but pass lightly over the reasons underlying his instruction. When we take someone to court, we have lost financially and emotionally, the church has lost its reputation, and Christ has lost our ministry.

While a multitude of biblical teachings instruct Christians on the character of their relationships, these three passages from Matthew and 1 Corinthians address specifically the proper response when conflict occurs. They define the process, instituted by Christ, which Christians are to follow in the resolution of conflict. The priority of reconciliation is clearly emphasized in Christ's teachings. Paul also taught that Christians are not to use the civil court litigation process—a position supported on both spiritual and pragmatic grounds.

Instead, within the framework of these passages are options for communication and dispute-resolution processes that can resolve conflict in a way that is effective, efficient, and respectful of those involved. The next chapter describes several of these process options.

# CHAPTER FIVE

## CHRISTIANS' ALTERNATIVES TO LITIGATION

THE MOST IMPORTANT DECISION facing someone caught in the midst of conflict is the decision about how to handle it procedurally. Thus, the most important help given by counselors, ministers, lawyers, and others involved in the ministry of reconciliation is assisting people in finding a process that holds promise for the resolution of their disputes and reconciliation of their relationships. When the counselor sets that as a first priority, the possibility increases that the disputants can be directed to a process and forum that will protect their individual interests while creating the opportunity for a collaborative resolution of their difference.

In many cases, such advice will direct those who are enmeshed in conflict to turn away from the courts and litigation.

While there *are* disputes that need the formality of courtroom litigation, in most cases it is neither necessary from a dispute-resolution perspective or appropriate from a Christian perspective. The use of litigation is usually the result of an overemphasis on the adversarial handling of conflict, an angry reaction without the awareness of better alternatives, and an admission that the two sides are not capable of resolving their own dispute.

Judge Wapner's "People's Court" television show is wrong. Instead of admonishing people who have a conflict to "take it to court," the announcer ought to advocate that those in conflict should select a process and resources that will allow them to resolve their dispute in a peaceful and collaborative way! Such an idea would not sell syndicated television shows, but it would guide people to more constructive and relationship-restoring forums for dispute resolution.

Christians have a choice of several alternative processes and resources that are consistent with biblical principles and that contribute to effective dispute resolution.[1] Figure 5–1 illustrates where these alternatives fit into a continuum of conflict-resolution processes that range from avoidance to violence. The illustration also shows which processes are categorized as collaborative, and which are described as adjudicative.

As we develop this repertoire of resources, a brief summary of each option is important.

**Continuum of Conflict-Resolution Processes**

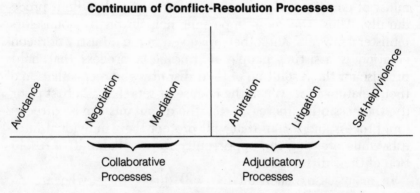

Figure 5–1

54

## AVOIDANCE

Often overlooked, yet almost always available, is the response of avoidance. As used here, avoidance is not seen as the suppression or denial of conflict as described earlier in a discussion of stylistic approaches to conflict. Rather, it is used here to describe a consciously chosen strategy in response to acknowledged conflict.

In a society that emphasizes individual rights, the possibility of deliberately walking away from conflict as a strategy for its management is often ignored. In his book *The Litigious Society*, Jethro Lieberman suggests that as a society we have moved away from any acceptance of wrong to a circumstance where virtually any act by another is actionable. We expect redress for events that in another time and place would have been both legal and accepted. Describing ours as a nation where litigation has become a "secular religion," he concludes:

> The democratization of our legal society, at least in theory, permits everyone to sue for anything—and bodes a revolution, still in the making and still largely unchronicled in the concept of justice.[2]

Former Chief Justice Warren Burger continued the theme in a 1984 address to lawyers attending an American Bar Association meeting:

> The entire legal profession—lawyers, judges, law teachers—has become so mesmerized with the stimulation of the courtroom contest that we tend to forget that we ought to be healers of conflict. For many claims, trials by adversarial contest must in time go the way of the ancient trial by battle and blood. Our system is too costly, too painful, too destructive, too inefficient for a truly civilized people.[3]

Conflict avoidance may be one alternative to this. Christ avoided conflict in a deliberate way. Often when the crowds were pressing, sometimes clamoring for miracles, he retreated to the hills and in doing so diminished the escalation of the crowd's demands.[4] In the Garden of Gethsemane, when he could have rallied not only his disciples but literally called down angels from heaven, Christ told Peter to put away his sword.[5] Finally, as Jesus anticipated his return to Jerusalem, it was obvious that he delayed that return, again avoiding what he understood would be great conflict.[6]

While recognizing the option and value of avoidance, there are numerous biblical examples where such actions were viewed as inappropriate. Christ did not avoid but rather addressed his conflict with the money changers at the temple.[7] The apostles did not avoid but rather addressed the conflict over the Jewish insistence on Gentile circumcision through the Jerusalem Conference.[8] Paul did not avoid but rather dealt with his conflict concerning John Mark prior to his second missionary journey.[9] In every instance, a decision about avoidance was made—a decision we also must make when confronted by conflict.

## NEGOTIATION

A second option available to Christians in conflict is negotiation. While this word may create mental pictures of formal peace talks, negotiation is simply using a communication process to resolve a difficulty, difference, or disagreement.[10] Most conflicts in most circumstances—families, communities, the workplace, and the church—are resolved through negotiation and communication.[11]

Negotiation usually depends on two things. First, it depends upon people's willingness to communicate, face to face, about the nature of their dispute. Until they are willing to talk about what separates them and what solutions there might be, there is no forum for dispute resolution.

Second, negotiation often depends on the individuals' willingness to make compromises during the communication process. At times, especially in the context of our faith, we have viewed such concessions as undesirable, a stance which often causes us to take extreme positions and dig in for the fight. Yet the study of conflict in churches suggests that doctrinal issues, those on which compromise might seem most difficult, are far down the list of issues in dispute. For instance, a recent study of conflict in churches completed by the Institute for Dispute

Resolution revealed that doctrinal issues were ranked lower than conflicts over methods, finances, and personalities—issues capable of compromise, which can be affected by creative thinking, and resolved through negotiation.[12]

In his excellent book *The Mediation Process,* Christopher Moore suggests a number of circumstances when negotiation is possible. Most disputes probably are amenable to this process at some point in their development. Think about conflicts in families, churches, or communities as you read the list.

1. Negotiation is possible when people in conflict rely on cooperation with each other in order to meet their goals and objectives.

2. Negotiation is possible when people are able to influence each other and can undertake or prevent actions that could harm or reward each other.

3. Negotiation is possible when people are affected by time constraints or deadlines and therefore have an impetus to settle rather than to prolong the dispute.

4. Negotiation is possible when people recognize that alternative procedures or outcomes are not as desirable as the procedure of negotiation which allows them to determine their own outcome.

5. Negotiation is possible when people can identify and agree upon the issues in dispute.

6. Negotiation is possible when the interests, goals, and needs of the two sides are not entirely incompatible.

7. Negotiation is possible when external constraints—reputation, costs, risk of an adversarial decision—encourage participation in a private, cooperative process.[13]

The challenge we face today is learning to negotiate—to communicate in ways that will lead toward resolution.

## MEDIATION

A third option available to Christians in conflict is the process of mediation. If one sees the admonition in the first part of Matthew 18 as an admonition for the parties to "negotiate" a resolution, mediation may be a description of the second phase of the process when "outsiders" are involved in the dispute. In its simplest form, mediation is facilitated negotiation. It involves

57

a third party who assists the conflicting individuals in moving from that conflict to resolution.[14]

Historically, mediation has been a major conflict-resolution process and is seeing a resurgence today. Jerold Auerbach's book, *Justice Without Law?*, describes how in colonial America, mediation, not litigation, was the dominant dispute-resolution process. In the religious colonies, conflicting individuals were brought together through the power of that community and the respect of its leaders. Law was not the standard, nor was litigation the norm when communities sought to resolve their conflicts in a way consistent with commonly accepted values.[15]

In other cultures, too, mediation has been a more common approach to dealing with conflict. Reports suggest there are only 7,000 to 10,000 lawyers in all of China, yet there are more than 300,000 mediators. Those mediators, largely community-based, bring the community's values to bear on conflict between individuals. In that environment, there is no need to move forward with more adversarial processes because facilitated dispute resolution is effective.[16]

Mediation has recently emerged as an attractive alternative to more adversarial dispute resolution in this country, as well. States such as California recognize the value of the collaborative dispute-resolution process, and have legislated that all disputes regarding child custody and child visitation be mediated.[17] As mentioned earlier, more that four hundred neighborhood justice centers have been established nationwide, largely as grass-roots efforts to offer those in geographic communities a forum for facilitated negotiation.[18] At the corporate level, major corporations are recognizing the value of a facilitated resolution of conflict and even signing commitments that they will attempt such processes prior to engaging in litigation.[19]

The church should not follow the world in all circumstances, but the explosive use of mediation as a dispute-resolution process throughout our society ought to create an environment in which the church's use of it is acceptable.

### ARBITRATION

The fourth process available to Christians is arbitration. Like mediation, arbitration involves a third party's intervention in the conflict-resolution process. But the role of the third party is different in the two processes. In mediation, the third party intervenes to facilitate a negotiated resolution. In arbitration, the third party intervenes with the power to make a decision.

While not described as such, the third step in the Matthew 18 process could be assumed to be arbitration. During the first stage, negotiation is attempted; and in the second stage, a third party assists, perhaps through mediation. But in the last stage, the two sides admit their inability to resolve the conflict and "tell it to the church." In a sense, the church, or its leadership, becomes the arbitrator who must make a wise decision regarding particular behavior and the nature of the fellowship.

### Differences in Focus

As one compares the adjudicative processes of arbitration and litigation with the more collaborative processes of negotiation and mediation, dramatic differences become apparent in the method's focus. (Refer again to Figure 5–1 to see how these methods line up along the continuum of conflict-resolution processes.) As with all forms of adjudication, the focus in arbitration is on the past. People present their views of what has occurred, and the decision-maker issues a ruling. While that ruling may impact the status or relationship of those people in the future, the process is largely one that determines the impact of events which already have occurred.

In contrast, the focus of the collaborative processes of negotiation and mediation almost always looks to the future. The primary question in mediation, for instance, is not who was right or who was wrong in the past, but what can be done to create a circumstance in which the conflicting people can resolve the conflict for a better future.

### Differences in Control

In addition to the differences of focus, the issue of control also distinguishes adjudication and collaboration. In arbitration, as an example of adjudication, it is the arbitrator who controls the process and the outcome. For a number of years, I have served as a hearing officer for a large Southern California city, essentially arbitrating disputes between the city and its employees. In that capacity, I have the power to determine when the two sides meet, when they take breaks, and when a hearing concludes. I have the power to accept or reject evidence presented, and the power to control the nature of the dialogue in my hearing room. In essence, I control the process.

In addition, I control the outcome. The decision is mine. I have the ability to substitute my judgment for the judgment of the individuals, and when rendering it, to impose remedies that are appropriate. Recognizing that power, the disputants bend over backward to demonstrate respect to me, knowing that such power can be used for or against them.

This stands in marked contrast to a collaborative process such as mediation, in which the conflicting individuals retain control of the process and the outcome. They decide if and when they will meet, what rules will be followed, and who will determine if an agreement will be made and the conflict resolved. The differences between adjudication and collaboration cannot be overemphasized.

## Attributes and Limitations of Adjudication

Before moving on, it might be helpful for counselors to understand some of the general attributes of adjudication. An adjudication process such as arbitration is especially appropriate when people are unable to resolve conflict in a collaborative way, yet want to resolve it in a process that is efficient and has great integrity. Arbitration is usually private, and is always predictable in the sense that a decision will be rendered. It is efficient, at least compared with litigation, and generally is quite satisfying to both sides, who see it as credible and fair.[20]

On the other hand, adjudication has severe limitations, including the potential to be divisive rather than collaborative. Because of the adversarial positioning, it can separate, rather than unite the two sides, producing a winner and a loser, rather than bringing about reconciliation. It should be used, then, as an alternative only when a more collaborative process is unsuccessful.

## THE IMPACT OF THE CHOSEN PROCESS

While counselors, ministers, and even lawyers might wonder how Christians ought to attempt the resolution of conflict apart from litigation, the reality is that Christians have a number of viable alternatives. The challenge is to educate ourselves about the alternatives and learn to use them. Again, it is the choice of process that is critical.

The dramatic impact of encouraging an appropriate dispute-resolution process was illustrated recently in a case handled by a Christian lawyer who represented a large religious private school on the East Coast. She had been retained when a disgruntled former employee, a Christian, had filed suit against the school and its headmaster for defamation and emotional distress associated with her termination. The lawyer outlined her work in leading the two sides of the conflict toward nonlitigation alternatives. Recognizing that she had little choice but to answer the lawsuit, the attorney nevertheless began immediately encouraging conciliation, another word generally used to describe a mediation process. She described her efforts this way:

In a letter, we outlined the potential legal claims the school had against the employee and the reasons it had not sought to resolve these through the courts. We proposed several alternatives to pursuing litigation including extending procedural dates to allow the parties, without counsel present, to seek to resolve their dispute between themselves. If that failed, the parties would submit the dispute to non-binding conciliation with the . . . Christian Conciliation Service. Follow-up phone calls resulted in much saber rattling and vehement objections to truncating a full-blown litigation war. In the opposing counsel's view, proffering conciliation as an alternative to litigation meant we considered our legal position weak.

Months of litigation followed—much of it hostile. A corporate lawyer by trade and nature, I found the process frustrating and discouraging. Telephone calls with opposing counsel invariably were acerbic and even lacking professional courtesy. We were in a war, and the guns were blazing. But we had different objectives. She wanted to win $2 million for her client. I wanted to see the parties reconciled to each other and to Jesus.[21]

After months of battle, the lawyer describing this case said she felt like a persistent suitor whose overtures were perpetually rebuffed. The opposing side finally agreed to meet with a representative from the Christian Conciliation Service, telling the corporate lawyer she was doing it to "get you off my back." The attorney described what then occurred:

[The] discernment and mercy of the [Christian Conciliation Service] representatives were like soothing balm on the wounds. Because opposing counsel was Jewish, [one] repeatedly explained how the conciliation process was rooted in the Old Testament. During that meeting, the conciliation process began, and opposing counsel and her client agreed to a non-binding conciliation.[22]

Thankfully, through a frank exchange of perspectives, a great deal of listening, and the sensitive creation of an acceptable solution, the disputes were in fact resolved. The attorney described what happened next:

At the end of the conciliation all of us, attorneys, conciliators, parties and insurance representative, joined hands in a prayer of a thanksgiving for what God had done to resolve the parties' dispute and renew their relationship. As I approached my litigation adversary, she came forward eagerly and asked my forgiveness for the way she had responded throughout the litigation process. I asked her forgiveness for the bitterness and resentment I had harbored towards her, and we parted as friends.[23]

The attorney summed up the effort to encourage a more biblical and humane process this way:

Because the issues are never clear, and the fault is often on both sides, our desire as peacemakers in the midst of the litigation process should be for faith that God can move even the most adamant opponents toward reconciliation.[24]

People in conflict will make decisions regarding the handling of that conflict either deliberately or passively. It may be their most important decision. Those assisting in this time of crisis can minister to them by encouraging the more creative and humane processes of negotiation and mediation—processes that are described later in this book.

# CHAPTER SIX

## CAPTURING THE
## VALUE OF RELATIONSHIPS

SEVERAL YEARS AGO, two businesses found themselves in the midst of heated and divisive conflict. While they had entered into a decade-long contract valued at more than ten million dollars, at the end of the first year they were embroiled in an argument over a thirty-thousand-dollar bill presented from one to the other. As is typical of much legal conflict, they began arguing over the thirty thousand dollars in light of provisions contained in their written agreement and were appalled that it gave little guidance to them for resolution. Lawyers were contacted, and the adversarial legal system took hold of their dispute. The attorneys aggressively prepared the case for trial as each side anticipated years of litigation and tens of thousands of dollars in legal cost in an argument over the thirty-thousand-dollar payment.

While the lawyers were digging in for the long siege, a student law clerk working on the case asked the simple question, "Why are these two businesses that have established a ten-year relationship going to battle over a nominal amount of money and a relatively unimportant principle?" His question caused the lawyers to reevaluate their actions; a short time later, they met to mediate a resolution to the claim. In less than six hours, a mediator found a way to draw upon the value of the business relationship to bring about a resolution to the dispute.

The principles of dispute resolution point to the importance and value of relationships—a value which motivates people to engage in the hard work of reconciliation. Those reconciled relationships in turn reflect biblical teachings and Christianity in an appropriate and influential way.

Before describing particular approaches to reconciliation later in the book, this chapter explores the characteristics of relationships that provide the basis for conflict management. The effective conflict manager seeks to develop these characteristics between the two sides, even while dealing with emotional and acute conflict. In addition to impacting the problem at hand, such characteristics also set the stage for opponents to handle future conflicts without assistance.

In marriage, the value of relationship in reconciliation is obvious. Counselors and pastors involved in the ministry of reconciliation among marriage partners recognize that a commitment to the relationship is the key to resolving many conflicts. When such commitment exists, it provides the deep well from which strength can be drawn and tremendous challenges overcome. When such a resource does not exist, too often it is impossible to find the basis for even an attempt at reconciliation.[1]

While adjudication focuses on the history of the relationship and thus decides which person might be right or wrong, collaborative dispute-resolution processes such as mediation focus on the future of the relationship. They emphasize the value of working through conflict so that the relationship is maintained. That focus on relationship is too often lost in the heat of an adversarial fight.

Acknowledging that a relationship can positively influence the resolution of conflict, what characteristics might that relationship have? Acceptance, communication, understanding, credibility, forgiveness, and sacrifice are among the most beneficial characteristics a mediator can help people develop as they work to resolve conflict.

## ACCEPTANCE

Simply defined, acceptance is the willingness of each person in a relationship to recognize the other's right to exist. It is also each person's willingness to recognize the merit of dialogue about the issues affecting them. This acceptance is essential to any conflict-resolution process.

Acceptance is in sharp contrast to the attitude which refuses to acknowledge the other's existence or to engage in communication regarding the conflict. Such an attitude makes any form of conflict resolution impossible.

Consider the generations of conflict between the Palestinians and the Israelis. For decades, Israel has refused to accept the territorial rights of the Palestinians, and the Palestinians have refused to accept Israel as a nation. Neither side considers the other worthy of negotiation. Regardless of the two sides' feelings about the issues of that conflict, reasonable people must question the long-term potential of policies that reflect such attitudes.

Unless the Palestinians and Israelis recognize the other as having at least a nominal right to exist, and unless they consider the other worthy of dialogue on the issues that separate them, the violence and death will go on and on. Resolution will not occur without the *acceptance* of each side by the other.[2]

The idea of acceptance may appear to demand more than people in conflict are willing to give; yet acceptance of their opponents may in fact be a genuinely self-serving decision. If the individuals conclude that they will be better off with the conflict resolved than with it continuing, they probably will want to make decisions that increase the likelihood of resolution. In that case, acceptance is a prerequisite for progress, and therefore reflects appropriate self-interest.

## Acceptance Is Not Concurrence

Acceptance should not be interpreted as concurrence with values or agreement between those locked in conflict. This is illustrated in numerous biblical teachings. One of Christ's primary attributes was his willingness to accept others. This provided the basis for calling Zacchaeus down from the tree.[3] It also allowed Christ to respond compassionately to the Samaritan woman at Jacob's well.[4]

Neither the publican, the woman at the well, nor any of us deserved acceptance due to our merit. Each fell short of the mark. But with each person, acceptance formed the threshold of reconciliation. By accepting Zacchaeus, Christ had the opportunity to teach. By accepting the Samaritan woman, he was able to minister. By accepting us, Christ provides the avenue for our salvation.

## Acceptance Must Be Complete and Unconditional

As defined above, acceptance must be complete and unconditional. What happens, for instance, if grown children turn their backs on their parents' teachings, values, or desired behaviors? The parents have two different options in that circumstance: One is to withdraw acceptance, even to the point of disowning the prodigal children. The other option is to continue to accept them, even though their children's behavior, actions, or values may be in great conflict with the parents'. The latter is difficult; but the former seems untenable.

Again, this acceptance does not demand approval of conduct, concurrence with values, or agreement as to how something should be done. Nor does acceptance in the context of conflict resolution suggest that conflict will be avoided. Acceptance does lay the foundation on which other aspects of the relationship can develop: the ability to communicate, an openness to understand, the willingness to forgive. When these attributes are in place, they become the basis for reconciliation.

### COMMUNICATION

When acceptance is established in the relationship, communication adds the next building block for reconciliation.

Communication is that process of verbal and nonverbal exchange that sends and receives messages between people. Communication can be effective or ineffective, constructive or destructive. Through the communication process, understanding is developed and credibility is enhanced—or perspectives are attacked, and relationships are destroyed.[5]

To create and maintain the type of relationships in which positive conflict resolution can occur, effective communication is mandatory. This does not mean that every member of the family, group, or community enjoys talking with each other. It only suggests that if a relationship is important, then effective, constructive communication must be maintained.

As the decade of the 1980s came to a close, events, especially those in Eastern Europe, brought about profound political changes, and declarations by leaders of both the United States and the Soviet Union that the Cold War had ended. As bitter as the relationship between those two countries had been during the previous decades, a wise decision was maintained to always have an open line of communication. Recognizing that a lack of communication could lead to nuclear war, diplomatic relationships were continued, even when the countries were at complete odds over political and military questions.

The power of communication is seen not only in its contribution to conflict avoidance, but also in conflict resolution. A surprising result of the four hundred neighborhood justice centers and community mediation programs mentioned earlier is that administrators report that many of the tens of thousands of cases handled monthly are resolved without a face-to-face hearing. The influence of a third party in starting the communication process between those involved in the conflict is often all that is needed to achieve resolution.[6]

It may be helpful here to evaluate communication in terms of the people, the substance, and the environment in which it occurs, and then to take a closer look at the actual process of communication.

**The People**

Those seeking to bring about reconciliation can help by asking who needs to be included in the communication process related to a particular conflict. In most cases, those affected by a decision ought to be involved. That may mean consulting with a much larger group than originally anticipated. But it is usually worth the effort, because if those people are not participants in the communication process, they will be less accepting of the result of such communication.[7]

## The Substance

Counselors should also consider what is communicated, as well as who is involved. As in all things, Solomon was wise regarding the substance of communication. In Proverbs 15:2, he noted, "The tongue of the wise commends knowledge, but the mouth of the fool gushes folly."

Especially in acute conflict, prudence should be evident. I have been impressed by the "Four Way Test" adopted by Rotary International that provides helpful guidance to its members around the world. Comprised of four questions about the substance of the communication, the test asks: 1. Is it the truth? 2. Is it fair to all concerned? 3. Will it build good will and better relationships? 4. Will it be beneficial to all concerned?[8]

## The Environment

As a mediator working with people involved in acute conflict, I have found that the environment—the location, physical surroundings, and atmosphere—has a great deal of influence on communication. For example, when dealing with lawyers on a business matter, the formality of a conference room seems consistent with the general expectations and needs. In other circumstances, however, I have found that more informal environments contribute to the communication process. The rose garden adjoining a state capitol building provided the environment in which a six-million-dollar dispute was mediated between a state government and a major corporation. In another dispute, early-morning breakfasts at a local coffee shop during a lengthy and complex mediation process provided needed distractions within an environment where the individuals controlled themselves. Moving my "office" to a public park for a mediation also has been an effective device. In that context, the people involved in the conflict were affected by the openness around them; as a result, their emotional, raised voices which would have been disruptive in a small conference room were almost insignificant.

The point is not to suggest a particular place or circumstance, but to encourage thoughtful consideration of the environment in which communication takes place, recognizing that it can help bring about effective exchanges between the parties.

## The Process of Communication

People in conflict must be given the opportunity to "tell their stories." This, of course, is basic to most counseling. People who need help to achieve reconciliation are involved in conflict—perhaps heavily invested in it. They need a forum where verbal expressions of that conflict can be carried out, not only with the other person, but also with a third party who will be an empathic listener.[9]

It is common for counselors to begin mediation by laying ground rules and establishing a framework for the process. But those first ten to fifteen minutes of the counselor's talk may not even be heard by the people involved in the conflict. They are waiting to get their stories on the table, and wise counselors, ministers, and conflict managers know that the conflict will never be resolved until these stories are told.

One's interest in telling his or her side of the story is usually balanced by the other side's disinterest in listening. Yet, successful resolution depends on both occurring, so it is critical to emphasize the value of listening skills. This means basic listening and counseling techniques are essential. I find an extremely helpful technique in mediation is to ask the listening side to summarize what the talking side has said. Typically, summarization never actually takes place, because the "listener" will admit to not listening, but then will be more attentive.

### UNDERSTANDING

After acceptance is established and deliberate efforts at communication begin, the potential exists for understanding. This occurs when the individuals gain sufficient insight regarding the conflict and each other to identify both their similarities and differences, and to have some sense as to where these attributes originate.

Roger Fisher and Scott Brown in their popular book *Getting Together*, which inspired this chapter, suggest that differences cannot be resolved without understanding them.[10] This may appear to be only a restatement of the obvious, but it is important. In situations of conflict, we typically expend great effort to persuade our opponents where we are "coming from," but we fail to invest in similar understanding about their side of the argument. In short, we don't understand them, and we don't understand the problem from their perspective—even though such understanding may be critical to solving "our" problem.

Corporations often fail to carefully understand a potential market and thus meet with economic disaster. Several years ago a Southern California retail drugstore chain, Sav-On Drugs, was bought out by Osco Drugs, a larger chain from another part of the country. One of the first moves Osco Drugs made was to change the name of all Sav-On stores to Osco. This was followed by an immediate and substantial drop in sales in the chain's Southern California outlets, especially those located in areas of substantial Hispanic population. Searching for the cause, company officials discovered that the word "Osco" is pronounced the same as the Spanish word *asco*, which is loosely translated "make me sick." No wonder potential customers were hesitant to continue trading at the store! Osco Drugs immediately restored the Sav-On name in many market areas, and continues to operate successfully. In that case, as in many others, the conflict was created by an innocent lack of understanding; it was resolved when communication made understanding possible.

Behind the suggestion that understanding is crucial in resolving or managing conflict is the admission that we simply do not "know it all." If we are to be successful in resolution and reconciliation, we must have a "learner's spirit."

In conducting training programs for thousands of people each year through the Institute for Dispute Resolution, I am always interested to note the contrast in spirit among participants. Most individuals are eagerly engaged in the learning process. Occasionally, however, someone attends the program not to learn anything but to teach us all! Usually this person—most often male—can't sit still. He must answer every question. He has great confidence in himself and an overwhelming view of how much others could benefit by his contribution. In reality, however, he never gets the attention and admiration he desires from other program participants, because he has failed to communicate any interest in understanding the others' experiences or insights.

Successful conflict resolution requires both sides to have a sense of exploration and inquiry that seeks to be educated by the other person as well as to educate him or her. This education is how individuals gain substantive knowledge and encourage others to become more responsive to them.

Fisher and Brown suggest that we focus our understanding in three areas: interests, values, and perceptions.[11] Each merits brief discussion as we add understanding to the building blocks of relationships.

## Understanding Interests

In a later chapter, we will examine the concept of "interests" and show how they may be most commonly thought of as needs—needs that are not always tangible, concrete, and easy to define, but are very real to the individual. Since needs drive conflict, they usually must be understood and addressed before conflict is resolved.

It is important to point out that disputants who have a greater understanding of their opponent's needs, goals, and motivations will be in a far more powerful position. They can then offer solutions that are more responsive and thus resolve the differences between the two sides.

A common dispute between a teen-ager and parent shows how understanding can help two people arrive at a creative solution to their conflict. Suppose the teen-ager is a boy who wants to use the family car on Saturday afternoon. This plan could quickly turn into an adversarial situation if the boy's parent—his father, perhaps—responds negatively. One can imagine them arguing as they deal with the issues of the conflict.

If, on the other hand, they seek to understand each other's interests in the matter, they discover that the son's interest is to

72

use the car to get to the mall, while the father's concern is being left without transportation. By understanding these interests, the two may come up with a number of ways to resolve their differences short of arguing. The issue causes them to argue, but understanding the interests causes them to be creative in finding a solution. As a result, they may decide that the father will drive his son to the mall. That way he keeps his own mobility, and the son gets to go to the mall.

## Understanding Perceptions

In addition to interests, we must understand perceptions— how people view a situation or circumstance. Obviously people view the same situation from a perspective that reflects their own experiences, background, and goals.

Several years ago, a major three-party dispute occurred that involved high emotion and acute conflict. Three separate groups were viewing the same objects quite differently, and their descriptions of those objects reflected great diversity. To one, the objects were characterized as "highway hazards." To another, the same items were "renewable resources." And to a third, they were "testaments to God." Can you guess what they were describing? Trees!

To the engineers who wanted to remove them for road construction, they were "highway hazards." To the timber industry, they were "renewable resources." To the naturalists they were "testaments to God." If something as simple as trees could generate such different perspectives, think what differences could occur in interpreting more complex events or relationships! Obviously, understanding perceptions is critical in building productive relationships.

## Understanding Values

In addition to interests and perceptions, we need to understand values, especially differing values that may impact our relationships. Values reflect our basic characters and the importance we attach to specific personal characteristics. Shared values become a resource the counselor can draw upon to help people manage conflict. On the other hand, when individuals involved in conflict have different values, especially values related to culture or religion, they can be great impediments to successful dispute resolution.

In teaching negotiation skills to business managers, it is extremely difficult to convince those who want to conduct themselves in a cooperative way that such methods will never be effective with a truly competitive opponent. This ineffectiveness is caused by the two sides' widely differing values. The cooperative negotiator values agreement and relationship far higher than the true competitive, whose highest value in this situation is winning. The cooperative person would like the more competitive negotiator to be won over to a mutually satisfactory agreement through respectful treatment, compromise, and fair dealing. Such clashing values bring great challenge to the negotiation arena.

Great contrasts exist in intercultural values. The Institute for Dispute Resolution is studying this contrast in seeing how conflict related to mass tort disasters—airplane crashes—is handled in different cultures. In this study we have discovered great contrast in the values exhibited after the August 1985 crash of a Delta jumbo jet in Dallas, Texas, followed by the crash of a Japan Air Lines jumbo jet in Japan ten days later. Reflecting the values of the Japanese culture, after the JAL disaster, the president of the company resigned, then personally visited and apologized to each family who had lost someone in the crash. The airline made voluntary settlement payments to each family within several months, and, reflecting the values of the culture, no lawsuits were filed in Japan by the families of Japanese victims.[12]

In contrast, after the Delta crash, responsibility was denied by the airline, and while some cash settlements were offered, Delta's insurers took a highly adversarial stance in the ensuing litigation. Years later, the litigation still continues at the federal appellate court level.[13]

These opposite responses reflect the different values that are important to these two cultures. Generally, the Japanese value a sense of relationship, and they don't want anything to fracture their community. So they are more willing to show responsibility and accountability—values which could protect the community from divisive actions.

In contrast, Americans seem to value a frontier-style approach to justice. We seem to believe that conflict should be resolved adversarially, so providing that kind of mechanism has become a priority for us, even though it can fracture relationships. We put the burden on the side bringing the action to demonstrate the responsibility of the other, as opposed to creating cultural values that encourage those responsible to voluntarily accept responsibility when something goes wrong. Our natural response is to defend ourselves against that proof.

Our values—who we are, how we prioritize basic personal characteristics—will influence our willingness to resolve conflict. So it is essential that consideration of values must be part of effective conflict resolution.

## Understanding History

It also is important to understand the history of the people involved in conflict, because that history provides a context from which their interests, perceptions, and values flow.

In mediating an angry dispute between two factions at a large church, I was puzzled by how unyielding and suspicious the leaders of the two sides appeared to be. Both were set in their positions regarding the minister; but as you can imagine, those positions were on different sides. To one leader, the minister had to go if the church was to continue. To the other, the minister had to stay if the church was to "weather the storm." Each grew red-faced and belligerent when dealing with the conflict.

In meeting individually with each of these two leaders, it became apparent that their histories, which in this case were quite similar, dramatically affected their handling of the disagreement. Both had extensive military and law-enforcement backgrounds, which led them to be decisive in their judgment, defensive when threatened, and highly committed to their positions. Historically, those characteristics had served them quite well—in fact may have helped them survive life-threatening career experiences. However, those same characteristics, molded

75

throughout their lives, prevented their resolving conflict in a completely different environment, one that demanded consensual decisions, cooperative treatment, and flexibility.

History, when understood, explains behavior and helps the counselor understand its impact on the process of reconciliation. Understanding interests, values, perceptions, and history adds to the foundation for relationships that can support resolution.

## Credibility

Another component of relationships is credibility. Unfortunately, by the time most conflicts have impacted relationships, whatever credibility each person had with the other has dissipated. Yet credibility is absolutely necessary if people are to trust, have confidence in, and be able to rely upon each other. Three concepts foster this credibility in relationships.

*Trustworthiness.* All of us have experienced moments when we question our ability to trust another person, or, on the other hand, when our ability to trust someone is greatly enhanced. Many times as we move through life our basic presumptions about how people will respond to a circumstance are either confirmed or denied.

This was demonstrated for me several years ago in the early-morning hours of a cold, snowy, January night. My dad was helping my family move from Minnesota to Oregon, and he and I were taking turns driving the diesel truck carrying our belongings. In northern Idaho, we faced the infamously steep "Fourth of July Pass" and recognized the absolute necessity for tire chains—which we did not possess. Luckily, when we pulled into a small, one-bay service station, we found what we needed.

The setting tugged at our emotions as the family of the station attendant slept in its car in the service bay, perhaps with no other place to go to avoid the winter night. While the attendant was finishing the arduous task of installing chains on a large truck, Dad suggested we pay him in cash, anticipating out loud that the attendant would probably pocket the money rather then ring up the sale. My outlook about human nature was strengthened, however, when the attendant methodically wrote up the ticket and placed the substantial cash payment in the register. By doing so, he showed the attribute most basic to credibility, the ability to be trusted. Without knowing him well, I felt better about how he might have installed those chains, based upon how he handled the money.

In a matter of moments, the attendant had demonstrated his trustworthiness—a value that even in this day of lengthy contracts, extensive written confirmation, and verbose documentation provides the basis for most good working relationships.

*Consistent Message.* Coupled with the evidence of trustworthiness is the need for messages that are consistent with the actions that will follow them.

In late summer 1990, the world felt the grip of danger as the nation of Iraq militarily took over the tiny kingdom of Kuwait. This book was completed before the crisis moved beyond a tense standoff between Iraq and virtually all nations of the world. Even so, the lack of credibility resulting from inconsistent messages obviously characterized the early difficulties of that international crisis. One day, the Iraqi government proclaimed that the thousands of Americans and other foreigners in that country were "guests" and would be treated accordingly. The next day, the world press reported that many of those same individuals were being transported to key military and industrial installations to serve as "human shields" against an attack by American forces. On another day, an announcement promised that foreign women and children would be released from Iraq; but the next day stringent conditions made such release practically impossible.

Regardless of the ultimate outcome, the inconsistency between Iraq's messages and its actions virtually eliminated any credibility for its government.

*Predictable Consequences.* Finally, credibility is built on predictable consequences—following through on what one says will be done. Predictability stems from a history of encounters and from the consistency of actions with words. Whether the consequences are positive or negative, when they are predictable, they become something to be dealt with in resolving conflict.

During my college days, I worked at a juvenile detention facility where the young detainees were told that if they left the facility before their stay was up, they would be brought back and their "sentence" would start all over again. After a couple of persons tested the system—and the fortitude of those who administered it—the outcome became most predictable. Sooner or later, those juveniles who escaped from the premises were in fact apprehended and returned. And then they started the program again at its beginning. The predictability of the consequences to the boys' actions became clear. This technique did not result in great regard for the administrators, themselves; but it did result in great respect for the administrators' credibility.

When applied to conflict, credibility is important for the disputants to have if they are to take each other seriously. Recently, I began work as the chairman of the construction committee involved with a major addition to our church. Such a job is neither an enviable position or a sought-after assignment. But as they say, "somebody has to do it." After a few weeks of work, it became apparent that the project as designed and already approved by the city was not the facility needed by the congregation. Nor would it be funded by the congregation. So my first task was to undo almost four years of work.

I recall one meeting with a key player when he was expressing his concern at the turn of events and his sense of frustration about the future—which included the possibility that someone else would be hired for the revised project. Since I represented the congregation—the main focus of his frustration—I knew that my only hope for establishing a relationship with him was to work slowly and methodically, developing credibility.

At one point in that conversation, I looked him in the eye and said, "I know your feelings about all that has transpired, and your suspicion about all the events that have taken place. I cannot instantly put everything back together. I don't control the committees in the congregation that are working on the project; but this I can assure you: I will always be available to discuss the matter with you, I will always be honest with you, and I will always represent things accurately to you." That promise did not result in any magical solution to conflict, or relieve his feelings of anger or frustration; but it did establish credibility as part of the foundation for our working relationship—and our new friendship.

## FORGIVENESS

In addition to acceptance, communication, understanding, and credibility, an attitude of forgiveness is very important in relationships where reconciliation can take place.

If we define life in its simplest terms, we might conclude that we cannot control a threatening future, and we cannot alter a troublesome past. So, as Christians, we turn to God as the one who can control, direct, and lead us, into whose hands we can put that future. We also turn to God in the hope that the difficulties of the past can be overcome, even though we know the past, itself, cannot be changed.

Ironically, while we cannot change our own pasts, we do have the ability to dramatically impact the pasts of others. We do that through forgiveness—which is only meaningful if there has been an event so damaging that it is truly needed. Most everyday conflicts that occur on the freeway, at the job, or in the home are not this damaging. In contrast, the events that need forgiveness are those that cause us to realize the depth of the hurt, sense the immorality of the action, and feel the unfairness of the result. It is when one is suffering through such an event that forgiveness becomes necessary for positive relationships.

Forgiveness necessitates a decision to slice out that part of our history—that event, that action which breached our relationship with the other person involved. We may not forget it, but we can decide that it will not preclude our future relationship. To the extent that the relationship has the potential for healing, such will only take place if we can isolate and eliminate the instance of abuse or unfairness.

Finally, forgiveness involves beginning again. It recognizes the potential to rebuild the relationship over time as the effects of the surgery heals. It may not be immediate; it may not be quick. And the relationship may be rebuilt in a different way than it was before the conflict. Nevertheless, a rebuilding process begins that can ultimately lead to reconciliation and a renewed relationship.

In assisting a group of attorneys to settle a major lawsuit between a corporation and a former employee who had been severely mistreated, I had the occasion, in private, to hear the president of that large corporation express his genuine sorrow that the company had not been more compassionate and fair with the employee. I believe his expression was motivated by his personal evaluation of the circumstance and not his interest in just avoiding legal action. At one point I asked him, "Have you ever shared those feelings with the former employee?" My belief was that such an expression, while not in itself resolving the conflict, would have a dramatic impact on the people involved, even those negotiating a resolution of the dispute. By his reaction one would think that this suggestion was a completely novel idea. Yet I wondered aloud, "What would it do to this conflict if you said those words your attorneys are afraid to say—'We're sorry. We were wrong. We want to make it right'?"

While an apology did not resolve the conflict which had gone on for years, there was a moment when the company president communicated with the former employee, not as an adversary in a lawsuit, but as a person who sincerely regretted his organization's treatment of that individual. It was a poignant moment, which lay the foundation for forgiveness, and will have tremendous meaning as that conflict moves toward resolution.

Forgiveness takes us off the escalator of revenge. Forgiveness creates the possibility of a new future. Forgiveness allows the relationship to be restored and the people to move forward to a new, more secure future.

We know the biblical instruction on forgiveness. In Matthew, we are instructed to forgive, and told that as we forgive, our Father will forgive us. If we fail to forgive, there is the clear indication that he will not forgive us. That is not an easy passage to accept, but it's one that reflects the necessity of forgiveness in our relationships.

## SACRIFICE

The last characteristic that sets the stage for reconciliation is sacrifice. The popular Christian sociologist Anthony Campolo admonishes us to be committed and to sacrifice when it comes to those in need.[14] Marriage and family counselors encourage commitment and sacrifice as the basis for a strong family. Church leaders hope those in a local congregation involve themselves sacrificially in giving and in service.

In turning to Scripture, we find numerous examples of sacrifice and its impact on human relationships. Jesus was in conflict with the Pharisees when, at the temple on the Sabbath, he wanted to heal a man. His desire and the Jewish law were in complete opposition, but Jesus was willing to sacrifice adherence to the law in order to minister to the man in need.

We see Christ as one who might have been a popular, successful, and even financially secure leader of his time. His priority, however, was to sacrifice those attributes, which so many in our culture strive for, in order to serve the poor, heal the sick, and bring spiritual riches to those who followed him.

When we think about God, the idea of sacrifice looms large in our consciousness. God was willing to sacrifice his son so that we might be saved.

The reality of sacrifice is brought down to its most personal level when we recognize that our most important relationships are those characterized by commitment and sacrifice. Think about the people you are closest to—your spouse, your family, and your friends. I would conjecture that many of those relationships were originally based upon acceptance, but that along the way commitment developed and even mutual sacrifice. Because those relationships are forged out of such sacrifice, they can withstand the challenges of time.

The power of sacrifice in establishing relationships under the most difficult of circumstances was made clear to me several years ago. My wife was enduring a very difficult pregnancy with our first child—one that had her hospitalized on numerous occasions and confined to bed for many weeks. That in itself was one act of loving sacrifice, as she took steps to protect the health of the unborn child. Meanwhile, at the church where we worshiped was a man with whom I disagreed about almost everything. We were from different church backgrounds. We were from different parts of the county. We had vastly different life and religious experiences, all of which led us to polite tolerance, but certainly not close friendship.

One day, late in the afternoon, there was a knock on our door. It was Larry, with a full dinner he had spent the afternoon cooking especially for us. The awkwardness in accepting his gift was only exceeded by the generosity of his spirit. His act of love caused me to change, forever, my view of him and establish what will always be, from my perspective, a Christian bond. Such a bond came not from our agreement on religious issues or common experiences in life, but rather from his sacrifice—that kind of sacrifice that leads to relationship.

Reconciliation does not take place in a vacuum. It stems from the relationships of those involved. While those relationships reflect the diversity of the people in them, the attributes necessary for effectively resolving differences are identifiable. When a relationship is established through acceptance, communication, understanding, credibility, forgiveness, and sacrifice, it has established that possibility.

These first six chapters were written to lay the foundation for the ministry of reconciliation. They were intended to provide reference points from which conflict can be addressed, and resolution and reconciliation can be achieved. The following chapters describe the processes and skills essential to conflict management.

# CHAPTER SEVEN

## NEGOTIATING AGREEMENTS

JUST AS A ROAD MAP IS NECESSARY for traveling in unknown geographic areas, a "map" is also important when negotiating the unpredictable and often unfamiliar area of conflict management. Some would suggest that this map could be a list of tactics to be pulled out and used on an opponent in an effort to "win" at the conflict-resolution table. While such tactics might be valuable in some circumstances, a more productive approach would be a road map of suggestions that could be used by everyone to move toward a common destination. This would allow the conflict to be resolved through mutually acceptable solutions.

This chapter provides a map of three suggestions for negotiating the way from confrontation to collaboration. They are equally applicable in addressing disputes in the home, church, workplace, or community. They establish the stage for efficient and effective conflict management.

## ADDRESS THE PROBLEM, BUT PROTECT THE RELATIONSHIP

When I needed to buy a new car several years ago I took my father and then ten-year-old son to a dealership. After selecting a car that was acceptable, I turned to the salesman and asked what I thought was a reasonable question: "What's your best price for the car?" He looked at me and said he could not give me a price for the car until I was seated in the showroom office. Somewhat surprised, I asked him why not. He answered that if he gave me a price I would leave the lot, take his price to another dealer, and he would lose the sale.

As we discussed his unwillingness to begin the discussion about price, my negotiation-teacher instincts started coming out, and I began suggesting better ways for him to sell cars. Our conversation went back and forth, with our discussion becoming more "enthusiastic," until it attracted the attention of his sales manager. He came over to us and joined in the conversation by asking me why I was being so "hard" on his salesman. I repeated my mini-lecture from Negotiation 101, and in time, the three of us were making quite a spectacle of ourselves—so much so that my son, unsure of what was happening, hid behind a pickup truck while my dad whispered encouragement to me. You can imagine the result of that conflict. The salesman lost a sale, and I left without buying a car—and also without a lot of pride in my actions.

This incident illustrates one common occurrence in conflict management: In many cases, what begins as a rational conversation about the substance of the problem changes into an unproductive, emotional reaction. When that happens, two results are likely to occur.

The first result is an inefficient process. Unable to deal with the substance of the conflict, the participants digress to the point where they have lost all ability to problem-solve and engage instead in personal warfare. Time and energy are spent on arguing rather than on working through conflict to an agreement.

The second result is the destruction of the relationship, which makes working together impossible. In the car incident, by the end of our discussion, I had resolved that I would not buy anything from that salesman, and frankly, I don't imagine he would be inclined to ever sell a car to me.

In order to avoid these harsh results, the participants must continually focus on the substance of the problem, and avoid attacking each other. By doing so, even at a time of great disagreement, relationships can be maintained and problems most effectively resolved.[1]

During his training programs in collaborative negotiation, a colleague, Professor Bryan Johnston, makes an important point about respectful relationships.[2] In examining the processes our society has adopted to resolve conflict, he notes that in courtroom litigation, great respect is shown for the one who makes the decision—the judge. This respect is reflected in the elevation of the judge's bench, the formality of the proceeding, and the participants referring to the judge as "Your Honor."

This show of respect for the decision-maker changes dramatically in less formal processes of dispute resolution, where participants are often verbally abusive, critical, and belligerent to each other. Professor Johnston points out that in the informal process of negotiation, both sides are really the decision-makers. So why, he asks, do they not act in a more respectful way, realizing that doing so would have a dramatic impact on their ability to resolve the conflict?

Scripture demonstrates an obvious focus on problems while protecting the relationships. Christ was critical of the prostitute's behavior, but gentle with her feelings. He detested the tactics of Zacchaeus the tax collector, but was willing to eat with him. Christ was burdened by human sin, but loved us enough to die so that we might have life. In each case, he valued people and relationships, even when the focus could have remained on behavior.[3]

To help carry out this biblical example, four related suggestions may help.[4]

### Recognize When the Focus May Be Changing

All of us have been involved in tense and emotional conversations. We have heard that single insulting or offensive comment that changed the course of the entire discussion. An awareness of such a change is the first step in protecting relationships. We must recognize the consequences of letting the course change from the substance to the people, and the damage which will invariably follow.

### Ignore Most Personal Attacks

In many cases, the movement away from the substance of the conflict begins with a personal attack. Part of the destructive value of such an attack is its emotional nature, so the ability to ignore such attacks will eliminate their dramatic effect and usually be enough to discourage their use.[5]

### Agree on the Process

When a change in focus is significant enough to seriously derail the discussion, the individuals may need to temporarily stop working on the substance of the conflict long enough to discuss the process to be used for the rest of the negotiation. This kind of time-out can be of great value in establishing the type of problem-solving communication process to be used. After agreeing upon the process, the parties can return to the substance of the particular problem at hand. This provides the opportunity to agree on a more productive use of time and energy. It may take a considerable period of time to negotiate on process, but it is essential if conflict resolution is to be effective.

### Steer the Talk Back to the Substance

The person who recognizes the change in focus simply may need to steer the other participants back to the substance. An invitation to again discuss the problem will usually be accepted, and the communication will then get back on track.[6]

### Benefits of These Suggestions

These suggestions offer several benefits. The first, most obvious benefit is achieving the end desired. Several years ago, while refinancing a house, I was late in making a sixty-thousand-dollar balloon payment, and I needed the help of someone at a lending institution to quickly process and approve my loan application. A friend referred me to the vice president of a savings and loan, and I made an appointment to see him the following week. I knew that he had the authority to look at my application and immediately approve it, if he so desired.

When I arrived at the savings and loan the next week, the vice president met me with a friendly handshake but said something had come up and he could not spend time with me that afternoon. Then he very quickly passed me off to a much younger employee, who was pleasant, but I doubted if she had been out of school more than a week or two. Literally, all she could do was quote me the current interest rate. I sat across the big desk from her and felt tempted to change the focus of the discussion from the sixty thousand dollars I needed to my dissatisfaction with the treatment I was receiving from that savings and loan. It was only by recognizing the potential risk of that move and then deliberately steering my conversation back to the substance that I avoided what would have been an unproductive focus on the people who were involved. A week later, I returned to the savings and loan and obtained financing for the house.

The second benefit of this process is that it will allow individuals the opportunity to negotiate again, because their relationship will be left intact. It is sometimes surprising to realize how often people find themselves working together again, after a separation of months or years. To a large degree, the ability to work together later is based on how they handled the relationship during their previous encounter. This is even true when the people do not think they will ever see each other again.

A young woman I know worked at a department store in Oregon. Like most employees, she parked across the street from the store and jaywalked across it to enter the side door. One day, after following her usual routine, she arrived in the china department and was at the cash register when a big, burly man walked up and started lambasting her for jaywalking. She stood there passively, just listening, as other employees stopped their work, customers turned and stared, and this individual expressed what seemed to be a world of frustration with her. After

87

he was finished letting her have it, he angrily marched out of the department store.

The man did not know that this woman also was a preschool teacher in the afternoon. At the beginning of each academic year at that preschool, the parents bring their children to meet their new teacher. You can imagine the look on the face of that same man a few days later as he and his three-year-old daughter were introduced to her new teacher—the woman who had jaywalked. After beginning a relationship on the least desirable terms, these two people were brought into a relationship where they would see each other daily and he would entrust his daughter to her care for the next nine months. Gingerly, the young woman and the child's father went forward with their necessary relationship, always feeling the burden of that initial encounter.

The fact is, we never know when we will have to negotiate again. Thus, the ability to focus on the substance while honoring the relationship becomes critically important.[7]

## FOCUS ON INTERESTS, NOT ISSUES OR POSITIONS

Any parent is familiar with hearing two children fight over a single object. A popular illustration which has been included in other books on conflict resolution describes two children who both wanted the only orange in the house. The parent's response to the conflict was to cut the single orange in two pieces, giving one half to each child. This solution appeared at first glance to have been logical and fair. The inadequacy of the approach, however, was revealed when one child peeled the orange, ate the inside, and threw the rind away, while the other child peeled the orange, threw the inside away, and used the rind in a recipe.[8]

The account illustrates an essential concept in resolving conflict. While this approach efficiently and effectively dealt with the *issue* of the conflict—which child would get what portion of the only orange in the house—the parent did not understand the *interests* of each child. A closer examination revealed that one child was interested in eating the inside of an orange; the other child was interested in using an orange rind in a recipe. Had the children's interests been understood, the parent could have increased the satisfaction of both children by dividing the orange in a different manner—without any additional resources. Separating issues and interests is essential in resolving conflict in churches, homes, and communities. It is the first step in reconciliation between people.

What *are* issues and interests? In *Collaborative Negotiation*, William Lincoln presents helpful definitions of these important terms.[9] *Issues*, he says, are those concrete items we discuss as we put deals together or resolve conflict. They tend to be measurable, tangible, and generally negotiable. We base our positions upon our perceptions of how issues ought to be resolved.

The usual response in situations of conflict is to define the issues—and then react to them. For instance, in a church context let's assume there is a movement by some members to remove the minister, withhold financial contributions, or promote the use of a particular version of Scripture. All are tangible issues—we can ascertain the minister's employment, the amount of Sunday's contribution, or the version of the Bible in the pew rack. Church leadership might react to such issues by arguing that the minister must be retained, financial contributions must be increased, or that a traditional version of the Bible must be used in all classes. Often such responses result in both sides digging in for a fight. Once begun, the fight escalates, becomes visible and disruptive, and threatens to harm both the people and the fellowship.

Lincoln suggests that *interests*, on the other hand, relate to needs—those items that are basic to each of us, but which tend to be difficult to measure. Included are items such as financial security, personal safety, recognition, and love—items that are not always tangible, or something we can touch, feel, or define. But interests are always present and very real to the people involved. Many times interests are not negotiable; we will not sell or give them away.

Our need for recognition is one example of an interest. As much as we may attempt to be selfless and even work to avoid attention, we still have a need for recognition. From time to time, we need to be told that we are important to our family, that our effort to serve our church is appreciated, or that our efforts at work are noticed.

In looking at recognition as an *interest*, however, a number of tangible *issues* may emerge, such as what people say to us (tangible expressions of support) or the financial compensation we receive. How such *issues* are handled will probably determine if our *interest* in recognition is met.

Making a clear distinction between the *interests* and the *issues* is essential in understanding conflict and its resolution. When conflict occurs, the issues usually are most easily identified. The interests, however, hold the key to resolution.

By understanding and focusing on the interests, the damage to relationships that often results from issue-focused conflict resolution may be avoided. Returning to the hypothetical church situations presented earlier, the *issue* of the minister's employment might stem from some church members' *interest* in receiving special attention from the current minister which he does not or cannot offer, rather than a personal dislike for the individual. Regarding the *issue* of increased contributions, the members might be minimally contributing because they have an *interest* in greater involvement in the budget process. Finally, concerning the *issue* of the Bible version to be used, some members may feel the *need* to offer children a more "readable" translation for classroom study.

In each of these cases, communication about the interests would take the discussion of the conflict in an entirely different direction than would a discussion of the issues. Dealing with the interests can resolve the issues, or provide ways to satisfy the interests that would be more beneficial to the people involved.[10]

## Techniques for Interest-Based Negotiation

Each year the Institute for Dispute Resolution trains hundreds of lawyers, church leaders, counselors, and managers to separate interests from issues.[11] Through the years, a number of suggestions have emerged for making such a distinction and applying it to negotiations. Interestingly enough, several of these suggestions are easily illustrated in Scripture.

*Resist the Initial Temptation to Discuss Issues.* In Athens, the apostle Paul was greatly distressed to see the city full of idols that had been erected to a variety of gods. The human reaction of Paul might very well have suggested an issue-based, argumentative response. He knew the behavior of the people was inappropriate. But note his careful response as recorded in Acts 17:22–23:

> Men of Athens! I see that in every way you are very religious. For as I walked around and looked carefully at your objects of worship, I even found an altar with this inscription: TO AN UNKNOWN GOD. Now what you worship as something unknown I am going to proclaim to you.

Paul did not immediately lash out at the Athenians by focusing on the issue of their worshiping false gods. Rather, he mentioned the interest in religion he shared with the people, and began his teaching from that perspective. In resisting the temptation to immediately discuss the issue, he found a common interest. While not totally successful in persuading all Athenians to stop worshiping idols, he was able to be heard and influence some who became believers.

*Seek Reasons for Positions.* When issues are raised, they are usually defined by the person's positions relating to them. For instance, if the issue is pay for a job performed, it may be described by how much pay an employee or union demands. If the issue is what color to paint the church classrooms, it may be defined by those who advocate particular colors. If the issue is planning a family vacation, it may be defined by family members taking positions on where each wants to go. Immediate reaction to these positions can cause disagreement or delay, or prevent a discussion of important interests. Interest-based problem-solving is only accomplished when people seek what is behind such positions. Instead of just reacting to the various positions, the effective counselor will attempt to explore their bases, seeking the interests that underlie them.[12]

Not long ago, a woman administrator at a university, angry and tearful, went into the president's office to contest her termination. Within the first five minutes, she made it known that she was extremely upset and intended to sue the university for sexual harassment, sexual discrimination, and unlawful termination of her employment. A typical reaction from many administrators

91

would have been to say, "Fine, we will see you in court!" The administrator might have hoped to discourage the woman's charges by pointing out it would be years before the issue would be decided by a court of law.

In this particular case, instincts were restrained as the lawyer-administrator searched for the reasons behind the woman's anger. In doing so, he learned that she really did not disagree with the basis of the termination, but she had several needs in securing her next position—needs that had not been recognized by those handling the personnel matter. She really was not interested in a lawsuit, but such a threat was the only way she knew to express her dissatisfaction and draw attention to her interests. By searching for the reasons behind the former employee's positions, the lawyer-administrator gained an understanding of her needs, which, in this case, could be satisfied without the university spending additional money.

Months later, she wrote the administrator, and after describing her new position, ended the note by saying, "Thanks for all the help." There is no doubt years of litigation were avoided as a direct result of the administrator's search for reasons behind the teacher's positions. Such collaborative resolution to problems holds far greater promise than an adversarial handling of such matters.[13]

*Ask Questions.* The Gospels describe a number of instances when Jesus opted to ask questions or make gentle statements rather than engage in criticism or argument. When he intervened between the crowd and the prostitute, Christ questioned the sinful nature of the accusers with his statement, "If any one of you is without sin, let him be the first to throw a stone at her" (John 8:7).

In considering the church issues posed earlier, one might ask, "What are the concerns of members about the minister?" or "How could support be increased for the church budget?" or "What reasons are there for using a particular translation of the Bible?" Answers to such questions will provide greater insight into the interests involved, and will ultimately lay the foundation for resolving, rather than escalating the conflict.[14]

*Be Alert to the Unstated.* We do not have the ability to look into people's minds, as Christ did; but we can be aware of both

92

their stated and unstated communication. Sensitivity, especially to what is left unstated, will assist in identifying the interests of the people involved, even if they cannot or will not verbalize those interests, themselves.

A common example of unstated communication is one's unwillingness to express need for recognition. Perhaps someone in an office needs to feel more valued by his or her colleagues. But it might seem too egotistical to march into the boss's office and ask for more recognition. Instead, the employee might start complaining about the location of his or her office, or the need for a bigger desk, issuing demands that escalate into conflict. If the employee's boss is alert to what is being left unstated—that the employee's real interest is in gaining greater appreciation for his or her efforts—a variety of ways might be found to bring the conflict to resolution, without changing offices or buying new furniture.

*Search for Both Common and Different Interests.* Obvious benefits result from discovering common interests and using them as a basis to forge new, creative solutions. Most illustrations in this chapter reflect such discovery. However, the possibilities of using *different* interests to everyone's advantage should not be overlooked. Frankly, different interests often contribute more to conflict resolution than do the common interests.

In the 1970s, two men struggled to resolve bitter conflict between their nations, conflict that had existed for generations. The issue was what to do with the strip of land between their countries. Finally, after ten days of discussions and with the help of a perceptive third party, the Camp David Accords between Israel's Prime Minister Begin and Egypt's President Sadat were announced. The solution to their conflict over the Sinai Peninsula would have been unlikely if both had wanted that piece of land for the same purpose. The key to the successful resolution of the conflict in that case was the discovery that Egypt's interest in the land related to sovereignty—it wanted to fly its flag over that territory. Israel, on the other hand, wanted the land for defensive military purposes, as a buffer zone between the two countries. The solution was to give Egypt sovereignty, but prohibit offensive weapons in that territory.[15]

Had there been common interests in either sovereignty or military control, an acceptable solution would have been more difficult to achieve. The different interests, defined only after several days of hard work, created the environment in which creative solutions could be developed.[16] When resolving conflict in the church, community, or family, counselors should look for the opportunity created by differences, as well as the power of common interests. Both can lead to resolution.

So far in this chapter, we've discussed two suggestions on our road map leading to reconciliation. First, we described the benefits of focusing on the substance of the problem while protecting the relationship; next we looked at the advantages of examining the interests of the conflicting individuals. Now, with the focus of the dispute-resolution process fixed on the substance of the differences and the identification of each person's interests, the stage is set to move the individuals toward agreement.

## SEEK CREATIVE, JOINT SOLUTIONS

Not long ago, I was browsing through an import store in Seattle—the kind you find in the warehouse district selling everything from dishes to rattan furniture. Pausing in the toy aisle to look for souvenirs for my children, my attention was drawn to a small, woven tube that was open at each end. I quickly recalled the challenge of this toy when, after putting my two index fingers in the holes, I could not pull them out! My anxiety grew as I became aware of others observing the predicament of a man in a three-piece suit who was unable to free himself. But the harder I pulled, the tighter the tube grasped my fingers; I could not pull them loose.

In time, I remembered how to escape. You may recall the toy, too, and know that the only way to free your fingers is to push them inward, releasing the hold of the tube. That is not the solution you think of first, however!

That tube offers a basic lesson in conflict resolution. After recognizing the issues and understanding the interests, we need to seek creative solutions, and not respond automatically to the obvious solution, which may not be the best—or even viable.

When my five-year-old daughter recently sat on my lap and shared the story of baby Moses—at least as she remembered it—I was struck by the creative solution Moses' mother developed to what was a life-threatening problem. As Exodus recounts, had Pharaoh discovered the baby, the law would have required that Moses be killed. Imagining myself in that position, I am not sure what I would have done if the life of my son had been threatened. Perhaps I would have tried to flee the country, or attempted to raise him secretly in my home. I probably would not have thought about the creative and daring approach which cast baby Moses adrift in the Nile River, to be found by Pharaoh's daughter and brought up by the baby's own mother in the king's palace.[17] That solution was either God-given, or the result of creative thinking—or both. It is the kind of thinking that goes beyond initial positions and reactions to discover a creative option.

To achieve creative solutions, people must first recognize that their perceptions dramatically limit their choices. When conducting training programs, I often ask participants to engage in a quick exercise which illustrates this point quite well. Below are nine dots. The task is to connect all nine dots by drawing four straight lines. You cannot lift your pencil once you begin. (Since this illustration has been used for several years, you may have seen the answer. Before getting too self-confident, though, remember that there are at least three solutions!)

· · ·

· · ·

· · ·

The answer appears in this chapter's endnotes.[18] The obvious lesson is that you must go beyond the mind-defined box if you are to be successful in completing the exercise.[19] The principle is equally true in conflict resolution. Possible solutions must reflect energetic and creative thinking. People must go beyond the obvious, past the certain, and into the realm of increased possibilities, rather than argue over shallow conclusions.[20]

## Invent Options

Creating helpful options may be easiest if a two-step process is used. The first step is to invent options. This brainstorming activity provides the opportunity to openly suggest ideas, no matter how practical or impractical, to increase the number of possible solutions. Given any problem, there is a multitude of possible solutions, many of which will not be considered unless there is a "safe" way for them to be expressed and considered. Brainstorming, then soliciting and listening without judgment, is an excellent technique.

**Develop Options**

The second step in creative thinking is to develop or assess the list of options to determine which are indeed possible. Disputants, perhaps with the assistance of a third party, should be encouraged to mentally examine each possible solution to determine if it realistically should be considered. It is important to emphasize here that this stage should be insulated as much as possible from participants' judgmental perceptions. The focus should be on the *potential* of each solution, not its desirability.

Developing ideas can be a homework exercise. It may involve contact with outside people who possess expertise in a particular area. It may require an investment of substantial time and energy, focused more on the solution and less on the conflict.[21]

In 1987, an incident illustrated the need to develop these kinds of creative options. The press widely reported that a city in New York attempted to dispose of garbage by loading 150 tons of it on a barge to be delivered elsewhere. Not surprising, after the garbage was loaded and ready to go, those in charge were unable to find a jurisdiction that would accept it. The barge then went on a three-month odyssey from New York, down the Atlantic seaboard, around Florida to New Orleans, and finally back up the East Coast to the same town in New York, where the garbage was then unloaded and buried. The town's first idea had not been developed before it was acted upon. It was a creative solution—but not a viable one![22]

Resolving conflict, or assisting others who need assistance in doing so, requires substantial creativity. Although it can be blocked by emotions or issue-based debate, when creativity is added to an environment where relationships are protected and underlying interests are considered, it can be the magic that brings the conflict-resolution process to a successful conclusion.

Perhaps one last illustration would be helpful in encouraging the collaborative negotiation approach to managing conflict. Several years ago a church instituted a separate worship period for young children during the Sunday morning services. It was designed to offer a vital and relevant experience for children. That innovation was met with considerable disagreement, however, because some members believed quite strongly that children should be present with their families during the entire worship service.

If stated as positions, those in favor and those against could have had considerable disagreement and watched that disagreement develop into serious congregational conflict. Churches have been known to split over less significant matters. The interest in meaningful worship experiences for children (and adults), however, was shared by all. Those interests, when recognized and discussed, provided the basis for a more creative and acceptable solution. In that congregation, the conflict was resolved by keeping the children in the "adult" worship during the time of praise, and offering children's worship activities during the minister's sermon. This was a seemingly simple solution to what could have been the catalyst for conflict. It was a solution that grew when interests were separated from issues, and creativity was encouraged.

In reacting to the central ideas in this chapter, many readers will conclude that the three suggestions are just common sense—and it is difficult to argue with that assessment. Yet in the midst of acute, emotionally laden conflict, how quickly disputants forget the ultimate value of relationships and gravitate toward the nonproductive argument of issues. These suggestions ought to raise our consciousness about the approach to conflict and set the stage for more successful conflict management.

An agreement reached in negotiation will always be compared with the disputants' other alternatives. The following chapter focuses on the power of having those alternatives in conflict management.

CHAPTER EIGHT

# THE POWER OF ALTERNATIVES

A YOUNG, ENERGETIC PRINCIPAL of a Christian school faced a dramatic conflict, probably a common one in many school settings. A group of his teachers had gone around him, directly to the school board, on a particular school issue. The conflict intensified when the board considered the issue and notified the principal of its decision in favor of the teachers and in opposition to the principal's administrative judgment. At that point, he pondered his choices: confront the board on the substantive and procedural issues, leave the school, or ignore the incident and anticipate a difficult year, expecting the incident to be repeated whenever a teacher-principal conflict emerged.

The principal was frustrated with the situation, angry at both the teachers and the board, and suddenly unsure of his place in Christian education. During our initial conversation, he inadvertently mentioned that while he felt helpless in resolving the conflict, he had received an offer from another Christian school in the same community. Even though he had no reason to consider it apart from this conflict, he was not opposed to such a move.

Not until our discussion did he recognize that he had a viable alternative—another job offer—and that the alternative provided him great power in the effort to cooperatively resolve the conflict. Now, instead of being overcome with feelings of frustration and lack of control, he could draw upon the power of his alternative and calmly seek a just resolution of both the substantive disagreement and the procedural difficulties. Instead of a relationship-damaging, confrontational meeting with the board, he could explain his perspectives and concerns, and know that if they were not addressed in an appropriate way, he could accept the other position. In thinking about his alternative, he discovered an important and powerful element of conflict resolution.

## GENERAL ALTERNATIVES

Alternatives are powerful because they check a person's perception of reality and provide an external measurement of his or her options. Every conflict provides the opportunity to develop and use alternatives. In most church and family situations, three broad, general alternatives are applicable. In response to conflict, people can: 1. ignore it, hoping it will go away; 2. separate from it; or 3. address it, and work through it.

### Ignoring Conflict

The style and strategy of avoidance discussed in previous chapters apply here as we discuss the alternative of ignoring conflict. But one should realize that conflict is only rarely resolved when it is ignored. As an alternative, then, people must be careful not to ignore conflict, believing this is an attractive alternative. They risk finding out later that they merely put off the inevitable.

## Separating from Conflict

Another alternative is separating from the conflict or withdrawing from the person with whom we disagree. This alternative suggests that there are times when attitudes, perspectives, or behaviors will not change and separation is necessary.

Families and churches are quick to elect this alternative—perhaps too quick. In the context of the family, ultimate separation from conflict means changing the family structure through divorce, and those who value marriage resist divorce as an alternative. In churches, the alternative of separation usually means some members of the fellowship leave. Those active in Christian churches are all too familiar with the tragic consequences of separation, both for the particular congregation and for its ministry.

However, separation may be an appropriate alternative. An excellent biblical example involves the conflict between Paul and Barnabas over John Mark. The biblical description is deceptively calm; but the dynamics are both interesting and important. After the Jerusalem Conference, Paul suggested to Barnabas that they go back and visit the churches they had established on the first missionary journey. Barnabas wanted to take along young John, also called Mark. Paul's reaction was quick and decisive. He refused to take John Mark because he had deserted them in Pamphylia. Acts 15:39–40 reports that Paul and Barnabas "had such a sharp disagreement that they parted company. Barnabas took Mark and sailed for Cypress, but Paul chose Silas and left, commended by the brothers to the grace of the Lord."

Few other details are known about this conflict, but the circumstances are clear: Paul and Barnabas had differing perspectives and values. Paul was the intense advocate for the proclamation of Christ. Barnabas was the concerned, emphatic minister. Whatever John Mark did, it had made a dramatic impact on Paul, generating clear and strong feelings. The question about John Mark was of great personal importance to everyone involved—it related to their views of ministry and their work for God. Paul and Barnabas disagreed sharply, and neither saw the potential for compromise. Separation was chosen as an appropriate alternative, and it was apparently handled in a way that acknowledged differences, but did not break their fellowship. Later, in his New Testament letters, Paul spoke highly of Barnabas and John Mark, and even asked for John Mark in his later years.[1]

Separation can be a viable alternative if it does not preclude continuing fellowship and relationship. It thus provides the umbrella under which a variety of ministries and approaches can be pursued.

## Working Through Conflict

A third alternative is working through the conflict to achieve resolution. This alternative is the focus of much of this book. It is based on the premises that conflict must be addressed to be resolved, and that it provides the opportunity for meaningful growth in churches, families, and communities.

### SPECIFIC ALTERNATIVES

If people decide to work through conflict, then additional, specific alternatives become critical. In this application, "alternatives" refer to those options that may be selected if a negotiated resolution is *not* achieved; some negotiators describe this as "the no-agreement alternative." For example, if no agreement had been reached between the school board and the principal described earlier, one alternative would have been for him to accept the other job.

Looking at specific alternatives is the only way to determine a person's strength in the negotiation process. Desirable alternatives result in the power to achieve objectives; less desirable alternatives provide the reality test necessary to encourage additional work in the conflict-resolution process.

Consider the simplistic, yet illustrative circumstance of selling a used car. Suppose, for instance, that you have purchased a new car and recently advertised your ten-year-old "transportation car" in a local paper for $1,500. Now you must decide what amount below $1,500 is a good offer. $1,000? $750? $1,300? $1,475?

Depending on the circumstances, any of the offers could be attractive. If you have waited for two weeks and no one has even called, a real offer of $1,000 might be worth considering. If, however, a first offer of $1,300 was made on the day the ad appeared in the paper, you might be inclined to wait and see if you could do even better. In each case, without a firm sense of a tangible alternative, you simply cannot know what to do, nor do you sense much power in choosing a resolution.

Now assume one modification of the scenario. Prior to advertising the car in the newspaper, suppose you took it to a local dealer who indicated a willingness to purchase it anytime in the next two weeks for $1,300. In this situation, how do you view the other offers? Obviously you have an external measurement and a greater sense of power. That power comes from the existence of a good alternative.

In a very positive way, alternatives provide the external measure we need to decide when to accept and when to reject proposed solutions. If there is conflict in a church over continued employment of the minister, one major consideration may be the ability to hire a better one. Yet in most cases the alternative of finding a new minister is usually not explored until after the previous minister is fired. In another case, if some members have a concern about their continued participation in the church program, the alternative of finding meaningful ministry elsewhere will impact the manner in which the conflict is handled. Most often, another church usually is not identified until after the separation in fellowship has occurred.

The existence of a good alternative provides the opportunity to handle a conflict with dignity and integrity. Anyone in the working world has, at one time or another, been in an environment of conflict. If no other employment options seem available, such conflict can be terribly stressful.

A number of years ago, a college administrator found himself in a situation where attitudes about his work, expressed by several colleagues, resulted in antagonism and a substantial disruption of his department. In sum, they disagreed with his qualifications and appointment to a particular position. Such conflict could have consumed him, as it had others before and after him, if he had not had an alternative. Simultaneously to the conflict, however, the administrator was offered a better position with a substantially higher salary at another university.

With that option, he was able to deal with the conflict without engaging in the kind of destructive and un-Christian response that was so tempting. The power of a good alternative made it substantially easier to respond in a mature and respectful way.

The following suggestions can be helpful when developing and considering alternatives.

## Develop Alternatives First

Preparation, especially in the area of developed alternatives, offers the greatest hope for a successful outcome. Yet most often, it is the area least considered. Usually, time is not invested in developing or assessing alternatives until they are urgently needed, and at that point, it may be too late.

An acquaintance of mine is the pastor of a church that has been in the midst of great conflict. Much of the conflict involves the fact that the congregation is undergoing a tremendous change in membership from Caucasian to Asian, and disagreements also exist between the older and younger generations within the congregation. Despite the wide diversity of the conflicts this congregation is enduring, the greatest intensity of feelings has been focused on the pastor. Some members earnestly desire his resignation, while others, equally earnest, want him to stay. This disagreement has resulted in secret meetings, vandalism to personal and church property, and intervention by denominational leaders.

During our conversations, the pastor kept wondering aloud when he would be forced to seek another church. My advice was to do it now. I suggested that he develop the option of another call as soon as possible, because that alternative, if developed first, will provide confidence and power in dealing with the conflict. But this option must be actively developed, not just threatened. An idle threat to seek another call if things do not work out is just that, an idle threat.

## Be Creative

While creativity in conflict management was discussed earlier, it must be emphasized again when discussing specific alternatives. Creativity in developing specific alternatives is just as important as it is in developing collaborative solutions. The same energy and inventiveness necessary for bold solutions is essential for good alternatives.

Creativity should be used to find alternatives that either provide power in conflict resolution or provide another acceptable outcome in case conflict resolution does not work out. In this context, the creativity of alternatives is designed to meet the individual's interests; thus the motivation should be great.

## Be Realistic

Usually, people assume that imagined alternatives are indeed possible, and they fail to explore them fully. It may or may not be realistic to assume that another church will meet my needs, that I can sell my used car for a particular amount on the open market, or that another employment position can be located. The only way to know for sure is to completely develop those alternatives.

In virtually all situations of conflict, people have an exaggerated view of their alternatives. When viewing litigation as an alternative, opposing lawyers, polled independently, said they considered it a viable option and evaluated their chances of winning as "excellent." Reality confirms that only half can be right; there is always a winner and a loser at trial. In developing alternatives, it is essential to be realistic.

The suggestions in this and the previous chapter are intended to provide a direction that will lead to more efficient conflict-resolution processes and more satisfying solutions. They describe the skills necessary to establish a collaborative, problem-solving approach, and outline the road map from conflict to reconciliation.

If everyone were skilled in using these elements of a collaborative negotiation process to address conflict, most would not need the assistance of counselors or others who can help with reconciliation. Unfortunately, however, the emotional involvement and the drama of conflict blunt our use of those commonsense techniques, making it necessary to seek assistance with the conflict-resolution process. The next two chapters describe ways a third party can facilitate collaborative conflict management.

# CHAPTER NINE

## THE VALUE OF MEDIATION

THE PHONE CALL TO THE INSTITUTE was like so many others received there. A young woman tearfully recounted the disintegration of her marriage and her immediate, critical need to resolve issues of financial support with her estranged husband. She knew one option was to hire a lawyer who would handle her case in a fairly traditional way—instructing her not to talk with her husband, filing motions in court for support and custody of the children, heightening the tension between the parents, and legitimately charging thousands of dollars for such services.

Her comments reflected a sense of tremendous loss and great fear; yet her voice also held a twinge of hope that there might be a better way to deal with the reality of her circumstances.

She sensed that, even if divorce was inevitable, the legal relationship should be changed in a cooperative rather than adversarial way. She wondered aloud if there might be any alternative to the television version of "Divorce Court" etched in her mind. She longed for any assistance, any process, any opportunity to protect at least parental relationships in the future.

The institute referred the woman to an outstanding family mediator who was instrumental in encouraging her husband to attend an initial meeting where the process of mediation was described. In that meeting and two others, the woman and her husband were able to establish a workable arrangement for custody and visitation of the children, agree upon financial support, and divide their property. They did so through mediation at a cost of less than twelve hundred dollars—thousands of dollars cheaper than a contested, judicially resolved divorce.

While that scenario is repeated thousands of times each month, it is not introduced here to suggest that divorce is the end result God wants from marriage. Nor do we imply that divorce is not a painful and traumatic experience for all involved. The description is here to suggest that, when faced with conflict, even one as severe as the disintegration of a marriage, the dispute-resolution process of mediation is a promising one.

While the people may change and the context of disputes may vary, what remains constant for most people in conflict is their difficulty in resolving it without some outside assistance. When their negotiations have broken down, their emotions are stretched to the limits, and they are exhausted from the physical as well as emotional strain of their differences, they need the assistance of a counselor or another helper to assist with the reconciliation process.

## THIRD-PARTY ASSISTANCE THROUGH MEDIATION

Mediation is a biblical idea. In fact, it is the essence of the gospel of Jesus Christ. In his first epistle to Timothy, Paul wrote:

For there is one God and one mediator between God and men, the man Christ Jesus, who gave himself as a ransom for all men—the testimony given in its proper time.

(1 Tim. 2:5–6)

Reconciliation between God and his children took place because a mediator came to a world trapped in conflict. Christ's life reflected a vision for his people's reconciliation. By great love and confidence not founded on reason, he was willing to get involved even to the extent that he put his life on the line for the reconciliation to take place. He did so as the go-between in the conflict between God and his people, just as those who mediate today go between people in conflict to facilitate their reconciliation.

Perhaps the simplest translation for the word mediation is "in the middle." A mediator is someone who places himself or herself in the middle of a conflict to bring about resolution of a problem and reconciliation between people.[1] The mediation process and its basic elements are evident in every circumstance where a third party attempts to facilitate the resolution of conflict. As we've mentioned before, arbitration also utilizes a person who works in the middle of a conflict. The difference is that an arbitrator usually has the power to resolve the conflict, while a mediator's role is to guide the two sides in coming to their own resolution.

One refreshing example of this mediation process can be observed in the city of San Francisco, where conflict management is a required part of the curriculum for sixth graders. On school playgrounds, sixth graders trained in the process of mediation wear T-shirts that say "Conflict Resolver" or "Fuss Buster."

Their function is to assist their fellow students when conflicts come up during school activities. They intercede right on the spot, using a simplified mediation process and listening to both sides of the dispute. They encourage the students involved in conflict to think about how their dispute might be resolved, while controlling their anger and emotions.

Because of their intuitive ability to understand the thinking of other students, their training in the mediation process allows them to be quite effective. Recent studies in some of these schools suggest that students trained in conflict management can reduce the violence that takes place on the playground by about 40 percent.[2]

Mediation is also seen increasingly in the workplace, where employee grievances that once would have been taken to arbitration now are resolved through the collaborative mediation process. In one statewide application, a sophisticated version of the same process used on San Francisco's elementary-school playgrounds was used to resolve teacher-administrator conflicts. In more than 90 percent of the cases where it was tried, the process provided the forum for resolution of disputes.[3] And in resolving their differences this way, the teachers and administrators arrived at their own solutions and returned to work, not as winners or losers, as would have been the case with arbitration, but as people who had successfully resolved the conflict between them.

Essentially the same process takes place in the arena of international affairs. As mentioned earlier, President Jimmy Carter used a form of mediation in the 1970s when he facilitated the resolution of conflict between Israel and Egypt over the Sinai Peninsula.[4]

### SEVEN STAGES IN THE MEDIATION PROCESS

The general elements of the mediation process not only apply to playground disputes, employee-employer differences, and international conflict, but also to disputes in our homes, churches, and communities.

Whatever circumstance exists, the mediator will find the seven basic stages in the mediation process, listed in Table 9–1, are important to integrate into the ministry of reconciliation.

---

**Seven Stages of the Mediation Process**

1. Prepare for mediation
2. Begin the mediation session
3. Communicate about the dispute
4. Define the issues and set the agenda
5. Clarify information and uncover hidden interests
6. Generate and assess options for settlement
7. Bring session to closure and settlement

---

**Table 9–1**

In the remainder of this chapter, we will examine those seven stages.

## Prepare for Mediation

A person cannot enter into a process to successfully resolve conflict without a certain amount of preparation. We cannot be embroiled in acute conflict one moment, and in the next be at the table working to resolve it. There must be a transition from the state of conflict to a readiness for resolution.

When working with Christians, one mediation organization, the Christian Conciliation Service (CCS) of Los Angeles, offers "Called to Conciliate," a Bible study which leads the participants into the word of God, and underscores the basic principles of our faith. As people go through that Bible study, they really do prepare for reconciliation. They are reminded once again of those values that are so easy to forget in the heat of battle. This CCS chapter's Bible study is included in Appendix A.

Also, in preparation for mediation with Christians, thought needs to be given to the role of prayer, a resource that is often overlooked. This is sometimes revealed when, during the early moments of intervention, the counselor asks how long the disputants have discussed the conflict, or how many meetings they have had. Often, they do not want to answer; but finally, after a long pause, they will say something like, "We've met six times already, at least two or three hours every time. We have been working real hard to get this resolved." Then the question can be asked, "How much time have you spent praying about it?" Usually the answer is not at all.

As people consider reconciliation, it is helpful to remind them that God can intervene and be part of the process. God loves his children and the church, and he wants his people to be reconciled. Given the opportunity to speak to his people through prayer, God will ready their hearts for the reconciliation process.

By helping people prepare for reconciliation, the mediator assists them in making the transition from investing in the conflict to investing in the resolution. Once that transition is complete, they will be ready for someone to minister to them.

*109*

## Begin the Mediation Session

At the beginning of the session, it is important to introduce the mediator and the participants, educate them about the process to be followed, and establish ground rules.[5] As mentioned in an earlier chapter, it is not uncommon for the mediator to spend several minutes describing these ground rules, perhaps even thinking, *They must really be impressed with my ability to do this.* But the reality is that the disputants rarely hear such admonitions. They are sitting there, anxiously waiting to tell their sides of the story, eager to proclaim the errors of their adversary and describe how the problem ought to be resolved. They are "chomping at the bit" to express their feelings about the matter at hand. The mediator should keep these thoughts in mind, and keep this part of the discussion brief.

A good friend who is an expert in community mediation begins sessions by describing the process of mediation, then asks the disputants, "What kind of ground rules should we have as we talk together? What kind of rules should guide our conversation?" Almost always, one side will suggest that they should not interrupt each other. The other side usually agrees.

That procedural agreement occurs in a moment of calm at the beginning of the session. But thirty minutes later, the two people are standing up, yelling and screaming at each other. After letting them go at it for a while, he raises his hand and calmly says, "May I just ask a question? Is the ground rule we established earlier still a ground rule?" The two people usually ask, "What ground rule?" And he reminds them of their agreement about not interrupting. They usually say, "Of course it still is," as they continue to yell at each other. Then he suggests that maybe they should handle this differently; then they think about it, and finally settle down and start talking in a more productive manner.

My friend's example illustrates the need, at the beginning of the mediation process when the individuals are more rational, to establish rules they will use when the conflict is more acute. That concept also works in a broader, preventive way outside the actual mediation process. A number of Christian organizations are now establishing guidelines, up front, describing how they will handle conflict over contracts or employment agreements. For instance, a Christian school and a teacher will agree, at the moment of contracting, that any conflicts related to their employment relationship will be submitted to the Christian Conciliation Service, or a board of elders.[6] At the beginning of a relationship, no one really pays much attention to such things; but when conflict emerges, that initial agreement becomes a powerful tool for constructive and respectful conflict resolution. Appendix C suggests language that can be added to contracts and wills to provide for mediation or arbitration of future disputes.

## Communicate About the Dispute

Obviously, people may need help from the mediator in managing their communication. The mediator should assure them they will both get the opportunity to talk, and remind them when they say things that are not productive or that might be harmful to the relationship.

Communication in conflict resolution operates in two ways, speaking and listening. The communication directed by one person to the other at times needs to be managed with help from the mediator. In addition, it is critically important for the two sides to hear each other—to listen carefully. The facilitator can be helpful in managing this communication so that talking is productive and listening is encouraged.

In the Christian context, the two sides may also communicate with each other through prayer to God. When people who are in conflict get down on their knees together and pray about the conflict, a kind of softening takes place. They may think they are praying that God will help their adversary see how it should be resolved—in favor of the person sending up the prayer. Nevertheless, in prayer, they are lifting up their adversary to God. And inevitably after prayer, a softening effect occurs, leaving the disputants more willing to help the resolution process succeed.

In a church dispute mediated a few months ago, the conflict between the two factions was intense. The people were very angry, and the mediator was hoping the Lord would help dissipate some of that emotion as they prayed. So they all got down on their knees together. Keep in mind that this is the first time these factions had prayed together—or done anything civil together—for months. As they knelt there together, each person in the room had the dilemma of what to say to God about the conflict.

It is a natural human emotion to want God to look down and see that the person who is praying is on the right side; so as each person prayed aloud that day, he or she said things to God that made that particular side look like the true peacemaker. As the disputants did that, they tended to be a bit more reserved and less offensive to the other side. Pretty soon, all were praying that the Lord would intervene and ease the conflict. They might not have recognized the significance of their actions at that moment, but they were important. As they prayed, they were doing something in tandem—cooperating with each other for the first time since the dispute began. Results of this kind of shared prayer can be subtle—or the genuine turning point in the conflict-resolution process.

The Lord does intervene through prayer. People enmeshed in conflict communicate and listen to each other very carefully as they pray. There is something healing about that process. In the church, we have the unique opportunity to utilize the dynamic power of prayer, and also through that mechanism to talk with each other in meaningful, unique, and helpful ways.

## Define the Issues and Set the Agenda

At some point, usually when a substantial amount of communication has taken place, the conflict and emotion have emerged, and the issues that need to be resolved are identified. This stage of the mediation process is the one that helps clarify the issues, reframing them in more objective terms, and setting the agenda for the problem-solving work.[7]

Typically, identifying the issues is a reasonably easy task. Parties know what the dispute is about and are able to identify those tangible items. Setting the agenda is not difficult; but it is important, because it diminishes uncertainty and provides direction for successfully conducting the session. Different approaches to setting the agenda include an ad-lib development—just creating it as you go, or taking issues in the order they are identified, or ranking the issues in order of importance, or letting participants alternate in the selection of items to discuss, or handling the less difficult items before the more difficult. Each approach allows varying degrees of control, but all provide a sense of expectation and direction.

### Clarify Information and Uncover Hidden Interests

While the issues are easily identified in most conflicts, the interests may be hidden. People bring to the table underlying needs which may be difficult for them to openly admit or describe. Yet addressing such needs is essential in resolving the conflict.[8]

As we seek to be ministers of reconciliation through our work as counselors, teachers, and church leaders, we can depend on the reality that something other than the obvious is usually driving the conflict. It might be psychological or personality problems within the two sides' relationship. It could be related to events in a person's past or his or her fears of the future. Sometimes, such underlying causes can drive the entire conflict, and many times their discovery will be the turning point in the conflict-resolution process.

An attorney shared the story of a woman who, while driving on a rural highway, had an accident involving a freight train. The amazing fact was, in broad daylight, she had run into the side of a parked boxcar blocking the road! Shortly thereafter, she contacted the lawyer to submit a claim against the railroad company. You can imagine the attorney wondering about the case. Boxcars are pretty big, and she had driven right into the side of one!

As they explored the case, they decided to file suit against the railroad. Actually, there was not much question about liability. Even though she had run into the train, it was really the railroad company's fault for parking the train across the roadway without putting out a flagperson, flares, or gates.

After weeks of negotiation, a favorable financial settlement was reached to compensate the woman for her medical bills and repair her car. The attorney recognized, however, that she was not satisfied. When he asked what she really wanted out of her case, the woman replied, "I want the railroad company to say it was not my fault." He was perplexed, and reminded her that this had been a legal conflict, that a lawsuit had been filed, and that the real issue was the amount of payment. But again she said, "What I need out of this is for the railroad company to say it was not my fault."

Finally, the attorney, who knew how difficult it is to negotiate an apology as part of a settlement, asked why that was so important.

"I am almost seventy years old," the woman replied. "I drove down the street and ran into the side of a boxcar. Now my kids are getting together and saying things like 'Maybe Grandma shouldn't be driving any more. Maybe we should take her car away. Maybe it isn't safe for her or other people.' They don't think I can drive."

Her underlying need, which would rarely be recognized in the court system, was a need for someone from the railroad to say, "Grandma, your driving really is all right. It was our fault for parking the train across the road." So, as the lawyer completed the negotiated resolution of the claim, he obtained a letter from the railroad saying it was not his client's fault. When she left the office after the next appointment, she was beaming, not because of the monetary settlement, but because of the apology. You can just imagine her the next time the family gathered, sharing the letter and saying, "See, it was their fault. I really *can* drive!"

That incident suggests what regularly goes on in conflict. At some point during mediation, information needs to be clarified and hidden interests uncovered. The participants need to be asked, "What else is going on?" The answer to the question is essential in solving the problem.

### Generate and Assess Options for Settlement

In the next phase of the mediation process, the people involved in the conflict create options that will meet their interests.[9] As recommended in a previous chapter, these options may be invented through a brainstorming process, then fully assessed from the perspectives of practicality and possibility.

These options must not only create a solution, they must include thoughts on how the solution would be put in place.

Often, people in acute conflict can see a solution but do not know how to back off from their positions and accept it. They may be able to visualize what they need to do, but because they have invested so much of their time, resources, and emotions in their position, it's difficult to leave it and move on to the resolution. Or they may be trapped in a case of tunnel vision, only able to see their original position, even though it's obvious that shifting that position could lead to satisfactory resolution. The mediator's role at that point is to expand their vision—open up the tunnel—so the alternative solutions are clear, and easily accepted.

An extreme example of this, but one that is not completely unique, took place several years ago. A colleague of mine, a retiring judge, left the bench and decided to start a career as a mediator and arbitrator. With the power of his former judicial office behind him, he was regarded as highly credible in that role.

The very first call he received was from a group representing the teachers in a collective bargaining dispute with a school district. The dispute had grown into a major conflict, with the latest developments reported each day in the newspaper. As a result, the teachers were angry, the school district felt abused, and the parents were upset. Clearly, the conflict needed someone's immediate attention and assistance.

The judge saw the case as a big opportunity. He would go in and help those people and in so doing, start his new career in a highly visible way. He arrived at the appointed time and found the teachers on one side of the room and the administrators on the other. He was ready to get to work.

The judge was a bit disappointed when one person turned to him and said, "We don't really want you to do anything, because we already have the dispute resolved. What we want you to do is sit here with us all day, drink coffee, and have lunch. We will keep the doors closed and pretend we are in here arguing with each other. Then, later in the afternoon, we want you to go out to the press and pretend like you have worked hard and finally have this resolved. You can announce *our* agreement as *your* resolution, and we will be supportive of it."

Surprised and somewhat puzzled, the judge sat there and

drank coffee all day, had lunch, and later in the afternoon announced the agreement to the media and the community. Now, for the first time, the two groups could leave, publicly agreeing to what they had privately agreed to days before. The mediator had intervened and provided what everyone on both sides most wanted—to save face before the public.

This kind of scenario may be difficult to understand if one is not familiar with a group's history of adversarial collective bargaining. In many cases, these organizations begin to thrive on conflict, as opposed to resolution. While the resolution represents compromise in most cases, all of the public conversation may have described highly adversarial positioning. After a group has created such a foundation, repeatedly describing how terrible the other side is, it is hard to move off that hard-nosed position to publicly agree with that opponent.

What the participants in that dispute probably wanted to say about the agreement which they, in fact, had created together, was something like this: "The judge strongly suggested that this agreement is the best we could get, so we're agreeing to it." That lets them off the hook. They have saved face, but still managed to preserve a position that will let them get the emotions going again when the contract is up for renewal in a couple of years.

Mediators must think about how to move the parties from the point of conflict to the point of resolution. Sometimes, they must be very creative so people can accept what has already been decided.

## Bring Session to Closure and Settlement

Finally, the mediation process must include a phase of closure and settlement.[10] Constructive dialogue has identified issues and interests, creative solutions have been proposed, and now it is time for the individuals to decide whether they will accept a proposed solution, or continue the conflict. The process has led to a crisis, and now it is the mediator who presses for a response.

Look how often Jesus found himself at the point of closure. In very few instances did he teach and then just walk away, saying over his shoulder, "Well, if that fits, fine; and if it doesn't, that's fine, too." There was always a sense of closure with him, a sense that he was saying, "Here is my ministry to you—my miracle that involves you. Here is my teaching to you. Now what is your response?" He brought the session to closure by forcing those involved to think about the reality of acceptance or rejection.

The mediator has that function as well. He or she must bring the disputants to the point where they say, "We have done all of this work; now what is keeping us from agreeing?" That question has to be asked so that they are in the position of saying yes or no—bringing themselves to reconciliation, or deciding to walk away.

Often, time deadlines force a candid look at the final bargaining and closure. Such deadlines can be established by external circumstances, or by the mediator if he or she can force the people to be very serious about either resolving the dispute within a given amount of time—or deciding to pursue other alternatives.

The seven steps described here will not always be handled as separately as they have been outlined here; nor will they always be followed in a particular order. But to one degree or another, they will be evident in every mediation.

People must prepare for mediation, a process that depends on the participants to control the outcome. It must be made clear to the disputants that communication should be open and respectful, that it should define the issues, and set the agenda. Time must be devoted to uncovering hidden interests so that the real needs of the individuals can be addressed. An environment must be created in which acceptable and face-saving options for settlement can be created and evaluated nonjudgmentally. Finally, the process must move people toward resolution—final bargaining, closure, and settlement.

The process of mediation is organized yet fluid, deliberate yet responsive, structured yet flexible. As Carlton Snow, an accomplished mediator, arbitrator, and founder of the Center for Dispute Resolution at Willamette University College of Law proclaims, "The magic is in the process!"[11]

# CHAPTER TEN

---

# SKILLS OF THE MEDIATOR

THE PROCESS OF MEDIATION is offered to a world in conflict. Whether carried out by a counselor, a pastor, a teacher, or a business manager, mediation is not needed unless there is acute conflict. As a mediator, every time you go to work, you go to a situation where people are not at peace, where a relationship has broken. The people you face have experienced conflict so severe that they cannot handle it alone. You will be the resource they turn to in their desire to move from conflict to resolution and reconciliation.

The challenge of assisting people through the stages of the mediation process, as described in the previous chapter, could at first appear overwhelming. But the role is not as complex as it may seem, although some technical mediation skills can provide great assistance. In fact, without ever describing yourself as a mediator, you probably mediate every day. If you are a parent, you are already an experienced mediator—at least if you are the parent of more than one child. If you live in a neighborhood, you may mediate conflicts and disputes there. If you are a supervisor in a business, you are a mediator anytime you facilitate a resolution of differences between two or more people. A mediator is simply the neutral or impartial third party who tries to help others achieve agreement.

## SEVEN MEDIATOR FUNCTIONS

Whether it's facilitating resolution of conflict in a family through counseling, mediating a landlord-tenant dispute at a neighborhood justice center, or assisting the negotiation of a major, multi-party environmental dispute, the role of the mediator remains essentially the same. The seven basic functions listed in Table 10–1 are essential to the mediator's role in effectively bringing about reconciliation.

### Conflict Assessor

The mediator's first role is that of a conflict assessor who evaluates the nature and degree of conflict.[1] The mediator can do this more objectively and successfully than can the people involved in the conflict.

Several years ago, a major dispute occurred that was related to airplane takeoffs at an international airport. Those in the

---

**Seven Mediator Functions**

1. Conflict assessor
2. Convener
3. Communication facilitator
4. Reality tester
5. Generator of alternatives
6. Expander of resources
7. Gainer of closure

**Table 10–1**

residential communities under the flight path were in conflict with the airport director over the time and altitudes of the planes taking off. As the conflict intensified, demands were made; yet no resolution was reached.

Finally, in the midst of the struggle, a mediator was asked to intervene. His first task was to assess the conflict. After hours of intensive conversation, the reason for the impasse was discovered. While the community groups demanded that the airport director resolve the problem, in reality, he was only one of dozens of parties related to the conflict. More than sixty airlines, several state and federal agencies, and other consumer and professional groups also were critical to the resolution. The possibilities for resolution increased dramatically when the mediator correctly assessed the conflict as one that the director and the airport-area residents could not make without assistance from at least some of the other parties involved in the situation.

In *The Art and Science of Negotiation,* Howard Raiffa lists a series of inquiries that are important for a conflict assessor to ask prior to negotiation. Some of those questions could be paraphrased as: Who are the people involved in the conflict? Are the two sides unified? What are the issues? Is this dispute-resolution process a one-time occurrence, or do these two sides meet repetitively to negotiate collective bargaining issues? Is the dispute-resolution process formal or informal? Is it private or public? How will values and mores impact it? What constraints will impact the dispute resolution? Is an agreement required? What happens if there is no agreement? Is ratification of an agreement required? Will an agreement be binding? Will it be enforceable?[2] The answers to these questions can provide information the mediator can use to evaluate the conflict and assist the parties in developing an appropriate dispute-resolution process.

## Convener

If in answering these preliminary questions it becomes apparent that mediation may be the appropriate dispute-resolution approach, the mediator may be charged with actually getting the parties to the negotiating table. In that case, the mediator's second role becomes that of the convener.[3]

On one occasion, I was in a city when it was embroiled in a highly emotional and public conflict. The city's largest hotel had agreed to host two very different kinds of conferences. On one side of the grand ballroom a meeting was scheduled for more than 180 law-enforcement officers who would come from five states to learn about terrorism. At the same time, more than 300 individuals focusing on peace and conflict resolution were to meet on the other side of the ballroom partition.

All of this might have worked, except the speaker for the law-enforcement conference had previously published a list of all "terrorist front" and "communist front" organizations he thought were operating in the area. Guess who he identified— of course, some of the peace groups on the other side of the partition!

The dispute had received wide public attention and caused quite a stir in the community. Public reaction to the incident was so significant, the state government withdrew as host of the law-enforcement conference.

As mentioned when we described this conflict in an earlier chapter, a colleague and I were asked to mediate the conflict. We began conversations with everyone we could find. We had coffee at a restaurant with community activists, we met with leaders of the various groups in the park, and we visited with ministers in churches. Finally those efforts resulted in identifying the people involved in the conflict and narrowing down the issues in dispute.

When we started discussions with each side about how the conflict might be resolved, we were surprised. The local sheriff, who was the new sponsor of the law-enforcement conference, was willing to make a lengthy series of concessions. But guess who would not meet the sheriff at the negotiation table to even discuss the conflict or its resolution—the peace groups! They liked all of the press and the attention they were getting as, for the first time in their organization's history, they were making front-page news. That was pretty exciting to them—more exciting than resolving the conflict and bringing peace.

Getting the disputants to the table is an important role for the mediator. Reports from community dispute-resolution programs suggest that if the mediator is successful in getting them to the table, 60 to 80 percent of the time the conflict can be resolved.[4] This is often difficult, however, and as illustrated in the example described above, sometimes impossible.

## Communication Facilitator

The third role a mediator plays is that of facilitating communication.[5] Sometimes the people, themselves, will take the initiative to communicate during mediation, and can do so without substantial intervention by a third party. When that occurs, the mediator can just sit back and let them work it out. All they need is somebody there to protect them in case the conversation gets abusive.

Most of the time, however, communication must be facilitated in a more direct way. In a recent case between a public school district and the parents of a student in that school, the parents were quite concerned that the student was being discriminated against because of the parents' business. They owned an adult video arcade and adult toy store—a business that was always controversial in their relatively small town.

So much animosity was involved in this dispute the mediator had to facilitate the entire communication process. At the beginning, the mediator had to tell both sides they could not talk to each other directly. The individuals sat on opposite sides of a conference table, only four feet apart; but he said to each of them, "If you have a question to ask the other persons, you ask me; then I will ask them." This went on for several hours, with one person saying, "I would like to know why this happened." Then the mediator would say, "She would like to know why this happened." The other party would give the reason, and the mediator would then repeat the reason for the inquirer, even though everyone at the table had heard everything that was said! Under most circumstances, such a system would be pure silliness. But it was not silly in managing this communication. It took about six hours before the emotions of the parties relaxed enough so they could talk to each other respectfully.

The mediator is critical in facilitating communication. Sometimes this is a very aggressive role, and other times it is a passive function. Always, though, it is important.

## Reality Tester

The mediator is also a reality tester, helping the individuals understand the consequences of not reaching an agreement.[6] Coming to grips with reality outside the specific conflict will usually influence how issues are handled inside the conflict-resolution process.

A number of years ago, the dramatic power of reality testing was confirmed for me through asking a series of thoughtful questions. I had intervened in an emotional conflict between some faculty members and an administrator at a public community college. The conflict was acute and there was little interest on the part of the faculty to participate in a facilitated process for resolution. During the assessment phase of the mediation, I recognized why this was so. The faculty members perceived that they had the power to get the administrator fired, and thus they had little incentive for a negotiated resolution.

Recognizing their focus on what they thought was an easy solution to the conflict, I tested their understanding of reality by asking a series of questions. I promised that I would withdraw from the mediation at their request if they would answer my four questions.

The first question was a simple query in response to their plan, which included going to the meeting of the publicly elected college board and demanding the administrator's termination. When I asked how they would get on the agenda of that meeting, they answered that they had a friend in the college president's office who would make sure they had an opportunity to be heard.

I then asked about the likelihood of the college board taking up a personnel matter in a public meeting. The faculty members responded that to their knowledge the board had never done so, but they were sure it would in this case.

I then asked how many of the faculty members would show up for such a meeting. Behind my question was an interest in ascertaining how solid they thought their power was with their own colleagues, especially recognizing that those who showed up would be putting at least their reputations—if not their careers—on the line. The faculty members responded confidently that not everyone would show up, but they were sure twenty-two or twenty-three out of the twenty-five department members would be there.

Finally, I asked the question that brought home the reality of the situation. I said to the three faculty members seated before me, "How would it affect your view of this option to learn that I have visited individually with all the faculty members in the department and asked them if they would show up at such a meeting? Only the three of you will be there." As you can imagine, they swallowed hard when they recognized that the plan, which had seemed so powerful to them, was simply not going to achieve the end they desired. That dose of reality was instrumental in encouraging their return to the bargaining table, where a more collaborative resolution to the conflict was achieved.

### Generator of Alternatives

The mediator must also generate alternatives.[7] Many times, people enmeshed in conflict simply cannot see other possible options or solutions. As described earlier, they view the conflict from their positions, which they have established after analyzing the facts a particular way. They may have great difficulty in imagining any resolution except the one they have proposed. As a result, their focus is advocacy, rather than problem-solving.

Into this context comes the third-party facilitator. This person is not part of the history of the particular conflict. He or she is not trapped in adversarial positioning. The mediator brings a fresh approach and perhaps fresh ideas aimed at resolution of the problem. It is the mediator who can direct people through the collaborative process of inventing and developing options that have the potential for mutual satisfaction. This direction can move people from the limitations of their perceptions to creative thinking.

Substantively, it is easy to see how a third party can bring fresh perspectives and help parties discover additional alternatives. Procedurally, however, it is quite important that such perspectives be introduced in a way that will be accepted by the people involved. In other words, it is critical that both sides "own" the solution to their conflict, so it must be presented in a way that lets them embrace it and honor their commitments related to it.

One approach is for the mediator to suggest ideas that come from his or her uninvolved analysis. In certain circumstances such ideas can be discussed, and on occasion, they will be accepted.

More powerful, however, is the presentation of alternatives in a way that lets the people feel as though they have been instrumental in creating them. Instead of pronouncing judgment, as is done in arbitration, the creative mediator will lead people to possible alternatives by asking a series of uninhibiting questions, such as: Have you considered . . . ? What if . . . ? What would your reaction be to . . . ? Could there be something in this realm that might satisfy your interest . . . ? Is there value in thinking about . . . ?

Such questions get proposals on the table in a way that assures the individuals of their freedom to accept or reject them. If accepted, almost always the process will result in feelings of greater ownership of the resolution.

## Expander of Resources

The mediator can also help by expanding resources, a role that is most often seen in conflicts involving an imbalance of power.[8] Divorce cases are frequently illustrative. One person in a divorce mediation may have all the information on the business and bank accounts, while the other person has no clue about those matters. If the parties are left alone to negotiate such items, they may come out with an agreement that is not very helpful, and may even be unfair to one of them. If that is a concern, the mediator becomes the person who expands resources. He or she might encourage the review of a tentative property settlement by a lawyer. If it is a particularly complex case financially, the mediator might suggest bringing in an accountant. If custody of minor children is involved, a psychologist may be appropriate.

Not long ago, the wife in a divorce case said her estranged

husband had earned all the money, so he should get all the pension. He also made all the house payments, so he should get the house, she reasoned. In fact, he earned all the money, worked hard, and always gave to the family, so she thought he should not have to pay her any ongoing support. The marital assets totaled about $800,000, so she was giving away about $400,000 to which she had a legal and a moral right.

Working as a resource expander, the mediator intervened to say, "Perhaps that is a good way to resolve this; but why don't you check it out with your lawyer and accountant and we will meet again next Friday?" In doing so, the woman learned what the court would do in a similar circumstance, and that information affected her bargaining stance. A fairer, and perhaps more lasting settlement stemmed from the mediator's use of outside resources.

### Gainer of Closure

Finally, the mediator is the gainer of closure.[9] This is a role that is not emphasized enough, perhaps because it is difficult. But at some point in the process, someone has to ask the tough questions, such as: "How are you going to resolve this? Do you want the conflict to continue, or do you want a resolution? You said you wanted resolution. You came to all these meetings. You have been working at it. But this is the moment when someone has to make a move."

The role of closer occurs at the moment of crisis—that stage when someone must say, "We have done all we can do. We have talked about the conflict in every way we can talk about it. We have explored every interest and we have been as creative as we know how. Now what are you going to do?" That is a tough moment, because the parties are about to give up the conflict. That means, in some cases, they are about to give up a part of themselves.

In a previous chapter, we described a conflict involving two Christian businessmen which had continued for a considerable time before the Institute for Dispute Resolution was asked to assist. At the end of months of work, the moment came when the question was asked, "Do you have anything else to say, because this is almost over?" I never will forget the look of terror on one of the faces—terror because this conflict, which had been so consuming and the focus of so much energy, time, sweat, and emotion, was about to end. Sometimes people simply do not know what they are going to do to fill the void.

Ironically, it is at this point during mediation when things can completely fall apart. So much work has been done and so much progress has been made, but now it is time to sign on the dotted line. Somebody has to be there to achieve that kind of closure, because the normal human response says, "Well, not quite yet. Maybe one more meeting. Maybe, if we talk about this aspect a little bit more, I will be ready." Someone needs to pull the curtain on this situation. The mediator does so as the gainer of closure.

The list of a mediator's functions could be much longer, but those described here form the basis for facilitating an effective conflict-resolution process. They are evident in most mediation processes, and provide the substance of the reconciliation ministry.

## CHAPTER ELEVEN

# ACHIEVING
# AGREEMENTS THAT LAST

PEACEMAKERS FACE THEIR GREATEST disappointments when the resolution of conflict does not last. People invested heavily in the process. The mediator or facilitator worked to put the resolution together, and those affected by it appeared to be pleased with the outcome. Then, a day, a week, a month, or a year later, the agreement disintegrates and the individuals are thrust back into conflict. At that point, the conflict may be more acute than when the process began.

This can occur in any conflict, whether it is an agreement regarding child visitation in a marriage dissolution, a decision about hiring a particular employee, or a treaty between two warring countries. The outcome most needed by those involved in any conflict is an outcome that will last!

William Lincoln, president of National Center Associates, describes three criteria he believes are important in evaluating the durability of an agreement.[1] All three focus on the satisfaction of the people involved. He suggests that in order to be supportive of an agreement, they must be sufficiently satisfied substantively, procedurally, and psychologically. They need not be thrilled with the agreement, but they must have sufficient confidence in and ownership of it that they will fulfill their responsibilities related to it.

## SUBSTANTIVE SATISFACTION

The initial criterion is that of substantive satisfaction: Are the people satisfied with the substance—that is, the terms—of the negotiated agreement?

The value of substantive satisfaction is most clearly demonstrated when it does not exist. You have probably seen situations where agreement was achieved, but not adhered to by one or both parties. The risk in such cases is that there will be "conflict aftermath" as a dissatisfied party expresses his or her real feelings about the agreement.

Marriage dissolutions often provide a good example of this. In a great number of cases, a fairly traditional pattern is established. The judge awards custody of the children to the mother, then requires the father to pay some type of financial support. Visitation rights on behalf of the non-custodial parent often are narrowly defined.

If the father is dissatisfied with the substance of that result, he really has only two choices. He can go back to court and petition for reconsideration and a different decision—an expensive and time-consuming process with slim chances of success. Or he can express his dissatisfaction with the substance of the decision to the mother and the children. Usually this dissatisfaction is quite obvious. Child-support and alimony payments begin to arrive late. In the first few months payment might just be a day or two late. Later, it might be several weeks late. Finally, payment stops altogether. Sometimes when that occurs, the mother and the children go on public assistance and the case is referred to the Attorney General, who goes after the father for reimbursement.

In response to this situation, a number of jurisdictions have begun using mediation as a process through which the divorcing couple establishes the terms of custody, visitation, and support, rather than having those terms determined by a judge.[2] Some studies indicate that in the majority of mediated divorce cases, couples who reach a settlement will honor their commitments, a proportion substantially higher than statistics related to court-decided cases. Surprisingly, in fewer than 40 percent of the court cases do the participants actually do what the judge orders regarding alimony and child support. On the other hand, in mediated settlements, more than 65 percent abide by their negotiated agreement.[3] In short, the higher the satisfaction with the outcome, the higher the commitment to abide by the agreement.

## PROCEDURAL SATISFACTION

In addition to substantive satisfaction, there must also be satisfaction with the process followed in the resolution of the dispute. Individuals who are not satisfied with the process may fail to support the resolution to the conflict, even though they agree with it.[4]

Some mediators have had to learn the lessons of procedural satisfaction the hard way. This was the case for an administrator who worked in the president's office of a private university. A small group of the administrators there decided over lunch one day that they should develop a new master's degree in public administration. They knew they could encourage the program's development through traditional faculty committees, but that could take months. The alternative was for a group of enthusiastic administrators to sit down and design it, then present it as a *fait accompli* to the faculty.

In a matter of just a few days, they did just that, developing everything they could think of to assist their teaching colleagues. Not only did they design the curriculum for the program, they set degree requirements, wrote course descriptions, and even decided which instructors would teach what courses. They thought they were being of great service to the faculty.

Anyone on campus the day the administrators presented their "helpful" work to the faculty could probably have heard the faculty's response. It is an understatement to say there was substantial acrimony. The meeting ended when the initiators raised the white flag, gave the bound proposal to the faculty, and quickly exited the conference room!

A number of months later there was a bit of irony, however, when the proposal came back from the faculty to the president for approval. That proposal had the substantial support of the faculty. As it was reviewed, it was somewhat surprising to see that 95 percent of it was exactly the same as the original proposal that had been presented to the faculty. In fact, much of it had not even been retyped! What was the difference? The "new" proposal had gone through the "proper" channels—the faculty committees. In doing so, it had generated procedural satisfaction among the faculty members, who had been given the opportunity to discuss it, put their imprint on it, and develop ownership. This anecdote shows that when people are not satisfied with the procedure that was followed, they may be unwilling to support the resulting resolution, even though they agree with it.

The lesson is easily applied in any area of conflict resolution. Satisfaction with the process is not something that can be instantly infused in participants. Rather, this satisfaction must be developed along the way. It is helpful to inquire at the very beginning of the mediation whether the process is acceptable, and then to ask repeatedly as the process is expanded to make sure that satisfaction with the process grows as the participants move toward a workable solution. If, for some reason, the process is not satisfactory, the mediator needs to know it so the discussion on substantive issues can be stopped and an acceptable process reestablished in which such issues can be resolved.

## PSYCHOLOGICAL SATISFACTION

People who have reached a resolution must be able to look back on the process and have a feeling that they were treated in a way that will allow them to support the agreement. The parties must believe they were treated with respect, their interests were acknowledged, their perspectives considered, and their contribution to the outcome was recognized. The exact state of mind may be somewhat nebulous, but the reality is extremely clear to people. When they stand up and shake hands at the end of the process, they must feel good about how they were treated, even if they did not achieve all they wanted. If, instead, they shake hands while holding an unstated feeling of anger about how they were treated, that anger may eat at their psyches until, eventually, they undo the deal that was made. On the positive side, however, there are situations where people disagree with the outcome, but because they've been treated well, they will support the agreement.[5]

Again, the need for this kind of satisfaction can be best illustrated by looking at instances when it did not exist. I once worked at a university where a group of employees organized a union. A year later, that union was decertified by those same employees. A year after the decertification, the employees again brought in a union. A year after that vote, they once again decertified it.

To anyone in labor relations, that is an interesting set of occurrences. When I began inquiring into the basis for those actions, employees quickly pointed to Sam, an employee whose job it was to run the university's incinerator. This was not exactly the place I would have expected to find a powerful leader and persuasive employee. As I visited with Sam, the story began to unfold. In the first year of organization, he was the force behind the employees organizing in a formal way; but when the employees had the election to select the shop steward a short time after organizing, he was not elected to that post. Consequently, he spent the entire second year suggesting to employees what a bad idea it had been to bring in a union. After some additional difficulties with the management, during the third year he was able to rally his colleagues to again bring in a union. After not being elected shop steward for the second time, he again spent the following year convincing his fellow employees what a bad idea it had been.

In essence, Sam perceived his election as shop steward as the way his fellow employees should recognize his effort to direct, rally, and advise them regarding their relationship with the institution. The employees' failure to do this created such psychological dissatisfaction in his mind he was able to turn 180 degrees against what he had been an advocate for only days or weeks earlier.

Sam's reaction was not substantially different from that of people in conflict. When emotions and psychological feelings are not handled in a way that is constructive, people express dissatisfaction. Psychological satisfaction is essential to outcomes that will be supported.

## BIBLICAL APPLICATION OF THE SATISFACTION CRITERIA

One illustration of the three aspects of satisfaction that are so vital to lasting agreements is shown in the way the early Christians successfully resolved a bitter conflict that could have split the first-century church. Paul and Barnabas, upon returning to Antioch from their first missionary tour, discovered that some Judean Christians from the party of the Pharisees had been teaching the Gentile brethren in Antioch that unless they were circumcised according to the law of Moses, they could not be saved.[6] The Gentile converts were, as can be imagined, less than enthusiastic about such a procedure, especially since they viewed it as a cultural rather than a doctrinal requirement. Seeing the great importance in resolving this crucial question regarding salvation, Paul, Barnabas, and some others appointed by the church went to Jerusalem to meet with the apostles and the elders to decide the issue.[7]

The first church council, called the "Jerusalem Conference," is described by Luke in Acts 15. It tested the ability of the young church to achieve a satisfactory solution. But in the end, through the guidance of the Holy Spirit, a decision was agreed upon, and followed through; and division in the early church was avoided. The success can be attributed, at least in part, to the substantive, procedural, and psychological satisfaction of the Christians as they left the conference.

### Substantive Satisfaction

It is clear that while the initial positions held by the opposing factions were distinct, the substance of the agreement they reached was at least minimally satisfying to both sides. The resolution stopped short of requiring circumcision, but insisted on the Gentiles' honoring many Jewish laws.[8] Those who advocated circumcision were reminded of the prophets' words regarding the Gentiles: "After this I will return and rebuild David's fallen tent. Its ruins I will rebuild, and I will restore it, that the remnant of men may seek the Lord, and all the Gentiles who bear my name" (Acts 15:16–17). The groundwork for agreement on the Gentiles' acceptance into the church was laid by this scriptural reference to the Gentiles' distinctive place in God's plan, together with Peter's explanation of Christ's teaching of salvation by grace, and Paul and Barnabas's relation of the signs and wonders done through them among the Gentiles. In addition, James explained the fear of burdening the new converts too much through the requirement of circumcision, but offered some alternative limitations—primarily the adherence to certain "kosher laws" mentioned in Leviticus 17–18.[9]

Because the council was able to center its decision on God's word and because the conference participants believed that the Holy Spirit had directed their decision—"It seemed good to the Holy Spirit and to us" (v. 28)—those who had sought the requirement of circumcision could overcome their fear of going against God's law. Due to the feeling that resulted from God's direction and the requirement of some limitations on Gentile activities, the circumcision group was able to obtain substantive satisfaction and therefore agree to and uphold the agreement.[10]

## Procedural Satisfaction

The Jerusalem Conference was also successful in achieving procedural satisfaction. Arguably, even if the people had concurred with the substance or with the agreement ultimately reached, the Christians from the party of the Pharisees, who held their position so strongly, might well have still gone against it if they had not been able to express their opinion on the important question regarding salvation. They were, however, given a voice in a well-structured conference instead of just being told what to do; therefore, they were satisfied with the process.

The foundation for procedural satisfaction was manifested in a variety of ways. First, the conference was held on "neutral ground" in Jerusalem, not in Antioch, where the dispute arose. Second, everyone met in one group, and apparently all were allowed to participate. Third, there was order in the proceedings and the Scriptures indicate that both speaking and listening filled the conference. It is apparent that people listened throughout the entire debate as others voiced their views. This order allowed for procedural satisfaction for all involved, rather than the chaos of a confrontational debate.

The final act that sealed the procedural satisfaction of both sides was immediately writing down the agreement in the form of a letter to the church at Antioch and sending it with representatives selected by all. This act allowed all involved to see the agreement and to be part of its immediate implementation. In this way, everyone felt satisfied not only with how the agreement was formed, but also with its administration.

## Psychological Satisfaction

Psychological satisfaction was essential in this situation because of the nature of the two sides. Both felt very strongly about the issue, as is evident from the very start of the discussion. An agreement had to be made which allowed for resolution while allowing those involved to feel that they had been respected and treated fairly.[11]

This psychological satisfaction was achieved through a number of wise decisions. First, the circumcision proponents were made to feel they were an important part of the entire group at Jerusalem. They were not excluded from the conference, but allowed to thoroughly participate. Their spokesmen helped decide the matter, write the letter, and select representatives to go with Paul and Barnabas. They also were represented to the church at Antioch in the letter expressing the council's decision—not as an outside faction, but as a group from among the whole.

In addition, it was made apparent throughout the proceedings and in the letter to Antioch that the Holy Spirit had been the driving force behind the decision. It was important for both parties to feel that God's hand was involved throughout and that the Pharasaic faction was not defeated but rather redirected by the Holy Spirit.

Finally, the greatest reason for psychological satisfaction was probably the dual message utilized in the agreement. The first part of the agreement resolved the issue about the necessity of circumcision that was troubling the Gentiles. The second part demonstrated appreciation for the concerns of the Pharasaic Christians by advising the Gentiles to accept certain limitations on their lifestyles which would make it possible for them to live a common life with Jewish Christians. The council was able to establish God's truth about salvation while showing those favoring circumcision that it was only their position that was rejected; they, themselves, were not.

Like most agreements involving the resolution of issues close to the hearts of people, the agreement achieved by the Jerusalem Conference was not without its future tensions. Paul later chastised Peter for his failure to embrace Gentile Christians, and no doubt there were others who were less than enthusiastic.[12] The durability of the agreement arising out of substantive, procedural, and psychological satisfaction, however, created a foundation upon which the decision was upheld and the church remained unified.

## Suggestions for Satisfaction

Substantive, procedural, and psychological satisfaction are important because agreements need to last. Several suggestions may be helpful in achieving such satisfaction.

### Watch for Signals of Dissatisfaction

If the mediator or facilitator is alert, people will provide their own signals of dissatisfaction. Silence, hesitancy, recalcitrance, or lack of cooperation may suggest that the level of satisfaction in some area is not sufficient for that person to be either involved in the process or supportive of its outcome. It is the mediator's job to listen and watch for such signs and incorporate a response to them into the dispute-resolution process.

### Recognize that Dissatisfaction Is Normal

In conflict resolution, some dissatisfaction is to be expected. If the individuals could themselves create a process that was meaningful and productive, they would not need a mediator. The challenge is to increase satisfaction to the level where the parties will support the agreement.

## Deal with Satisfaction Problems as They Arise

Many times dissatisfaction can be dealt with immediately. If it is obvious one side is having trouble, stop the process long enough to bring everyone back on board.

## Specifically Inquire About Satisfaction

Specific inquiry about satisfaction should be made both during mediation and at its conclusion. If, at the conclusion, there is not sufficient satisfaction for the people to move forward with the agreement, one must decide either to "chance it," or to turn and begin all over again. The latter is often difficult to elect because of all that has been invested. Yet it is essential if the goal of a durable agreement is to be achieved.

The ministry of reconciliation is most fruitful if it creates the environment for long-lasting agreements. Achieving substantive, procedural, and psychological satisfaction will set the stage for durable agreements and effective service.

## CHAPTER TWELVE

# COUNSELORS AND MEDIATORS: COMPARING PERSPECTIVES

RECENTLY, I SPENT SEVERAL HOURS talking with a counselor who served on the ministry staff of a large church. The focus of our intense conversation was the acute conflict in his congregation. That conflict was no different than that which often occurs in churches: dissatisfaction with leadership, differences between the senior minister and staff over direction and priorities, and disagreements among congregation members regarding the church's decision-making process.

Most satisfying in that encounter was my sense of "connectedness" with the counselor as he summarized his impressions of those involved in the conflict and I described how they might participate in a dispute-resolution process. We seemed to be talking about the same characteristics of the people and identifying similar approaches to the conflict environment, but we were using somewhat different languages—languages that reflected our separate backgrounds in counseling and conflict management. Upon reflection, that should have been no surprise.

It has been said mediation "has been derived and synthesized from diverse fields of practice." The theory, practice, and technique of mediation have been borrowed from the fields of labor negotiation, law, social psychology, and the psychological disciplines that provide the basis for psychotherapy and counseling.[1]

As a result, counselors find themselves on familiar turf when studying mediation. Most of the concepts and much of the language of both counseling and mediation derive from a similar sociocultural tradition.[2] Counselors often employ techniques used in mediation, such as active listening, issue reframing, and reality testing. Counseling multiple clients, such as couples therapy and family therapy, inherently involves some facilitation of negotiations among the parties—in a sense, mediation.

The purpose of this chapter is to identify some of the differences and similarities between the processes of counseling and mediation. Its purpose is not to describe completely all the forms or applications of counseling and mediation, but to provide the reader a sense of these two fields that, in practice, complement each other. Necessarily, generalizations and some abbreviated descriptions are used.

Four major areas of distinction can be made between counseling and mediation. They include: 1) primary focus and goals, 2) the depth of psychological exploration, 3) control of the process, and 4) emphasis on negotiation. In the following pages, each of these areas will be discussed.

## DIFFERENCES IN FOCUS AND GOALS

One observable difference between counseling and mediation is a contrast in focus and goals. Three differences are notable.

### Focus on the External Versus the Internal

Depending on one's school of psychology, individual counseling may explore the clients' past, examining the events which shape their psyches, usually with a goal of personal and interpersonal growth. This occurs through some form of psychotherapy in which a bond between therapist and client is established. It is designed to give the client an opportunity to examine relationships and events in the nurturing atmosphere of the client-therapist relationship. Therapy with couples and families may investigate the relationship between and among the clients to determine shared behaviors which contribute to their negative interaction. Obviously, considerable expertise and substantial time are required to ensure that this therapy is properly carried out.[3]

In contrast to most counseling, mediation is a "goal-focused, task-orientated, time-limited process."[4] Rather than a primary concern with the person's internal self, the focus of mediation is on the external. The goal of mediation is to create a workable solution to a problem or conflict being confronted by the clients. This is done in concrete (contractual) terms, usually without an extensive examination of the psychological bases underlying the problem.

For example, when an angry landlord and a frustrated tenant caught in acute conflict over an apartment show up at the Van Nuys Courthouse in Los Angeles, many times the judge will refer them to a mediator who immediately seeks to help them resolve their problem. As emotion fills the small conference room down the hall from the courtroom, the dispute becomes clear—rent is late and eviction is the landlord's answer. However, the landlord knows about the tenant's financial trouble, does not look forward to having a vacant apartment, and is convinced that the tenant may "trash" the apartment if forced to leave. So in a strange sort of way, the tenant and the landlord are dependent on each other. The tenant needs a place to live, and the landlord needs to protect and receive income from the property. Even though such dependence is overshadowed by angry words, disturbing threats, and great emotion, it is still very real to both parties.

While each person in such a conflict may bring to the meeting a variety of psychological problems, diverse personal histories, and uncontrolled emotions, those components are not the subject of the mediation process to be carried out by, in this instance, a volunteer for the Christian Conciliation Service of Los Angeles. Granted, therapy might allow the individuals to resolve their long-held psychological problems, change who they are, and equip them with skills for future relationships. That is probably needed! But the challenge of the moment is conflict over the impending eviction, and this issue must be settled in the next hour, either through the mediation process or by the judge.

Thus, the mediator's goal is resolution of a concrete and very acute conflict. The task is to find a mutually acceptable way for the landlord and the tenant to continue what should be a basic business relationship. The time to carry out the task and achieve the goal is limited not to days or weeks, but to minutes. As such, the focus is on those items one would perceive as external: the contract, the law, the facts, and the immediate relationship of the individuals involved. This focus almost exclusively on the external and the concrete is normal for mediation—but may be different from most counseling.[5]

## Focus on the Past Versus the Future

While counseling and therapy have a substantial focus on the past, in order to prepare for a better future, mediation is directed more toward the present and future as a way of resolving the past.

Generalizing again, the counselor's activity, at least initially, explores a client's past to prepare him or her for dealing effectively with the future. Understanding the past naturally allows the client greater resources to use in addressing what is ahead. For instance, the daughter of an alcoholic uses the history of alcoholism in her family in addressing what might be her own tendency to become an alcoholic in the future. A history of being physically abused may be important for the client to address to avoid being the abuser in the future. Understanding past events that triggered serious depression may be a key factor in controlling depression in the months to come.

While such a focus on the past provides substantial information that can be helpful in resolving intrapersonal and interpersonal conflict, it is a luxury not usually available in mediation. In the environment where mediation is most important, there

141

typically is an acute conflict and either: 1) an ongoing relationship between the people involved, or 2) recognition that the people cannot resolve their differences themselves and their alternative (perhaps litigation) is undesirable. The expectation is that the mediation process will expeditiously help them reach an acceptable resolution.

Returning to the landlord-tenant dispute as an example, there certainly is an applicable history; it has resulted in the parties being on opposite sides of a potential eviction order issued by a judge. The past, whether it was the late rent payments or the failure to repair the stove in the apartment, brought the tenant and the landlord to this moment in their relationship. About all the court can deal with is who was right, who was wrong, and who gets his way now. Counseling may be helpful in educating the individuals about the development of conflict in their relationship, but what they need now is practical assistance and immediate resolution. In such a case, mediation will *address* the past, but *focus* on the future.

If the mediator can get the individuals to look at the future, at how they envision living in the same apartment complex, as well as the characteristics of their business and personal relationships, an agreement can be reached, and many times the importance of who was right or wrong in the past diminishes— sometimes it even evaporates. Through a new system of accountability to each other, developed in the mediation process, the disputants refocus from the past, and a fault-oriented resolution of it, to a future of greater mutual benefit.

## Focus on Tools Versus Resolution

The primary goal of mediation is to accommodate different perspectives in a problem-solving process which results in meaningful conflict-resolving decisions, whether or not there is emotional growth, release, or complete internal peace. Taken to the extreme, the goal of mediation is settlement. Mediation's objective is to create confidence that the disputants can reach agreement on substantive issues and make settlement a reality. If settlement can be used as a motivating factor, it may cause both sides to compromise from their positions, thereby moving toward resolution. Reconciliation of a relationship may not be achieved in mediation, but cessation of conflict is accomplished.

The experience of a federal mediator who had been called in to resolve a contract dispute between a large teachers association and a school district is extreme, but it illustrates mediation's emphasis on settlement.

One member of the bargaining team was cautioned by its chief negotiator, "Remember, not everything the mediator says will necessarily be true, especially when she describes what the other side is thinking. But the mediator's job is to say and do anything that will help bring about a settlement." While this admonition is overstated and *not* representative of mediation in the context of families, churches, communities, or even many collective bargaining circumstances, it does validly state the importance of settlement in mediation, and it sharpens the distinction between the goals of counseling and mediation. In contrast to counseling, which is intended to reduce emotional distress by examining and resolving its causes in order to achieve behavioral or interactional change, mediation is only pragmatically interested in the causes of conflict and how this conflict might be reduced. Settlement is mediation's primary purpose.

The counselor therapist may find the mediation approach to be antithetical to his or her training, because, after a thorough investigation of the root causes, many counselors usually seek to give clients tools rather than solutions to their problems. It can be very difficult for counselors to switch orientations for fear they may miss some important issue or fix something that is not broken.

A benefit of mediation's goal orientation, however, is its attractiveness to clients who are reluctant to risk self-examination, or who do not need to do so in order to reach agreement with others. The businesslike approach of mediation can reduce the threat level some clients experience in human interaction.

Another benefit of mediation's goal orientation is the hope it provides that issues can be resolved. It achieves that benefit by creating the expectation that at least small changes can reduce if not eliminate conflict. Accepting the notion that a procedure like mediation can be useful in resolving conflict may encourage people to change other aspects of their lives. Clients can rediscover their own skills involving the decision-making process, and apply them with fresh enthusiasm.

Counselors may be pleased to recognize that the decision-making process in mediation often results in the emotional equilibrium sought by the more exploratory methods of counseling and psychotherapy. As the result of task-oriented problem-solving, anxiety, depression, and anger are frequently reduced, and self-actualization and communication skills are often improved. Many times, a successful mediation may even result in less resistance to deeper psychological reflection, and bring about the actual reconciliation of relationships.

### DIFFERENCES IN DEPTH OF
### PSYCHOLOGICAL EXAMINATION

The second major difference between counseling and mediation relates to the depth of psychological explanation. Again this is best illustrated by an example.

Outbursts of anger punctuated the atmosphere as mediation began with a young woman and her husband regarding their conflict over keeping a pit bull terrier in their home. The young woman's husband wanted to keep a pit bull that already had bitten one of their children twice. The woman was angry about the dog being there, but did not want to confront her husband. In mediation, the fear of the future was addressed not in terms of the woman's unwillingness to confront her husband, and the psychological basis for that, but in terms of the safety for the children. Both parties could agree upon the value of safety. They were able to decide to give up the animal without exploring the dynamics of the marriage relationship. Significant counseling issues became somewhat less important as they discovered they could make and enforce decisions.

This illustration is not put forth to suggest that the underlying psychological and relationship issues should not be addressed. The long-term prospect for their marriage may demand it. The point is that, in dealing with the acute crisis, the pragmatic and decisive approach of mediation may be helpful, even if carried out, as it usually is, without deep psychological examination.

## Examining the Past

The pragmatism of mediation does include a limited examination of the past and present relationship. This examination is needed to identify the basis of the dispute, as well as to know the parameters in which an agreement is likely to last. No mediated settlement will endure if there is not at least a reasonable resolution of emotional issues. Also, no one should feel he or she was somehow hoodwinked into agreement without having had a fair airing of his or her concerns. Thus, the mediator must be aware of both the substantive and psychological history of the dispute. Any settlement must be placed within that history so that it provides sufficient psychological satisfaction.

Unlike the counselor conducting mediation, who must rein in his or her instincts to pursue a deeper examination of the psychological causes for the dispute than is necessary, the mediator will seek to contain the emotions, rather than explore them, by focusing on the concrete issues. The better the mediator understands the psychological causes, the more likely a satisfactory settlement can be reached; but the mediator will limit this examination to what is necessary to achieve a lasting agreement.

## Too Much Psychological Exploration

The danger for mediators, especially those with great sensitivity to counseling issues or those with counseling backgrounds, is the overinvestment in psychological exploration at the expense of an efficient, businesslike facilitation of the mediation process. As in counseling, disputants may attempt to draw the helper into the inter- or intrapersonal conflict. They can take up vast amounts of time describing their feelings about the circumstances of conflict. They may focus on the genesis of the conflict, which may or may not be feasible to address in the context of mediation.

In one recent case, two family members who were in conflict over the conduct of a family business were quick to invite the psychological exploration of their relationship and, particularly, their relationship to their parents. They had different views of how their parents had treated them during their youth, and it

145

was obvious by their conversation that they attributed their current conflict to lifelong events in their family. Without diminishing the value of counseling in such a circumstance (and in that case, encouraging both parties to seek counseling so such psychological dimensions of their lives could be explored), the issue on the table was much more tangible. How would they manage their family business? Getting distracted with the psychological exploration would have prevented them from coming up with the immediate, realistic, and concrete approaches to management that both could commit to so they could move forward in a productive way. Understanding the nature of the mediation process explains why the psychological exploration is appropriately limited.

## Inappropriate Psychological Exploration

Finally, psychological exploration may be inappropriate, depending on the qualifications of the mediator. While some mediators have a counseling or psychotherapy background, many mediators, especially those working outside the context of domestic relations, come to the field of mediation with backgrounds in law, business, or other fields. They need to recognize the limitations of their particular preparation and not engage in activity that is beyond their abilities. Again, those involved in the conflict will not respect the nuances of the mediator's preparation. It is up to the mediator to limit his or her involvement where such would be inappropriate, or even harmful, and to utilize counseling professionals as a complementary resource.

## CONTROL OF THE PROCESS

The third major difference between counseling and mediation relates to the way the counselor or mediator controls the process. Once again, keep in mind that a substantial part of this difference reflects the circumstance of the respective process. In most counseling, there usually is only the counselor and one other person. The process generally involves rather straightforward conversation between the therapist and the client. While at times emotional, the management of the process involves little more than the management of their conversation.

In mediation, the third party always works with two or more other individuals. Activity in mediation that relates to control of the process involving an increased number of individuals and several conversations is more prominent.

Mediation also demands more intense conflict management and process control from the initial stages of contact with clients. As described in an earlier chapter, substantial time may be invested in helping the parties arrive at a procedural agreement for their conduct and the conduct of the mediation process. In reality, many times the mediator establishes a certain control of the process by imposing procedural structure such as the time, place, and rules of communication to be observed. The mediator may make it known, for instance, that he or she will control who talks and when each person talks. The obvious element of control may be most prominent as the process begins.[6]

## Active Intervention

While it is acknowledged that there is a broad range of intervention activity among counselors, mediators tend to be very active as they intervene in the conflict. Such may reflect the increased control of the process described previously. In fulfilling the mediator's tasks and roles, the mediator will actively help the individuals identify the issues in their dispute, as well as propose solutions to the conflict. Unlike the perception that the mediation process involves people sitting on pillows and drinking herbal tea, negotiation when conflict is acute may demand substantial intervention by the mediator in controlling and directing the process.[7]

## Balancing Power and Tension

Mediators also control the process by balancing power between disputants. Because the essence of the mediation process is the disputants' negotiation, it cannot be effective if the power is so imbalanced that one side is simply not able to negotiate. In these cases, the mediator may very well work to balance the individuals' power through private meetings, the sensitive inclusion of information, or the inclusion of outside resources, particularly experts in fields like law and accounting.

Certainly counselors balance power. Usually, however, it occurs through the empowering of one of the people involved in conflict. Since often counselors are working with just one of the two or more people involved, they can assist that person in developing characteristics that will create a more powerful negotiator: assertiveness, effective communication skills, and greater knowledge of the matter to be negotiating. However, it is a longer-term approach to balancing power through the development of personal characteristics. Mediators must create a more balanced atmosphere almost immediately for the usually short duration of the dispute-resolution process.

In addition to balancing power, the mediator must make critical decisions regarding the level of tension to allow during the mediation process. Often, mediation sessions allow more tension, hostility, and perhaps fear than the usual counseling and therapy session. While too much tension can cause people to pull back from full participation, some tension can be a highly motivating factor keeping people focused on the task of coming up with a workable solution to their conflict.

## Acceptance of Stress

Finally, the mediator must be prepared to experience considerable stress, which the disputants may focus more on the mediator than clients might direct toward a counselor. In counseling, the counselor might put that stress of the circumstance back on the individual so the client comes to grip with reality. The counselor simply cannot afford to take personally the anger and anxiety of every counselee. In mediation, the mediator might accept a certain amount of stress, recognizing that, if absorbed by the mediator, such is not then directed by the disputants at each other. In a sense, the mediator becomes an alternative recipient of the conflict, thereby pulling from the conflict what would otherwise be destructive to the people involved.

Overall, one may get an accurate sense that controlling the process in mediation may be somewhat more assertive and manipulative than dealing with the same issues in the context of counseling. That is probably a correct assessment based upon the particular use and focus of the mediation process.[8]

## THE IMPORTANCE OF NEGOTIATION

Negotiation is the element that most distinguishes mediation from counseling. Following the gathering of information, mediation differs from counseling in preparing viable proposals, manipulating such proposals, keeping the process moving, keeping disputants from being locked into positions from which they find it difficult to move, and working toward creative and acceptable compromises. In mediation, the third party is not like a counselor asking questions, managing a communication process, and leading the individuals to helpful conclusions about themselves or their relationships. Rather, the mediator is actively involved in helping the individuals negotiate a resolution that is acceptable to them. Holding settlement out as a carrot, the mediator must encourage the disputants to leave behind the psychological sources of their dispute and build a new relationship unhampered by the destructiveness of the past. The task of the mediator is to make the settlement real and achievable in a manner that lets both sides obtain some portion of their objectives.

The mediator goes beyond communication to help the disputants find a way they can "win" or at least discover a solution that is more attractive than the alternatives. Many times that will mean they engage in difficult negotiations that only rise to the level of being acceptable, not thrilling. Counseling skills are an important element in the overall process; but it is knowledge of the process of negotiation and techniques at facilitating it that become most important.

### SIMILARITIES BETWEEN COUNSELING AND MEDIATION

While some differences exist between counseling and mediation in their focus and goals, psychological examination, control of the process, and importance of negotiation, there are also a number of similarities.

### Skills of Conciliation

A broad view of mediation includes at least four phases: conciliation, data gathering, proposal generation, and negotiation. Conciliation has been defined as the process of "correcting perceptions, reducing unreasonable fears, and improving communication to an extent that permits reasonable discussion to take place and, in fact, makes rational bargaining possible."[9] Conciliation has also been described as "the psychological component of mediation in which the third party attempts to create an atmosphere of trust and cooperation that is conducive to negotiations."[10] This stage is especially amenable to counseling skills.

At the outset, the mediator must usually employ counseling skills to examine the disputants' history enough to understand the issue being addressed. The mediator must also facilitate the communication between the disputants, even though it is possibly quite hostile. One of the mediator's goals will be to establish trust and mutuality between the individuals while weighing against any power imbalances. This will require active listening by the mediator and, even more important, active listening by the disputants as they lay out their separate positions. Achieving this kind of listening will likely require tenacious encouragement by the mediator.

The strong feelings typical of a dispute are a major hurdle to agreement, and it is in this area that the mediator must determine the depth to which psychological exploration will be a prerequisite to problem-solving. Mediation research indicates the more emotionally based the dispute, the more difficult settlement will be.[11] A destructive emotional component may take two forms: Either the disputants are overtly hostile, or ironically, they may focus on facts to avoid emotions which are too raw to express. While the mediator will use focusing on facts later as a conflict-management technique, in the beginning, a prolonged rehashing of facts may signal insufficient emotional resolution to allow the two sides to prepare for negotiation. If this occurs, the mediator must clarify for the disputants what is happening[12] and suggest that it will be necessary to process the emotional component of the dispute before mediation can truly begin.

Because processing highly charged emotional conflict or extreme hostility is beyond the goals of mediation, some form of outside therapy may be necessary. The mediator's task is to balance the level of emotion sufficiently to maintain the disputants' motivation to resolve the conflict without letting that emotion become destructive. The highly intuitive communication skills of many counselors and therapists should be most useful in this regard.

## Approach to Short-Term Assistance

It is important to acknowledge that there are forms of counseling and psychotherapy which focus on the shorter term, either because the client prefers it, or by design of the therapist. Counseling clients often seek to limit their expense by setting a goal of achieving some level of resolution in a relatively few number of counseling sessions. Other clients may simply want to solve a problem without extensive psychological probing. Involvement is often very short in a typical crisis-counseling situation—even as short as an anonymous telephone call to a crisis hot line. Generally, counselors who practice more directive techniques in counseling may be more comfortable in the mediation process.

To illustrate, there are parallels between aspects of mediation and a practice some therapists call "Brief Therapy." Brief Therapy is characterized by four steps: 1) outlining a clear definition of the problem in concrete terms, 2) investigating solutions previously attempted, 3) clearly delineating the change to be achieved, and 4) forming and implementing a plan to produce this change.[13]

Some brief therapists describe their work as an effort to achieve "second-order" rather than "first-order" change. A first-order change is the one which results from most therapies: a change of the person within a system while the system—family, marriage, etc.—may or may not remain intact. A second-order change is directed at the system itself and seeks to *reframe* the context in which the problem exists.

Jesus provided what could be considered an example of this approach in John 8:7 when the Pharisees brought an adulterous woman to him and asked what should be done with her. The system in which Jesus operated was well established; the Old Testament has strong admonitions against adultery. The Pharisees sought to force Jesus to condemn the woman to death. Rather than succumbing to this trap, Jesus said, "If any one of you is without sin, let him be the first to throw a stone at her." He simply reframed the issue. How the woman had come to her predicament was not relevant. The future was the only issue. With his admonition, Jesus thrust upon the Pharisees a call to self-examination. The woman could not be condemned by those present because, as humans, none of them was sufficient to the task. This was, indeed, brief therapy among those present; the focus, as in mediation, was on the solution and short-term assistance.[14]

The purpose of this chapter has not been to describe counseling and mediation with great specifics. It has been to point out that there are at least four general differences between much of the counseling that is offered and most applications of mediation, as well as two significant similarities between the processes. An awareness of the differences and similarities between the processes should provide a clear perspective and aid those seeking to refer individuals caught in conflict.

# CHAPTER THIRTEEN

# MANAGING CONFLICT IN FAMILIES

"AND WHERE DO YOU THINK you're going, Vincent?" Mary asked as her fifteen-year-old son zipped up his tattered leather jacket even though the weather was warm.

"Aw, you know, Mom, . . . out," he muttered. She folded her arms and stared at him hard as he continued. "Me and the guys, we're goin' down to the arcade and then maybe out to a movie," he said, moving toward the door.

"And then maybe out looking for beer is more like it," Mary replied, stepping between him and the exit. "Vince, I don't want you going out with those boys. Last time you kept me waiting up till two o'clock, and I need my sleep. Maybe you don't want to work around here, but I have to. You've got homework, and you and I both agreed with the school counselor that if you're going to pass this year some changes have to be made."

"Aw, screw the counselor," Vince said under his breath.

"What did you say?" she shot back, raising her right hand. As Mary backed against the door, Vincent's sleepy-eyed younger sister came out from the bedroom carrying a stuffed animal.

"I said I ain't doin' my homework and you ain't stoppin' me from goin' out," Vince said, both his anger and his voice rising. He turned and headed toward the kitchen. Mary lunged after him, grabbing his jacket by the collar. He was still only about as tall as she was, and she wasn't about to back down. Suddenly he turned, catching her across the shoulder with his forearm, knocking her to the floor. From across the room the little girl began to cry.

"Leave me alone, Mom!" shouted Vincent over his sister's crying, his voice cracking with both fury and hurt. "You married a bum, and now you've raised a bum. Dad's gone, and soon I will be, too; so you won't have to worry about me anymore." He turned on his heel and headed for the back door.

Mary picked herself up and started toward the kitchen after him. She saw him open a drawer and pull out a large carving knife. "I said leave me alone!" Vincent shouted again, turning, tears starting to form in the corners of his eyes. The frustration of failure was too much for him. He had to get out, get away. Still holding the knife between them, he raised the window with his other hand and stepped out onto the fire escape. "Don't bother waitin' up," he said, tossing the knife through the window onto the kitchen floor. "It won't do no good anyway." He turned and started down the cold metal stairs.

Mary sank to the floor, crying, pounding the linoleum with her fist. She felt hopeless and helpless. She was losing another man in her life, perhaps the last. The little girl shuffled up behind her, clutching the stuffed animal. Slowly Mary stood up again, raising her daughter in her arms. Her family was turning out just as her own parents' family had. She wondered what her daughter's life would be like, but felt powerless to make a difference.

## CONFLICT IN FAMILIES

The tragic instance described above may seem extreme; but in reality, it represents what is all too normal in many families. While relationships among family members—husbands and wives, parents and children, siblings, or even more distant relatives—can be the wondrous source of joy and encouragement, all too often they create a terribly stressful arena of hurt, anger, frustration, and even violence. These are the results, at least in part, from the challenging realities of families and family relationships today.

In a report on the family to the president of the United States, a White House working group made the following conclusions regarding the 3.6 million children entering school for the first time in 1986:

- 14 percent were part of families in which the parents were not married.
- Between 25 and 33 percent were "latchkey" children. They returned to their homes after school each day with no one to meet them—no day care, no supervision, no parental guidance.
- Almost half would live in a single-parent home before they were eighteen years old.[1]

Another prominent observer of the family has collected the following collage of statistics on the events related to family members—events that are expected to occur during a typical year:

- 500,000 children will attempt suicide.
- More than a million children will run away from home.
- 275,000 teen-age girls will give birth to illegitimate babies.
- 12 million teen-agers will take some form of narcotics and regularly use drugs.
- 3.3 million young people will experience a serious drinking problem.

- 5 million children will become victims of broken homes.
- 4 million children will be beaten, molested, or otherwise abused by their parents.[2]

While a variety of factors may contribute to this tragic portrayal of families, including poverty, limited educational opportunities, and psychological dysfunction, each of those results can be caused by conflict as well. It may be the intrapersonal conflict of a young mother trying to finish high school with a child, or the interpersonal conflict of a husband and wife who simply do not possess skills necessary for effective communication. Such conflict disrupts the operation of what could be a healthy family system, and sends those who are members of it into circumstances for which they are not prepared. Without knowing the personalities, all of us can sense the existence of conflict in the circumstance described by Chuck Swindoll in his best-selling book, *Growing Wise in Family Life:*

> During my forty-plus years on this old Earth, I have been allowed to witness firsthand the disintegration of several families. . . . All of the homes involved were once what you and I would call fairly strong—meaning both parents were ordinary, in love with each other, and the children were wanted, loved, and seemed well-adjusted. For all outward appearances, there were healthy and agreeable relationships among the family members. In none of the homes was there any sign of poverty, abuse, physical affliction or mental disorder. . . . Each home seemed a happy place to be. But each eroded so drastically that the hope of recovery and rehabilitation faded from view.[3]

One does not have to go to extremes of shocking statistics or personal recollections to confirm the reality of differences within families. Even families that are accurately portrayed as loving, supportive, and healthy experience conflict. In my own family, when Friday night arrives, we all know the potential for conflict arrives along with it. Dad is tired after a long week which usually has included cross-country travel. Mom is also tired after successfully maneuvering her way through five days of work encompassing everything from 100 miles of carpooling for the soccer team to deciding on what termite service to hire. The kids—three of them who range from post-toddler to pre-adolescence—reflect the stimulation of their week with an energy level that is unbelievable to Mom and Dad. All of these experiences converge on our home at 5:00 P.M. Friday. The one last challenge of the week is to decide where we're going to eat that night.

Such a decision should not be an insurmountable task. There are dozens of restaurants from which to choose. But the decision quickly becomes the week's most difficult, as differences and conflict jump to the surface.

After buckling the kids in the van, the journey down the boulevard begins, along with a chorus from the back seat: "We want to eat at a kids' place." Everyone knows what that means— a restaurant where the attraction of the jungle gym far exceeds the attraction of the food. Mom quickly responds to the back-seat chorus by saying, "We've eaten at those places all week! Tonight we're going to an adult place."

This does not solve the problem, however, for as soon as that threshold decision is made, the conflict intensifies over the choice of the "adult" restaurant. John wants fettucini at Bodducco's. Tiny Melinda advocates Mexican food at Lupé's. Janet is convinced that Chinese food at Hunan is the right choice. Any of these would be fine with Mom if the family could just eat together in peace. Keep in mind now, as the conflict continues, the van with the Friday-night family is traveling down the boulevard, passing dozens of restaurants!

Finally, after hearing enough and concluding that a negotiated resolution is probably not possible, I pull the van into the parking lot of my favorite deli, looking forward to its great food and a relaxing meal. This is not to occur, however, because even though I had the power to make the restaurant choice, my adjudication of the conflict left in its path dissatisfaction at all levels, including both the process and the outcome! As a result, the real conflict may just be beginning, and will last through dinner. It may even be brought up the next day. And certainly it will be remembered the next Friday night when we again pile into the van and head for dinner!

Such conflict does not pose a serious threat to the family. But it, and a host of similar conflicts, present themselves daily, and provide constant challenges to even the most healthy families.

## CONTEXT OF FAMILY CONFLICT

While differences, disagreements, and conflict are evident from time to time in all relationships, conflict in the structure of a family has special, sometimes unique characteristics. Several are worth noting here.

### Lifelong Relationships

At one time, most of us would have assumed that the family could be compared with a dinner selection from a restaurant menu. We made our choice, and all the parts of the meal simply "came with it." Increasingly, though, there is a sense that we can pick and choose, bring together and easily separate family members, and define our families like the *à la carte* selections at a cafeteria. Now, the family is a collection of different individuals with different, yet generally long-term relationships.

A generation or two ago in a more rural society, extended family members such as grandparents, aunts, uncles, and cousins were nearby; but today it is not uncommon for our mobility to have separated family members by thousands of miles. As a result, the number of those with whom we share vital family relationships is whittled down dramatically. In addition, the impact of divorce, children born outside of marriage, and the rise of single parents have caused us, with justification, to define the family unit differently than the stereotypical family comprised of Mom, Dad, and the kids.

In some circumstances, the choosing of family has extended beyond the individual's acceptance of a particular person as his or her marriage partner. It now includes women who abort babies prior to birth, and even parents giving up children who are born with imperfections and disabilities. *Newsweek* magazine recently published a story which described in alarming detail the attitudes of many who simply found a baby's disabilities too great an interference with their perception of life, so they gave up the child to institutions or more compassionate adoptive parents. What was so incredulous in the description of such parents was not the fact that in many cases this painful decision is necessitated by economic need or psychological inability to cope, but the sense that family is defined by selfish convenience.[4] Harvard professor and psychiatrist Robert Coles in his book *Harvard Diary* reacts with dismay to the current situation of abortion; many people might react the same way to divorce or giving up children to adoptive parents or shuffling off aged parents to nursing hospitals:

> I can't forget what I see all around me now—abortion has become an everyday fact of life, a mere routine, and oh dear God, a "right" part of the program of "entitlement" a self-centered population lottery demands.[5]

While the developing sense of family may include the ability to define who is included and what the family's structure might be, in a real sense conflict must be addressed within relationships that last a lifetime. Take, for instance, the illustration in Figure 13–1 of a traditional family. Each large circle represents half of the marriage partnership, as well as that person's parental role. One person is a wife and mother; the other is a

**Traditional Family Structure**

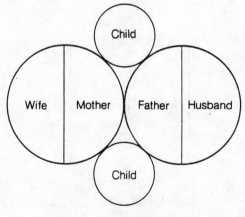

**Figure 13–1**

159

husband and father. The two smaller circles are the children. If all goes according to God's plan, that illustration would continue to accurately present the family, and any expected conflict that arose would be handled within its structure.

What if, however, the wife and husband end their marriage? Figure 13–2 shows how the structure of the family changes. There are no longer complete circles, and everyone feels the pain of that loss. While husband and wife can change the nature of their relationship, they are the only biological mother and father those little circles will ever have! Like it or not, their relationship will last a lifetime.

In working with divorcing couples with children, many pastors, counselors, and other helpers find that the spouses view the divorce as an end to conflict, and to some extent it may be. But the reality is that their ability to productively and respectfully manage conflict related to them and to their children is a lifelong challenge. They will continue to deal with a variety of parenting issues, support needs, and demands required by their relationship. The question becomes whether they want to handle such issues in a highly adversarial and destructive way,

**Family Structure After Divorce**

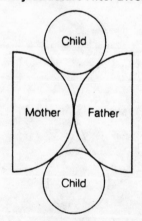

**Figure 13–2**

usually through the courts, or whether they can learn to handle it in a respectful way with each other.

The same is true in other family relationships. Estrangement between parents and children, as well as brothers and sisters, will not be resolved through avoidance or the passage of time. Relationships between family members last a lifetime, and so too will unresolved conflicts.

### Serious Concerns

In addition to the reality that most family relationships are lifelong relationships, many family conflicts are related to family members' serious and important concerns.

We argue over money because it is essential to our existence. Conflict between spouses occurs when each is challenged to be selfless rather than selfish. Differences between teen-age children and parents take on ultimate importance as teen-agers move from adolescence to adulthood and, in doing so, face the issues of who they are and who they are to become. As these and similar concerns are faced by families, they bring to the surface challenging conflicts.

To put these issues in perspective, it might be helpful to compare them to conflict generated by less-serious matters. Having spent years as part of several university faculties, I have seen my share of conflict over globally *un*important issues. We have argued over the wording of catalog descriptions for the courses we offer. We have vigorously discussed whether the minutes of the last faculty meeting were correctly recorded. We have engaged in dramatic debate over grade inflation, registration policies, and the proper role for the dean to play in fund-raising.

While of some importance in the context of higher education, such issues pale in comparison to the functioning of the family system, the development of values, the rearing of children, and the permanence of family relations. This is just part of the list of family concerns that keeps many parents awake at night wondering and hoping that they are doing at least part of it right. As Charles Swindoll concluded in his book, *Strengthening Your Grip*, "When you boil it down to the basics, the pulse of an entire civilization is determined by the heartbeat of its homes."[6]

## Great Emotion

In addition to lifelong relationships and serious concerns, conflict in families is characterized by the great emotion that surrounds it. The amazing picture described in the first verses of Genesis of a divine God creating the world quickly gives way to a description of human emotions as Cain and Abel—two members of the same family—confront their conflict. Cain's jealousy of his brother Abel's acceptance by God went to the essence of their relationship, calling forth the most passionate emotions. It cannot be described more visually than in the passage itself:

> Then the LORD said to Cain. . . . "If you do what is right, will you not be accepted? But if you do not do what is right, sin is crouching at your door; it desires to have you, but you must master it."
>
> Now Cain said to his brother Abel, "Let's go out to the field." And while they were in the field, Cain attacked his brother Abel and killed him.
>
> Then the LORD said to Cain, "Where is your brother Abel?"
>
> "I don't know," he replied. "Am I my brother's keeper?"
>
> The LORD said, "What have you done? Listen! Your brother's blood cries out to me from the ground. Now you are under a curse and driven from the ground, which opened its mouth to receive your brother's blood from your hand. When you work the ground, it will no longer yield its crops for you. You will be a restless wanderer on the earth." (Gen. 4:6–12)

In other circumstances the Bible identifies numerous causes of marital and family conflict: envy,[7] greed,[8] stubbornness,[9] adultery.[10] Even in the family which feels close to God, human nature may cause love for each other to be lost. The story of Adam and Eve's eating from the Tree of Knowledge tells us we cannot be human, separate from God, and knowledgeable in the ways of the world, without struggling with our failings. Our inadequacies often result in conflict, even with those we love most.

These inadequacies are reflected almost daily in the headlines of local newspapers. Within the family unit, differences occur, passions are aroused, emotions get out of control, and the conflict results in violence, injury, or death.

## Underlying Causes

The real issues and values underlying family controversy may be hidden among false problems and irrelevant arguments. The true sources of anger and pain may be so bound up in family and marital history, even in subconscious or early-childhood events, that the disputants may be unaware of the genuine causes of their discord.

As many helping professionals recognize, issues such as those between Mary and Vincent in the example used at the beginning of this chapter may appear commonplace when, in fact, they hide more serious concerns. The dispute may focus on issues such as homework, grades, and mildly delinquent behavior when other, less obvious, issues are the real causes.

Like many teen-agers, Vince may be confused about who he is and what he wants to do with his life. Part of him may want to become more powerful, while another part wants to remain a child. He may find that failure gains him attention and becomes a refuge from responsibility; in a sense, failure may give him power to control the adults around him.

At the same time, Vincent's behavior likely causes Mary to feel both angry and ashamed. Being a single parent, she is probably not able to spend the kind of time she wants with her children. She may be frustrated that most of her communication with Vince concerns his poor performance in school, the length of his hair, or where he goes at night and when he will be home. She probably feels she is in a constant struggle over her authority and her son's willfulness. While she may truly care about Vince, all their conversations may still end in shouting matches over issues as trivial as what television channel the family will watch.

Mary and Vince probably do not understand the real sources of their rage and distress. Mary may be unconsciously angry because Vince reminds her of her ex-husband, and the divorce which left Mary with little money to raise their children. Or she may see in Vince her own failings and may, by focusing on his unsatisfactory school work, be transferring to Vince her anger at herself for not completing school. Vince, on the other hand, may be hurt because his father left him as a young child; he may blame his mother for driving his father away. Or he may be struggling with the process of separating emotionally from his youth and his mother; he may find their arguments a means of asserting his independence, reassuring himself that leaving home will eventually be a good thing.

Are these or any other important underlying issues likely to be revealed during their nightly fights? Probably not. Mary and Vince may be completely unaware these issues even exist, much less the importance they have in their relationship. They may simply find it too difficult or painful to discover and deal honestly with such issues—issues that lie behind each day's conflict.

## Lack of Preparation

As a teacher, my life is committed to preparing students for their future careers. College students pay thousands of dollars in tuition to study dozens of subjects for several years. Finally, they are awarded a degree and sent off to contribute to the working world.

Contrast that preparation with what most people engage in before beginning the all-important marriage relationship or the task of rearing children. For most people, less time is spent preparing for either of those challenges than is spent getting a driver's license, which at least requires exposure to some rules and successful passing of a basic test! The result, years later, is obvious in failed marriages and failed parenting. In his book, *Parenting Isn't for Cowards,* Dr. James Dobson reports the results of his study of 35,000 parents. More than 30 percent responded to his inquiry regarding their performance in the parental role by saying, in effect, "I am a failure as a parent!"[11]

While there are many areas of family life where education and training could make us more effective partners and parents— including education about communication, financial management, sexual relationships, and discipline—one area of great need is problem-solving and conflict-management. As has been stated throughout this book, if conflict and differences are inevitable, we need to learn how to address them.

In his insightful book *How to Enjoy a Family Fight,* Will Cunningham describes the need well:

> Whenever two or more people have a continuing relationship, there will eventually be conflict. Are you married? There will be conflict. Are you single and living at home with your parents? There will be conflict. Are you the parent of a single son or daughter living at home? There will be conflict. . . . And whenever there is conflict, there can only be one of two outcomes: We will either hurt—even destroy—each other, or we will build up each other and benefit from the experience. It all depends on whether we fight wrong or fight right. . . . Fighting wrong comes naturally. But rarely are we given instructions in how to fight right.[12]

The family is a unique environment for conflict. It is in that environment that lifelong relationships, serious concerns, great emotion, underlying causes, and lack of preparation all affect the development and resolution of conflict.

## RESPONSES TO FAMILY CONFLICT

Our culture considers a strong marriage and secure family the bedrock of our society and culture. As a result, many current religious and political programs seek to revitalize families and marriages in the face of growing divorce, juvenile delinquency, and extramarital sex.

Traditional approaches to resolving family and marital conflict, however, place considerable pressure on families and couples to solve problems in the home with only occasional support from church and community. This pressure on parents and spouses has increased as society offers an increasingly tempting panoply of distractions that can tear families and couples apart.[13]

To meet this challenge, history would place responsibility on the father and husband, expected to be a pillar of strength, a hardworking provider, generously furnishing his family the wealth and protection it needs in a dangerous world. The ideal-ized wife and mother is equally under pressure to be the fam-ily's source of comfort and love, attentive to her spouse and children's individual needs, never thinking of herself, always putting the interests of her family first. Within this utopian environment of love and support, the family is expected to maintain sufficient stability to care for its members. Any failure to meet these needs is seen as a personal dereliction, a short-coming in character, especially in the parents.

Even though this model has been considered the ideal, it has dramatically diminishing relevance for today's families and couples who are struggling with materialism, changing values, and confused identities. The stereotypical family with a bread-winning father, a full-time homemaking mother, and two chil-dren now makes up only 15 percent of the family population.[14] To counterbalance the pressures of single-parent families, dual-income families, and blended families, society is expanding its support of the family from churches, schools, mental health facilities, and professionals through counseling and conflict resolution.

## Helping Troubled Families Through Counseling

Counseling is probably the most frequently used method of offering help; and mediation, if it is used at all, is employed only during the divorce process. Our purpose here is to show how mediation can be used to help resolve conflict in marriage before it escalates to divorce or conflict in other family rela-tionships before it becomes estrangement and violence. Again, generalizations are necessary to describe the process choices, even though they may not be as apparent in specific cases.

Counselors often find a variety of characteristics in troubled families and couples: poor communication patterns, lack of negotiation skill, uneven power, an unclear decision-making system, and a pervasive tone of depression and cynicism.[15] To address these problems, counselors and other helpers are begin-ning to perceive the family not as a collection of individuals, but as a unit which must be dealt with as a whole.

Traditional counseling efforts directed at family conflict and divorce often focused on the member who was acting out the most—whose behavior was the worst, whether it was a delinquent child, an irresponsible parent, or an adulterous spouse. Such approaches might occasionally involve other family members; but the focus was often on the individual and how his or her behavior might be changed to become less disruptive to other family members.

Counselors now direct their attention not just at individuals within the family but at the entire family structure and all family members. A family counselor addressing the conflict between Mary and Vincent, for example, would not fall into the trap of focusing only on Vincent. The counselor would recognize that Vince's negative behavior takes place in a context of support, not only from his friends, but also from Mary, although it is doubtful she recognizes how her behavior contributes to his. Mary and Vincent's relationship, like all family relationships, is characterized by a balance of power and by habits which encourage each other's behavior, both positive and negative.

To deal with a family or couple holistically, many counselors begin by learning how the particular family functions, its members' normal daily activities, and the role each family member plays. Counselors recognize the need to be sensitive to the diverse lifestyles families and couples choose, and then to be willing to operate within a values context different from the counselor's own values.[16] By examining individual roles, the counselor can identify each member's codependent behavior—those behaviors which support negative interactions within the family and between the spouses.[17]

Codependent systems are usually very subtle. One spouse may deny the other spouse's compulsion for overwork, or may unconsciously cause the stress that results in a spouse's drug dependency. One child may instigate arguments among siblings in order to be perceived as "the good child" by the parents. Wherever there is continually negative behavior, there is almost always codependent behavior which disingenuously supports it, even by those who may appear least culpable. Family members and spouses choose behaviors either because they believe they are trying to help (for example, Mary's nagging at Vincent about his homework) or because their current behavior is the only way they know (for example, parents who

167

rear their children the way the parents, themselves, were reared).[18] Even as the counselor identifies the negative results of codependent behavior,[19] he or she must affirm the positive rationale that motivates it.

Many different counseling approaches may be used to examine the psychological bases of conflict in an effort to work through these issues. These approaches can be quite effective; but they are not the only process resources available.

## Helping Troubled Families Through Mediation and Conflict Management

Considering mediation's success in other group contexts, it is a logical process to use in resolving conflict in a family or marriage.[20]

As described previously, the approach of the mediator will likely differ from that of the counselor, particularly in emphasis. Rather than exploring the psychological causes of marital and family conflict, the mediator takes a more problem- or task-oriented approach, with the goal of assisting the family in negotiating its differences. Indeed, it is the mediator's ultimate goal actually to train the family or couple in negotiation skills so that future conflicts can be addressed without the involvement of a third party.

As a caveat to these suggestions, it must be noted that many conflicts in marriages need the effective, thorough work of therapeutic counselors, as well as the guidance of biblical pastoral counselors. For many spouses, their problems are too ingrained, too tied to great personal needs, or too solidified in the historical operation of their family to ignore the resource of the counseling profession.

Counseling, however, is not the only resource; nor is it the only helpful approach to family conflict. There is great need for the pragmatic, goal-focused, task-oriented, time-limited process of mediation and conflict management which can help people create workable solutions to everyday problems.

The mediation process as a form of facilitating a collaborative approach to problem-solving was described in previous chapters. Its use may or may not be as formal as the process described there; but its application in the setting of the family holds great promise for the effective resolution of conflict. The following discussion will describe some of the possibilities.

*Marriage Conflicts.* If future spouses can successfully "negotiate" aspects of their relationship to give them sufficient confidence to marry, shouldn't they continue that negotiation *after* marrying? If estranged marriage partners can successfully negotiate the emotional issues connected with divorce, couldn't they also negotiate during marriage to resolve differences in a way that honors their commitments to the marriage relationship?

In a real sense, infusing a couple's relationship with the skills of negotiation and the resource of mediation equips the spouses to manage marital conflict and be successful in their marriage. Excellent advice is provided in well-known resources such as H. Norman Wright's *Communication: The Key to Your Marriage,*[21] and David Augsburger's *Caring Enough to Confront.*[22] Cunningham also makes some helpful suggestions in his book, mentioned earlier. While not described here in detail, the following collage of Cunningham's advice gives one a sense of how marital conflict might be constructively managed.

1. Pick the right time to fight
2. Learn to listen.
3. Don't bring up the past.
4. Give your opponent a sporting chance.
5. Control your hands and tongue.
6. Don't drag in outsiders.
7. Manage your stress.
8. Give value and consideration to the interests—the goals and desires—of each person.
9. Don't walk out.
10. End a fight with an act of love.
11. Be aware of your differences—and accept them.
12. Be willing to forgive.
13. Express your feelings truthfully.
14. Woo your opponent.[23]

*Conflicts between Children.* The approaches of negotiation and mediation can also be valuable to children in conflict with

169

each other. One understands and expects repeated instances of sibling rivalry in any family with more than one child. Common sense tells us that kids can't always get along. But kids can be taught and encouraged to solve their differences in respectful ways. This is true when they are still young, and perhaps more importantly, when they are adults.

Courts see spouses and siblings at their worst—generally either during divorce proceedings as the marriage relationship is terminated, or at the probate of an estate, when family members fight over the estate of a deceased family member. Both instances of family conflict are so expected, we have institutionalized special courts to deal with them: divorce court and probate court. It is in the latter, probate court, where adult siblings have their most pronounced conflicts. At times it seems they will invest any amount of money in lawyers, even their entire inheritance, trying to get a bigger share of the estate, or preventing someone else from having any share at all. The conflict over money can quickly become a relationship-severing experience that can never be repaired.

Mediation and conflict-management techniques can be important at each stage of children's relationships. As young children, they can be taught how to manage differences respectfully; a mediation resource (usually parents) can be provided if their negotiations are unsuccessful. As adults, mediation ought to be implemented in probate proceedings in an effort to resolve immediate conflicts while preserving lifelong family relationships.

As uncharacteristic as it may seem, children can incorporate negotiation and conflict-management techniques into their relationships. While relaxing one evening, I became aware of my oldest daughter and young son arguing in his bedroom. It was obvious by the volume of their voices and the words being spoken that their conflict at that moment was intense and needed dramatic intervention from an outside source. I moved down the hall toward the bedroom, adrenaline rushing, and determined to adjudicate the dispute with the posture of a federal judge! As I swung open the door, surprising them with both my presence and the fire in my eyes, my then-seven-year-old daughter held up her hand, and in defense of the commotion, quickly explained, "Daddy, Daddy. It's okay. We're just negotiating!"

Well, as an advocate of collaborative problem-solving, what could I say? It was not my idea of the negotiation process. But I had to give her credit for at least thinking about a productive and respectful conflict-resolution process. We all shared a laugh, which broke the tension; then we shared a hug. I hope she will always remember the process—and become better at implementing it!

*Conflicts between Parents and Children.* As children mature, the opportunities for parents to engage with them in collaborative problem-solving and mediation grow as well. Not every parent-child conflict is negotiable. In our house, for example, the request to spend time "hanging out" at the shopping mall has a predictable answer: "No!" Because of the environment at the mall, that is nonnegotiable. Most requests, however, fall into the category of "negotiable," and we spend substantial time working on ways to satisfy the interests involved.

Recently I saw an example of such a circumstance. After church one Sunday evening, a couple with whom we were going out had to deliver their daughter back to their home. Even though that meant travel in two different directions, the couple's nineteen-year-old son, who also had a date later that evening, was not interested in being helpful. His response when exposed to the dilemma was that he just didn't have time to take his sister home. A few moments later, he decided he just *had* to have the family's new car for his date. That is when the negotiations with his father began. During the ensuing discussion, his father said, "I'll make you a deal. You can have the new car, which is want *you* want, if you take your sister home—which would help *me* out." Minutes later, as the son drove off in the new car with his sister sitting beside him in the front seat, the result of effective, collaborative negotiation become apparent. Instead of the father imposing his will, the father and son had used a communication process to resolve a conflict.

In a more acute circumstance, mediation was an important process to manage the conflict between parents and a difficult teen-ager. After running away from home and spending several weeks on the streets of Los Angeles, the seventeen-year-old girl wanted desperately to go home. Everyone realized that the homecoming would be tense, emotions would run extremely high, and it would be a critical time in the relationship between parents and the child.

Someone wisely suggested that the counselor who had been seeing the family in a therapeutic role be present in the home as the "mediator" when the homecoming occurred. Stepping out of her counseling role, the helper was present to direct communication, manage any acute conflict, and help the family members commit to constructive dialogue for their first few days together. This was a unique use of mediation, one that was extremely valuable to that family in crisis.

Every application of mediation and conflict management cannot be described here. What has been put forth are several descriptions that suggest the possibilities available. As a complement to the resource of counseling, dispute-resolution techniques can contribute to family relationships that are durable and cherished.

One of my real loves is country music. While many of my professional colleagues believe themselves to be more sophisticated in their musical tastes, I know what kind of music reflects the spirit and soul of this country—it's America's music. Now, I must admit a good bit of country music reflects what has gone wrong for people in life: bad marriages, broken relationships, and a host of personal problems. But every so often there is a song that reflects what can be right in a relationship.

Recently, Michael Martin Murphy recorded a hit song that describes what families can be like with commitment to solve the problems along the way. It begins by chronicling the conversation between a father and son as the son expresses his agony over whether to commit himself to marriage. The father responds by describing the tradition of deep, enduring love in his family. He concludes with the affirming statement, "Son, you come from a long line of love!" That kind of love endures through tough times and serious family conflicts.

Wouldn't it be great if families took advantage of resources such as mediation that could assist them in working through differences and conflicts instead of moving to the dissolution of family relationships? Wouldn't it be great if families overcame the expectation of broken relationships and instead were recognized as representing a long line of love?

## DIVORCE MEDIATION

Ideally, conflict in troubled families will be adequately addressed and resolved through counseling and mediation. In the perfect world, such processes would bring about reconciliation within families and restore them as the enduring and supportive institutions that God intended them to be.

We know, however, this is not a perfect world. Even with the best efforts of counselors, therapists, ministers, and friends, a substantial number of marriages are going to be fractured, ending in divorce. The impact of that event will be long-lasting; in most cases its effect will be felt by everyone in the original family for a lifetime.

In their book, *Second Chances*, Judith Wallerstein and Sandra Blakeslee describe the general impact of divorce when they write:

> With divorce comes an erosion of commitments to our partners and to the institution of marriage itself. With divorce comes a weakening of our unspoken moral commitments to our children. Today we expect more from marriage than previous generations did and we respect it less. The divorce-marriage mirror reflects an image that is shockingly different from any we have seen before, and we cannot hope to break the mirror or to make it reflect the time that was.[24]

The dismantling of the traditional family through divorce is accomplished, in a technical sense, through our legal system, which utilizes an adversarial process. I remember as a small boy in the 1960s the afternoon television show "Divorce Court." There, in black and white, angry divorcing spouses would trade accusations in an attempt to establish fault, which then became the basis for the dissolution of their marriage. Shortly thereafter, their marriage was terminated before the television audience.

While the courtroom drama did have sufficient entertainment value to capture a television audience for 30 minutes each afternoon, the effects on the couple enduring that process would last forever. Those effects could have been exacerbated by the nature of the legal process. Attorney Freya Ottem Hanson and pastor Terje C. Hausken in their book *Mediation for Troubled Marriages* accurately describe the legal system's involvement in divorce:

> The legal system is not equipped to save the American family; nor does it claim that saving families is its mission. It often centers its focus on the past instead of providing creative means for couples to restructure their lives after divorce. In many cases, the adversarial system has prevented the family from reaching any positive outcome so that all that remains is isolation, hostility and revenge.[25]

While acknowledging that the legal system has done what it does fairly well, especially considering the demands placed on it with the escalating number of divorces since the 1960s, the same authors describe the limitations of divorce in the adversarial forum of the courthouse. Among the limitations they note are:

- Cost for legal services
- Fear of the legal process and its outcome
- Delay of months or years in court resolution
- Blame of those involved in the process—lawyers, judges, counselors, friends, and family members
- Need to win the battles over property, child custody, and support[26]

In response, there are significant movements in both secular and religious institutions to effectively deal with what seems to be the inevitability of divorce. As stated in the first chapter of this book, many states have instituted a mandatory mediation process that diverts all cases involving disputes over children and property to a more collaborative forum.[27] In Los Angeles, the Conciliation Court is staffed by professionals in mediation who assist thousands of families as they move from one family structure to another while avoiding the detrimental effects of courtroom litigation.[28] It is in such a circumstance that the advantages of the mediation alternative are most evident:

- Financial costs for lawyers are dramatically decreased.
- Settlements are more creative because the divorcing couple has more latitude in coming up with solutions best suited to their personal situation.
- Focus is more oriented to the future and how the family will exist in a new structure, than oriented to the past and determining who was right and who was wrong.
- Divorcing spouses have greater commitment to the agreement. Amazingly, only a small fraction of the fathers ordered by the courts to pay child support do so on time, or at all. However, if the agreement for child support comes out of a mediation context, that figure jumps dramatically. In fact, compliance with mediated agreements is reported to approach 80 percent.[29] Mediated agreements are three times less likely to wind up in court with compliance problems according to Hugh McIsaac, director of the Los Angeles Conciliation Court.[30] There seems to be a strong correlation between the process used to establish the obligation and its fulfillment.
- Relationships are treated with greater respect—not because the conflict is less acute, but because the environment in which it is handled promotes respect. This setting also encourages productive contact and recognition that long after a divorce is final, some aspects of the relationship will continue.

### Divorce Mediation in the Church

A novel and largely untried idea being discussed in the Christian community is the church's role in divorce mediation. Even suggesting that there might be a role for the church in divorce brings to the surface the church's general discomfort with the entire idea of divorce and remarriage. But that discomfort is not justification for avoiding the issue, or for refusing to consider the church's possible role in its members' divorces.

Fundamental to any involvement by the church is the concern that ministry at the time of divorce is not understood as

175

condoning, supporting, or encouraging divorce. The traditional response to that concern has been to sever all relationship with the divorcing couple and their family so that what one believes about the commitment to marriage is not misinterpreted.

That approach by many in the Christian community, however, fails to acknowledge two competing realities. First is the reality that those who are divorcing are just as governed by Paul's writings to the Corinthians as others in the Christian community. Paul wrote:

If any of you has a dispute with another, dare he take it before the ungodly for judgment instead of before the saints?

The very fact that you have lawsuits among you means you have been completely defeated already. (1 Cor. 6: 1, 7)

His admonition is often forgotten when it comes to divorce. The Christian taking family matters before a secular court reveals the same shortcomings of our relationships and our community as other cases taken to that tribunal. It's time to acknowledge that Paul made no exception in the case of marriage dissolution, property division, or child custody. Those issues can and should be handled within the Christian community rather than outside it.

If two people going through a divorce are sincerely interested in not going to court, where do they go to resolve the many issues between them? One option is secular mediation. Structured either through the court or through private practitioners it is tremendously better than courtroom litigation. It can bring financial savings and a respectful environment, as well as foster a creative outcome. But even secular mediation falls short of what could be available in the Christian community.

The second reality in the Christian community is the emphasis on reconciliation. Christ described its importance when he included in his Sermon on the Mount the instruction to seek reconciliation, even prior to worship. He did not exempt anyone, even divorcing spouses, from that admonition. If there were a Christian mediation option, one of its objectives could be reconciliation. Occasionally, such reconciliation might take place, so divorce is avoided. But more often, it would encourage reconciliation of the people after the divorce has occurred. Mediating family issues in the context of Christian values can resolve the immediate issues in a changing family structure and set the stage for post-divorce reconciliation—reconciliation that may not bring back a marriage, but can allow the former spouses to co-exist in the world together.

So often when a divorce involves a couple within a church, one or both spouses leave the congregation. In doing so, the spouses leave some of their closest friends—the people to whom they would have turned with any other problem, and those with whom they shared the most intimate personal and spiritual relationships. Perhaps a great deal of the responsibility for that separation rests with the divorcing couple. But some of the responsibility also rests with those of us in the Christian community who just do not know what to say, or how to respond, or what role to play. And so, as members of the church community, we let the tragedy of divorce sever our relationships rather than viewing the reality of divorce as another opportunity for the great expression of love, personal support, and grace.

We need a process within the Christian community to assist people who are moving through a divorce. Such a process would help them avoid the secular courts and establish the possibility for reconciliation, but this process would also necessitate a different and perhaps less comfortable involvement for church members. Other observers have described the potential for mediation of divorces within the Christian community this way:

> The church mediation process claims its position as that of a caring body whose job it is to demonstrate Christ's grace and love. We are called to care for people on every level: physical, financial, spiritual and so forth. This is our chance to say to families going through this type of painful trauma, "We care about you. We love you. We desperately want to help you if you will let us try."[31]

The anecdote that began this chapter described hypothetical conflict between Vince and his mother. But such tragic circumstances also exist for many children in real families, or in the continuing destructive changes resulting from divorce. When such conflict occurs, families and the individuals who comprise them desperately need the rewards of reconciliation.

Conflict-management assistance can be most beneficial in the context of lifelong family relationships, areas of important personal concerns, and an environment of great emotion reflecting only minimal preparation. Through counseling, innovative conflict management, and even divorce mediation, the family can be a more functional and supportive entity.

## CHAPTER FOURTEEN

# MANAGING CONFLICT IN
# THE CHURCH

IN HIS BOOK, *WHEN CHRISTIANS CLASH*, Horace Fenton, Jr., makes a penetrating statement to all who belong to Christ's church. He contends, "We can hardly call the world to peace while the church falls short of being the reconciled community God intends it to be."[1] His statement addresses the challenge of our mission—calling the world to peace—by directing us first to examine ourselves as members of Christ's church. Fenton's words portray a body of believers who need to experience reconciliation themselves so the message they proclaim is credible.

Sadly, numerous signs point to the reality that the church is *not* reconciled and *not* unified. In fact, we see examples of the church in conflict at all levels. A large church takes its local

179

neighbors to court to establish its right to purchase and tear down neighborhood homes for expanded parking. Members of a large denomination hold a collective breath awaiting the outcome of annual church-officer elections which will determine the doctrinal line of the church's seminaries. A local church body is divided so deeply over the role of women in the church that the church splits, resulting in a lawsuit between factions to determine who gets possession of the building.

These are only samples of the conflicts that emerge in churches, inflaming the emotions of church members, diverting precious resources, and distracting the church from its central calling of proclamation and ministry. Each has immediate significance to the people actually involved in the church—and eternal significance to those who may be observing from afar, judging the credibility of the message by the behavior of the messengers.

While numerous references to conflict in the church have been made throughout this book, this chapter is included to address several issues that are unique to church-related conflict. It identifies the nature and impact of conflict in the church, describes the limitations of two common approaches to dealing with it, and suggests a strategy for effective management of conflict in the body of Christ.

## THE UNIQUE NATURE OF CONFLICT IN THE CHURCH

As an organization, the church is a unique environment for conflict because it is comprised of individuals with differing backgrounds, diverse needs, and personal concerns. And it provides the setting for the "spiritualization" of conflict that emerges within it.

### A Group Comprised of Individuals

Like other organizations, the church is a collection of dozens, hundreds, or even thousands of individuals. While these individuals might agree on some matters, the fact that they are individuals means they bring to the organization diverse backgrounds, experiences, and perspectives, and their own preferred ways of doing things. Drawn together as a group, these members still maintain their individualism, thereby setting the stage for differences and conflict.

## Diverse Needs

In addition, church members present a variety of needs. Some members practice "restaurant Christianity," wanting to select from a menu of spiritual entrees for their religious enrichment. Others are called to service, and desire opportunities to carry out that service in a way they see as appropriate. Many look to the church as a spiritual hospital from which they can receive care and comfort. Still others view the church as an institution that does and should provide a range of education and social services with few, if any, demands connected with them. Some members bring to the church long traditions of family and cultural values and need the predictability of the church's traditions. Others, newly connected or joined, bring limited perspectives of tradition and need the vitality of change and development. The demands of such diverse needs and the viability of any church to meet them all of the time sets the stage for conflict.

## Personal Concerns

The church provokes passion. That is the reason for the often-quoted advice to avoid politics and religion in conversations with certain people. Religion is one of these areas in which beliefs are held dear, emotions are highly invested, and passions are great. When conflict emerges in the church for some reason, it often escalates quickly, far beyond what one might anticipate in another setting.

Many of the most acute conflicts in churches would be insignificant to many other organizations. Announce plans to tear down a corporation's previous facility for the construction of a new housing development and no one cares. Announce plans to tear down the church's current building for the construction of the same housing development, which then will allow the church to build a new facility at a different location, and rebellion takes place. The act may be the same, and the purpose may even be to advance the church; but the response is passionate! Because spiritual feelings are so personal, and concern for them is so great, threats to our views about them evoke more extreme responses, and many times they then result in conflict.

## Spiritualizing Conflict

Finally, conflict in the church is unique because it is "spiritualized." Only in the church can interpersonal conflict be described in terms that call forth the drama of a holy war between good and evil, with each side proclaiming that the justification for an adversarial response is to defeat the evil on the other side. It is not uncommon for a church caught in litigation with someone outside the church to go far beyond the normally expected sense of winning, all the way to describing the lawsuit as an "attack on God" which necessitates an all-out response in order to protect both God and the church. When such a perspective takes over, compromise or settlement is rejected. After all, who can compromise God?

As the result of portraying the conflict in spiritual terms, the church becomes overconfident (believing God is on the church's side) and continues the conflict far beyond the point that is rational. This is not to say that there are not legitimate threats to the church, or that the church cannot respond to them. Instead, it points out the tendency of the church to interpret conflict in spiritual terms, and to react in a spiritual manner, which may satisfy the emotion of the moment, but may not reflect spiritual attitudes or the priority of peacemaking.

In essence, the characteristics of the church environment—a collection of individuals with diverse needs, important personal concerns, and the tendency to spiritualize differences—increases the challenge to the church in effectively managing conflict.

### TRADITIONAL RESPONSES TO CHURCH CONFLICT

A continuum of conflict-management approaches, including avoidance, informal problem-solving, negotiation, mediation, arbitration, litigation, and self-help, was described earlier in Figure 5–1. While churches occasionally use each of these methods, two processes tend to be overused: avoidance and adjudication (some version of arbitration or litigation).

## Avoidance

The church board wrestled into the night with the dissatisfaction with the youth minister some members had expressed. Things had gotten off to a rocky start—several parents had been alienated by the youth minister's attempt to "relate" to the kids through his dress rather than provide an example of maturity for them. The conflict escalated when the youth devotional at the beach turned into an unstructured and unsupervised event with many of the couples in the group getting "lost," and disappearing for the evening. Finally, the youth minister's cavalier response when questioned about the incident pushed the limits of the parents' patience . . . and trust. Several demanded that the church board replace the youth minister without waiting for more serious incidents to occur.

Unfortunately for the church board, the youth minister was the son of one of the congregation's long-time and financially generous families. An attack on the son would most certainly be perceived as an attack on the family . . . something that would increase the number of individuals involved in the conflict.

Such a setting called for thoughtful dispute-resolution process—but the church-board members chose avoidance instead. They thought that by "lying low for a while," in time, all would be forgotten and they would not have to confront the new employee, anger his family, or deal in any more depth with the parents of the church youth. While not an irrational approach, this avoidance actually increased the risk of substantially more serious conflict in the future. The problem had not been adequately addressed and would lie in wait for the next incident involving the youth minister, when it would emerge in a more vocal, more dramatic, and more harmful way.

According to Speed Leas and Paul Kittlaus in their insightful book, *Church Fights*, there are legitimate reasons to avoid conflict: when time is short, if individuals involved are so fragile and insecure that they cannot participate in a conflict-resolution process, when addressing conflict is likely to result in violence, and when the priority of dealing with another conflict takes precedence. But, as those experts suggest, ". . . avoiding conflict creates more problems than it solves." In avoiding it, people use energy to get away from the conflict or the other people involved in the conflict. Resources are directed at avoidance, rather than resolving the substantive issues, and church leaders spend time getting around issues rather than facing and resolving them.[2]

## Adjudication

In contrast to avoidance is the choice of adjudication as a means to resolve church conflict. Like avoidance and other dispute-resolution processes, there are times when adjudication—a decision by an individual or group—is an appropriate way to resolve an issue. If the disputants cannot achieve a collaborative resolution and are committed to supporting the decision once it is made, it is quite possible an adjudicatory approach will be effective.

On the other hand, what if there is some question regarding the commitment to the "win-lose" result in adjudication? What if the system of adjudication limits the involvement of the people or translates the process into a more formal setting than is necessary? What if adjudication can effectively decide the issue—for example, does the minister stay or go?—but cannot address the real interests of people caught in the grip of conflict? What then?

A number of church denominations that would quickly advise members not to handle their conflicts in a secular court setting have created a similar system within the church to handle church-related conflict. They have a system of complex rules and procedures, use the language of the courts, such as referring to the disputants as "plaintiff" and "defendant," and create the certainty of a decision but not the outcome. As a result, one side wins and one side loses.

By incorporating a model of adjudication, the church automatically brings to itself the benefits—and detriments—of such a system. On the benefit side, adjudication allows the church to control the dispute-resolution process; it also makes a decision a certainty and sets up the decision as a precedent for deciding future cases. At the same time, on the detrimental side of adjudication there are likely to be emotional and financial costs imposed by the system. In addition, the disputants may feel a lack of ownership for the result, and reconciliation may be difficult when one person experiences victory and the other feels the "agony of defeat."

In *Interpersonal Conflict Resolution*, Alan Filley suggests the characteristics of those win-lose approaches to conflict— typically represented by adjudication. As you read the list, think about the last time you were in a setting where someone or some group could decide between competing positions. Based on that circumstance, Filley observes:

1. There is a clear "we-versus-them" distinction separating the individuals, rather than a "we-versus-the-problem" orientation.
2. Energies are directed toward the other person in an atmosphere of total victory or total defeat.
3. Each person sees the issue only from his or her own point of view, rather than defining the problem in terms of mutual needs.
4. Conflicts are personalized with a focus on the people rather than depersonalized with a focus on the substance.
5. Disputants are conflict-oriented, emphasizing the immediate disagreement, rather than relationship-oriented, emphasizing the long-term effect of their differences and how they are resolved.[3]

Such win-lose approaches to conflict often result in lose-lose endings. Adjudication usually is not the best alternative.

## STRATEGIES FOR MANAGING CHURCH CONFLICT

After acknowledging the reality of conflict and educating appropriate people in the skills of resolving conflict through collaboration, it is essential to establish mechanisms, processes, and structures to deal with the conflict this way.

Every church has some structure for making decisions. It may be a vote of the congregation or a decision by the denominational hierarchy. In many cases conflict is handled in the same decision-making system without recognizing the impact of doing so. For example, if conflict over a pastor in a church is handled by a vote of the members, the issue of whether the pastor stays or goes may be resolved. But what about the relationship between the two factions that caused the vote to occur? It still exists, and if not resolved may prevent the next pastor from being successful.

If a church hierarchy makes a decision regarding the appointment of a pastor to a new church location, how does it address the conflict in the pastor's current congregation? How does it deal with the impact of the change on the pastor's family and on the spouse who is employed in a professional position? Again, the structure through which the initial decision is made is not necessarily the structure that resolves the related conflict.

Churches need to establish resources and processes through which decisions can be made—but also through which conflict can be handled. They may be the same, but they probably are not.

As I've spoken with church leaders across the country, I have continually been asked, "What needs to be put in place so that conflict can be managed in the local church?" The question usually is the result of having lived through divisive and harmful conflict and a deep commitment to avoid having to do so again. The answer is not complex. From hundreds of conversations with church leaders and dispute-resolution professionals, a ten-point strategy has emerged that can make a great contribution toward more effective conflict management. Components of this strategy are listed in Table 14–1 and are described in the following pages.

## Seek Consensus on the Basics

As a foundation for conflict management in the church, there must be an agreement or consensus on the basics. Congregations are held together by some sense of agreement, a belief system that generally is shared. Unless such agreement or consensus is achieved and communicated, there is no perspective from which people can decide whether or not to be involved with that congregation. If the basic belief system is defined and communicated, decisions by prospective members about joining the congregation can be based on that system, and those

---

**Conflict-Management Strategies**

1. Seek consensus on the basics
2. Develop positive attitudes toward conflict
3. See conflict as normal
4. Educate to manage differences
5. Emphasize process as well as substance
6. Intervene early
7. Institutionalize conflict-management systems
8. Develop congregational resources
9. Use outside resources
10. Keep in touch with the spiritual

---

**Table 14–1**

choosing to join can do so. The result is a congregation of people who are joined together because of agreement as to who they are, what they stand for, and what priorities they have as a group. Unity on those items will not eliminate all conflict, but it will set the stage for the members' work together.

One congregation had recurring conflict over the style and practice of worship. Some members wanted change—new music, diversity in order, and variety in format. Others wanted to conform with that congregation's tradition—a worship format that had been essentially the same for a generation. Neither was inherently right or wrong, but both contributed to conflict that was substantial enough that several members had left the congregation during the previous year. While innovative changes in worship may bring about controversy, much of that controversy could be prevented if new members had been told to expect occasional changes when they joined that congregation. Expectations would be clearer and tolerance among those who chose membership in that congregation would be greater as a result.

The need for such clarity and agreement on basic purposes, goals, and priorities is increased when the mobility of Americans is recognized. Approximately one-half of the population changes addresses every five years. In the congregation described earlier, more than 40 percent of those attending today were not part of the fellowship three years ago. The challenge

*187*

was described well by church-conflict experts Larry McSwain and William Treadwell when they wrote:

> To the degree a congregation is effective in ministry to mobile Americans, it must assume responsibility of fostering an acceptance of church goals by newcomers or continually involve non-mobile members in reassessments of their missions in light of changing needs.[4]

## Develop Positive Attitudes Toward Conflict

As stated earlier, conflict is a reality in the Christian community and will continue to be a force influencing the church. It is time we acknowledged it and focused on its possibilities rather than its burdens. When we do so, not only will we change our attitude toward conflict and those enmeshed in it, but we will also increase our willingness to be involved with it, ourselves.

As a consultant, mediator, and trainer, one of the realities my family and I must face is my almost constant travel. Almost every week, I am away from my home and family at least part of the time. To those who do not travel, it may appear glamorous—visits to new cities, luxury hotel rooms, great restaurants, and loads of adventure! To those of us doing the traveling, the reality is quite different. We equate travel with the stressful demands of tight schedules, crowded airports, and being treated more like cattle than human beings. When we think of travel, we think of long lines, bland food, and monotonous evenings in hotel rooms that all look the same. Everything combines to extract any perceived enjoyment nontravelers might have of it.

After an especially long trip, I was complaining to my wife, who, justifiably, had heard enough. During a spirited discussion, she helped me realize that the travel was going to be a part of our existence, something that was necessary for the work we have agreed I will do. She suggested that each of us could look at my traveling as an undeserved burden, and bad-mouth its impact on our lives—or we could recognize it as a part of our reality and decide to gain from it all that it has to offer.

Her advice changed my attitude and approach to my work. The travel is still quite demanding and generally boring; but my outlook is more cheerful, and as a result, the stress for both of us has been reduced.

The same is true of conflict in the church. Since it is going to be a part of the community, why not change our attitudes and approaches to it? While always demanding, it, too, can become less stressful as we accept it and effectively deal with it.

## See Conflict As Normal

Ron Kraybill, former director of the Mennonite Conciliation Service, gives rather unique advice to churches with which he works. He recommends that if they want to have less conflict in their church, they should have more of it. At first that does not appear to be sound advice, especially given by one who was asked to assist in resolving conflict. One expects the conciliator's task to be the elimination of conflict, not the encouragement of it.[5]

Upon reflection, however, there is wisdom in his advice. Churches that admit having conflict on a regular basis—conflict that occurs in the normal course of events—rarely have the kind of conflict so acute that outside assistance is needed or which threatens to divide the congregation. It is because such churches acknowledge and deal with conflict regularly that the deep-seated, unresolved, more serious conflict rarely emerges.

The comment that frightens me most as a consultant on conflict and cooperation is the declaration, "I've been at this church for more than twenty years and we never have conflict." It frightens me because my experience tells me that either this congregation has not done anything for twenty years, or it has failed to admit those instances where conflict has in fact existed. The conflict probably did not go away, but is there, waiting for that moment when it will emerge in an acute and harmful way. As suggested by McSwain and Treadwell in their book, *Conflict Ministry in the Church*:

Conflict occurs most often in congregations in which there is a deep commitment to the church, the more deeply ingrained is the sense of ownership about what is happening, the more possible the conflict. Apathy is a sure guarantee of a conflict-free setting. Persons who do not care about their faith are unlikely to exhibit enough energy to act upon it. Corpses do not fight![6]

Much more productive is the admission, "We have dynamic people, dynamic ministries, and programs which produce their share of conflict. We use the conflict to move each of us toward growth and the congregation toward even greater service." That is an exciting circumstance that can harness the energy of differences to move forward in creative ways!

Leas and Kittlaus summed up the spirit of this suggestion in the conclusion of their book, *Church Fights:*

. . . conflict in itself is not a bad thing. . . . Conflict, though it may be experienced as painful and frightening is the fire in which a healthy organization is tempered. On a number of occasions we have asked individuals in churches to tell each other what is currently happening in their lives where personal growth is taking place, and it is a rare occasion when someone will mention a non-conflict situation that is bringing growth to his life.[7]

Such is true in the church as well.

## Educate to Manage Differences

If there is sufficient maturity and confidence to admit that conflict is a reality and that its existence can contribute dynamically to the Lord's people, it is imperative that people learn to manage it effectively and respectfully.

Who would think of hiring a pulpit minister who had not studied the Bible and the art of communicating it through a sermon? Who would leave the management of the church's finances to one not knowledgeable in accounting? Who would engage the services of a hospital chaplain who was not skilled in counseling? If no one would consciously do any of the above, why do we engage the services of ministers and other church leaders who may spend a majority of their time managing interpersonal conflict without equipping them with skills to be successful?

If the church is going to be the reconciled community God intended it to be, we had better equip its leaders and its servants in the ability to understand and facilitate the resolution of conflict!

Just as we've talked about students in some public schools who are being taught an alternative to violence in dealing with conflict, we should recognize that students in Christian schools and in church education programs need to be taught those skills. After all, they are called to be peacemakers!

Just as managers of major corporations and public agencies are trained to deal with conflict in the workplace, so should those who "manage" the most precious institution on earth— the church—be trained to manage differences between people.

Just as diplomats and arms negotiators are given the skills to resolve conflicts in the global community, so should Christians be given the skills to bring peace to their communities, churches, and families.

A church that is educated and skillful is diagnosing conflict, responding to it in a deliberate yet compassionate way, will move closer to being a reconciled community of believers— reconciled not only to God, but its members to each other. Perhaps the familiar Proverb could be adapted, "Train up a child (or any Christian) in the way he should handle conflict and even when challenged, he will not depart from it."

Or, as other experts in church conflict declared:

How ironic that we place such high expectations for healthy personal relations with so little training to achieve them! The congregation which wishes to minister effectively to persons is one which plans for training experiences which will help it cope with its struggles.[8]

## Emphasize Process As Well As Substance

In chapter 11, three criteria for durable agreements were introduced, one of which is procedural satisfaction. The suggestion was that the conflict-resolution process is so important that even agreement on substantive issues will not overshadow

191

dissatisfaction with the way things were done. Strategically, it is essential that churches become sensitive to the dynamics of *how* issues are decided.

Emphasis on process will demand a different investment of time and energy than emphasis on the problem, itself. Thought must be given to the nature of the dispute-resolution process, as well as to those who are involved in that process if it is to be successful. Discussion usually reserved for determining the substantive outcome—the decision—needs to initially be refocused in order to develop sufficient satisfaction with the process that the result will be supported.

Over and over again, studies have shown that people will uphold decisions if they were arrived at in a way that reflected fairness and the opportunity for individuals to be heard. For example, churches are faced with the annual challenge of putting together a budget that represents the priorities of ministry of those in the congregation. This budget is usually the result of much conversation and committee work. It is to be expected that not everyone will be completely pleased with the outcome. Some may want more money spent for foreign missionary work and some may want to emphasize ministries in the inner-city. But reality requires that eventually, all members need to come together and be supportive of that church's priorities for the next twelve months.

This can occur to the extent that individuals have had the opportunity to share their perspectives, and their opinions have been respectfully heard and seriously considered—even if their own priorities are not completely reflected. But if they are satisfied with the *process* of the budgetary decisions, they usually will make the financial commitment to the church. Thus, part of their willingness to let go of their own positions, be supportive, and give money every week may be related as much to the process as it is to the final decision, itself.

In the most extreme cases, where a decision is made in adjudication by a judge or arbitrator, the decision—even a decision that is opposite to what one person desires—will be accepted because of the credibility of the process.[9] Our judicial system and the fabric of our society depends on such procedural credibility. So does peace in our churches.

**Intervene Early!**

Avoidance, which is the approach most often used in responding to church conflict, moves away from instead of toward the conflict. Within any church body, there are individuals in conflict—a marriage is enduring unusual stress, a family is at wit's end dealing with a teen-age child, or several families are having private meetings to decide on actions regarding their dissatisfaction with the minister. In each case, and dozens of others, those in leadership know what is happening, but they resist intervening to help—they seek to avoid the conflict. But many find that it is no easier to address the conflict later, when the marriage partners separate, the teen-ager runs away from home, or the dissatisfied faction leaves the congregation.

The sensitive, caring, and skillful intervention by those who are called to the ministry of reconciliation can have tremendous impact if involved early enough. The church leader, minister, counselor, or other person trained in conflict management can be especially effective in bringing needed skills and in moving people from conflict to collaboration if such assistance catches the conflict before it becomes acute.

An example of the impact of early intervention occurred in a large congregation on the West Coast. The leadership recognized that after several years of substantial growth, significant differences were emerging between groups in the church. Some of the members who had had lifelong commitments to the church's tradition were reacting quite defensively to the suggestions of young adults for a freer and more openly emotional style of worship.

The conflict was being defined as the particular activities of Sunday-morning worship were discussed. The older group wanted biblical expository sermons, formal hymnals from the traditional hymnal, a predictable format, and a reverent spirit. The younger group, generally made up of young professionals on the fast track to career success, wanted inspiring, topical messages from the pulpit, energetic and spontaneous musical choruses, a format reflecting diversity, as well as an informal and upbeat spirit. There are few churches that have not dealt with similar issues.

193

In that setting, the initial response from the leadership, as the differences in perspective evolved into definable conflict, was to attempt to make decisions about each aspect of worship. Then the leaders worked to "sell" those decisions to the various constituencies. That response was consistent with the church's leadership pattern in the past, when continued attempts were made to "keep a lid on things."

Signs of the imminent failure of that approach arose early as the leadership recognized its own weakness in trying to make decisions for the congregation and advocate their acceptance. No longer was it a congregation of followers with unquestioned commitment to the church's tradition. Instead, it was a diverse and dynamic group of Christians who, in this case, openly articulated their differences.

For the first time in the congregation's history, the church asked for help—help that came *before* the institution of two separate worship services or even a church split. This was help that assisted the leadership avoid making decisions on the issues—what types of sermons would be preached, which songs to sing, or the level of formality in worship. Instead, it created a new process through which the differing groups were given the responsibility of resolving their conflict.

When the groups left the argument on *issues* and focused on the interests represented by their positions—fear of change on the one hand and a need for vitality on the other—they began moving toward more creative and acceptable solutions. But more important, they gained a greater regard for each other. The last circumstance was a result completely unlike what would have resulted from a more autocratic decision-making model. The key was the timing—early intervention is almost always an attribute in successful conflict management.

## Institutionalize Conflict-Management Systems

In addition to a strategy of early intervention, conflict-management mechanisms can be institutionalized in the structure of the church. G. Douglass Lewis, in his book *Resolving Church Conflicts*, suggests that people and organizations need an "early warning system" to remind them that a particular conflict situation has the potential to be serious and destructive,

194

and also a structure institutionalized to deal with it. It is such a system that moves people away from avoidance to confidently addressing conflict in its early stages.[10]

Lewis describes a particular church situation where two staff people were in conflict, with one wanting desperately to avoid it and the other frustrated because it could not be dealt with and resolved. In response, they institutionalized a simple new process to deal with differences. They committed to communicating about their perspectives at the beginning of their weekly staff meetings. This was not especially comfortable at first, especially for the one who wished to avoid it all; but it did serve as the mechanism through which conflict would be addressed and a more effective ministry team developed. We need to create in the church an effective system for such conflict management.

## Develop Congregational Resources

In every congregation, people should be called to the ministry of reconciliation. Just as some are called to teaching, some to benevolence, some to administering programs, and so on, these individuals should be called to peacemaking. They would be trained to serve in a mediation capacity and thus assist in the resolution of interpersonal conflict within the church and its families.

Such a ministry should be publicly designated and acknowledged. It should be funded as a priority, just as the ministries of education, benevolence, evangelism and others are funded. Those who accept the ministry of reconciliation should coordinate their efforts with church leaders and staff members. But the independence and confidential nature of the ministry should be retained as appropriate. In that way, the ministry not only becomes a work of the fellowship, but also a resource for it.

## Use Outside Resources

In many circumstances conflict within the church cannot be managed by someone from within the same body. The minister of a congregation cannot mediate when he or she is involved in the conflict. If involved in a conflict, church leaders are limited in their ability to bring about reconciliation, because of their leadership role. A member of the congregation, even if well trained, may not be appropriate as a dispute-resolution resource because of past or future relationships. In short, even those who might be thought of as physicians ready to bring about healing may not be able to do so if they are connected with the dispute.

At such times, it is important to be able to look outside the church congregation for assistance. Organizations such as the Christian Conciliation Service, the Alban Institute, the Mennonite Conciliation Service, and the Institute for Dispute Resolution regularly help churches as outside consultants and mediators. Their addresses are included in Appendix B.

While it may seem foreign to many church bodies to consider a resource outside its congregational or denominational structure, obtaining the services of such an organization can be advantageous in a number of ways. The person intervening will be highly experienced in conflict management and dispute resolution. The consultant, adviser, or intervener will be free from the politics of the situation. The outside resource person will be able to keep the focus where it should be—on the people involved in the conflict and not on the intervener. Those who are experiencing difficulty will be assisted, and when a successful resolution is reached, they will be the ones credited with resolving the conflict.

In addition to outside organizations that provide conflict-management assistance, many churches are instituting a resource that operates within their overall structure but is separate from any particular congregation. One group has "Committee on Ministry" that regularly assists churches in conflict. Another has its "Committee on Adjudication." Still another denomination has given one of its denominational staff members responsibility for intervening in conflict.

While such arrangements are commendable, great care must be shown in the approach used. A Committee on Adjudication focusing on decision-making, for instance, may not be as effective as a body using some other process. In addition, if the committee established by a denomination will ultimately decide an issue, one would question the long-term effectiveness of any informal assistance that might be offered. It might not be effective in generating confidence in individuals involved in conflict, because the disputants might be reluctant to share information, knowing it might come back to haunt them later if the committee has authority to decide the issue in dispute. Such an outside resource needs to be perceived as independent, nonbiased, and capable of making a neutral evaluation.

Perhaps a better model would be a free-standing team with no obligation to or standing with the church hierarchy. The team would be comprised of highly trained individuals without obligation or function in the church hierarchy to be available to assist in the resolution of conflict.

A sort of mediation "SWAT" team approach could be very valuable. The SWAT team, like a police department's Special Weapons And Tactics squad, would have to be gutsy enough to move into volatile situations. Such a mediation team would use "weapons" of reconciliation instead of guns and ammunition; team members would be highly trained Christians, available on short notice, with the courage to intervene in turbulent situations. The group would be subtle and quiet in its work, and careful not to draw attention to itself. It could be affiliated with a denomination, but outside the hierarchy of the church; or it could be affiliated with an independent, nondenominational ministry such as the Christian Conciliation Service. Such a group could be effective in reducing the immediate hostility and anger so the problem, whatever it might be, could be dealt with efficiently.

This outside group, like the resources of an attorney, accountant, or church fund-raising consultant, would be utilized on an "as-needed" basis. But using such a group would be as normal as going to a lawyer for legal advice about the church bylaws or an accountant for a church audit.

## Keep in Touch with the Spiritual

The suggestions offered in this chapter, and in this book as a whole, are largely practical in nature, drawing upon knowledge of how we interact and how we can improve that interaction. Less has been stated about the spiritual dimension of conflict resolution, primarily because it is covered with great expertise in other books.

Let it be known, however, that the spiritual is critical. The church is Christ's church, not man's church. It is Christ we seek to honor and Christ who sent his spirit to guide and comfort us.

Our ability to find unity because we are tuned in to God will be far more powerful than our ability to relate, however well, to each other apart from God. A. W. Tozer stated it well in his book *The Pursuit of God:*

> Has it ever occurred to you that one hundred pianos all tuned to the same fork are automatically tuned to each other? They are of an accord by being tuned, not to each other, but to another standard to which each one must individually bow. So one hundred worshipers together, each looking away to Christ, are in heart nearer to each other than they could possibly be, were they to become "unity" conscious and turn their eyes away from God to strive for closer fellowship.[11]

It is that unity and spirit Paul had in mind, and we should have in mind, as he wrote to the Colossians. His counsel to them is still counsel to those of us today who seek strategies for dealing with conflict.

> Therefore, as God's chosen people, holy and dearly loved, clothe yourselves with compassion, kindness, humility, gentleness and patience. Bear with each other and forgive whatever grievances you may have against one another. Forgive as the Lord forgave you. And over all these virtues put on love, which binds them all together in perfect unity.
>
> Let the peace of Christ rule in your hearts, since as members of one body you were called to peace. And be thankful. Let the word of Christ dwell in you richly as you teach and admonish one another with all wisdom, and as you sing psalms, hymns and spiritual songs with gratitude in your hearts to God. And, whatever you do, whether in word or deed, do it all in the name of the Lord Jesus, giving thanks to God the Father through him. (Col. 3:12–17)

When the church has in place these ten strategies— strategies that accept the reality of conflict, encourage productive conflict, educate the church to manage its differences, and create resources for the church to use in resolving conflict—the church will be prepared to move forward in a dramatic way. It will go beyond traditional approaches to conflict, acknowledging the unique nature of its environment and accepting the challenge to be the reconciled community God intended it to be.

A note to counselors: While the strategies contained in this chapter are written for consideration by all who work in a reconciliation role, the counselor can be especially effective in carrying them out. He or she may be the first person in a congregation to see its dysfunction. The counselor is usually qualified to understand and diagnose the cause for such dysfunction. He or she is professionally prepared to assist people in the congregation, both in their individual and group healing. The counselor probably has a personal commitment assisting people who need to grow and mature in their relationships with each other.

The strategies described here are neutral in respect to who carries them out. But counselors will be a prime resource for the effective management of church conflict.

# CHAPTER FIFTEEN

# MANAGING CONFLICT IN THE WORKPLACE

AN ADMINISTRATIVE ASSISTANT STOMPS out of the office declaring, "I don't have to take it!" after being bombarded with work and torn between the demands of two supervisors. An aerospace engineer, believing a government-contracted product does not meet specifications raises the issue—and is summarily fired. A corporate personnel manager is fired when he comes to the aid of a woman who is being sexually harassed. A church secretary works in terror, anticipating the next time the pastor will make a move on her.

These anecdotes describe real cases, and represent thousands of similar incidents that occur daily across the country. They show how conflict occurs in the workplace—whether that workplace is a factory, retail store, educational institution, professional office, or church. This chapter will focus on the nature and impact of that conflict. It also will examine the traditional, adversarial responses to workplace conflict, and share how the skills of collaborative negotiation and mediation can resolve such conflict differently—in a way that is respectful and productive.

## THE WORKPLACE—A HOTBED OF CONFLICT

Anyone involved in work recognizes that conflict is a part of it. As interaction takes place on the job, people seek to accomplish individual and organizational objectives, and workers carry out a variety of workplace roles: supervisor/subordinate, laborer/foreman, staff assistant/senior manager, teacher/administrator, executive/board member, and many others. Conflict comes with this territory; and at times, it gets out of hand.

It is important to note that some conflict in the workplace is beneficial, even necessary. The wise manager realizes that the staff's unanimous agreement with his or her every idea may result in harmony, but it will not result in the best ideas and approaches to solving problems. Conflict that results from the expression of differing viewpoints, innovative proposals, and diverse expressions will often yield far better results. That kind of conflict promotes growth and in the end, serves the organization well.[1]

On the other hand, conflict also can be highly destructive to the organization and the people in it. This kind of conflict often results from communication failures, personality clashes, differing values and goals, lack of authority, frustration and irritability among employees, and competition for limited resources, as well as noncompliance with rules and policies.[2] It can impede creativity, distract the focus of the employees, disrupt the organization's culture, and bring its work to a standstill.[3]

In every case where conflict moves from being productive to destructive, it dramatically impacts the organization. In the United States each year, there are more than three million involuntary job terminations, and 800,000 voluntary resignations.[4] Many are the result of conflict that was so extreme it could only be "resolved" through the employees' separation from the workplace organizations.

Unresolved conflict affects employee productivity. This, in turn, affects the productivity of the organization, whether it is a teachers' group refusing to have its members stay past a particular time in the school day to work with students, or employees of a public-sector agency willing to only work "by the book," or a city's transit drivers slowing down just enough to disrupt every bus schedule. At that point, conflict affects the organizations' customers or the recipients of its services. The results can be minor—or catastrophic. Some news reports have even indicated that the Challenger space shuttle disaster in 1986 was caused largely by an unresolved conflict among decision-making employees.[5]

Workplace conflict is also costly. When it results in dismissal or resignation, the turnover cost, considering the disruption of work in a supervisory or skilled technical position and the expense of recruiting and training a replacement, may reach the equivalent of the employee's annual salary.[6] Another cost, as was mentioned in an earlier chapter, is the estimated 25 percent of a manager's time that is spent responding to conflict; that means 25 percent of his or her salary is invested in conflict resolution.[7] Add to those costs the expense of stress-related illness, as well as the possibility of substance abuse resulting from unresolved personal conflict, and a more complete, and expensive, picture appears.

Finally, on a personal level, nearly everyone is familiar with the traumatic impact of conflict with a co-worker or supervisor. For most of us, work is the single largest weekday investment of time. Conflict in that setting can affect every part of our lives, resulting in sleepless nights, high anxiety, and increased hostility toward the work environment.

## TRADITIONAL APPROACHES TO WORKPLACE CONFLICT

Traditional responses to workplace conflict are often heavy-handed, unsuccessful, and unsatisfactory. Despite the costs of finding and training replacements, many employers perceive the employee enmeshed in conflict as an expendable commodity, easily replaced, and not worth the time or emotional energy necessary to change him or her into a contributing organizational member. Unfortunately, termination is not merely a traditional approach, it is still very much a staple of American employment practice. The U.S. Bureau of Labor Statistics indicates that during the average month in 1988, 2.2 million people were unemployed because they had been fired, a figure which was up 28 percent from twenty years previous.[8]

Other traditional approaches may be somewhat more complex, but are often no more satisfactory. The restrictive contracts of classic unionism, for example, sometimes protect the employees' jobs, while leaving unmet their need to find meaning in their work. As a result, conflict in that workplace goes unresolved. Even well-meaning union personnel and company executives may be limited in their options for problem-solving by collective bargaining contracts that specify how conflicts will be resolved. The inflexibility of a required formal grievance process may prevent them from approaching conflict in a more creative, humane way.

Typical organizational grievance processes do not fare much better. Traditionally, these approaches have been mostly adjudicatory, and have brought to the organization the disadvantages of adjudication described in an earlier chapter. Such processes have given employees the right to appeal certain management decisions, especially those connected with personnel issues; but many times these appeals are unsatisfactory because they create an adversarial forum in which there is usually a winner and a loser. Even in the context of traditional labor arbitration, which has the integrity of neutrality and fairness, the result is the confirmation of one position in the conflict and the rejection of another.

These descriptions apply not only to the secular workplace, but also to much of the religious world. In conducting a recent training program in Christian conflict management, I visited with a minister who was highly involved with his church's dispute-resolution process. The group's title—Committee on Adjudication—gives you a quick idea of its orientation. The minister described the committee's dealing with a personnel problem at one of the denomination's seminaries. The process was conducted by lawyers and was highly adversarial in nature, even to the extent of calling the appealing employee the "plaintiff" and the seminary the "defendant." In short, that church has adapted the trappings of secular courts in its dispute-resolution process, and unfortunately, may also feel the disadvantages of it.

While such approaches have been institutionalized and in many cases are successful, there is growing recognition that the high-handed, adjudicatory approaches leave much to be desired. In many cases, they are not successful in ultimate dispute resolution. They offer little hope for reconciliation and productive future relationships; and they are becoming increasingly expensive, time-consuming, and inefficient.

## NEW APPROACHES TO RESOLVING WORKPLACE DISPUTES

In response to the escalating costs of organizational conflict, and the inadequacy of existing processes to deal with it, a number of new approaches have emerged. Three are discussed in this chapter: prevention, collaborative negotiation, and mediation.

### Prevention

The concept of prevention may seem contrary to this book's basic assumption that conflict exists and must be addressed. It is not illogical, however, to think of prevention as an approach to resolution, especially if what one is preventing is the continuation of unresolved, destructive conflict, rather than the elimination of all conflict.[9]

For instance, consider a Christian elementary and secondary school. It would be irrational to believe that serious conflict will not occasionally emerge in the employment relationships of its teachers, administrators, and board members. The initial question then is, How can destructive conflict among those in such roles be prevented?

*Recognize Workplace Conflict as Normal.* While statistics cited earlier may underscore the fact that workplace conflict is normal, many employees and employers treat all conflict as if it were an unexpected and certainly unwelcome guest.

Whether we perceive conflict as normal or unexpected is shown by our response to it. If we view conflict as unexpected and a serious breach of the organization's culture, we most likely will respond in panic by trying to either avoid it entirely or deal with it forcefully. On the other hand, when we view conflict in the workplace as normal, we will more likely respond to it in a calm and deliberate fashion. If treated as normal, conflict's impact on our emotions will be diminished and our response will be more deliberate, sophisticated, and confidence-building.

Managers and others who can intervene in a neutral capacity when conflict emerges should do so with an attitude of deliberation and confidence. Acknowledging that such intervention is never easy, it is of great importance that the intervener reflects the attitude he or she would like the people in conflict to possess.

*Cultivate a Willingness to Address Conflict.* In addition to an attitude about workplace conflict that perceives it as normal, there must be a willingness on the part of the organization to address conflict in a deliberate and productive way.

A number of years ago, I completed a study of student attrition at a major Christian university, to find reasons students left that school. I found it very interesting that in almost every case, the students who left did so because of a problem that could have been resolved had there been a mechanism or a willingness on the part of the institution to address it.

Without scientific data to back up my suspicions, I believe the same thing is probably true in workplace conflict. Relatively few conflicts cannot be resolved if there is a willingness to address them. What typically occurs, however, is a reluctance to deal with such conflicts until they have escalated; then, they are often dealt with in a highly adversarial and nonproductive way.

Corporate America seems to have recognized this circumstance, and during the last decade has made a substantial investment in employee support, even support for employees undergoing tremendous personal challenge. While it is an extremely humane approach for corporations to provide counseling services and a variety of mental and physical health services, as well as specific treatment programs for tobacco, alcohol, and drug dependency, in many cases the organization does so with its own self-interest in mind. Its leaders recognize that these programs address a wide range of personal and interpersonal conflicts, and increase the likelihood that such conflicts will decrease, rather than grow, in the workplace. Such corporate thinking reflects a willingness and an investment in preventing conflict.

*Be Committed to Early Intervention.* Conflict in an organization is very much like a tomato. Many conflicts are not "ripe" for resolution because they are not observed by management or expressed in any way by employees. The most sophisticated conflict-management resource in the world cannot address conflict that is not yet known to the parties or to management. At other times, conflict is allowed to "over-ripen" until it is beyond the point where informal processes can resolve it. In this circumstance, employees know it is there, and managers know it is there; but the avoidance approach is taken until it is virtually impossible to address the conflict in a collaborative way.

Without question, the sooner conflict is identified and addressed, the greater the opportunity for finding a face-saving, acceptable, and efficient way to resolve it. A deliberate, early-intervention strategy should be institutionalized to address apparent conflicts.

*Establish Processes for Dealing with Conflict.* Finally, in preventing conflict—or at least in preventing conflict's escalation—processes must be in place to deal with it. Many organizations's failure to plan for conflict management is apparent too late—after a bitter or hostile conflict has emerged. In contrast, what needs to happen is the thoughtful establishment of a dispute-resolution process long before any particular conflict emerges. Then when conflict occurs, the process helps handle it as if conflict were a normal occurrence within a culture that is willing to address it.

The company should establish processes that have already been proven successful, then communicate their existence to employees and be prepared to assist the employees in using them appropriately.

These processes can be internal or external. For example, some organizations find that an institutional ombudsperson usually allows conflict to be handled within the corporation—but by someone who is specifically trained, has sufficient authority, and is well respected by his or her colleagues.[10]

At the same time, other organizations rely upon outside resources to provide that kind of intervention service. Most notable is the Christian Conciliation Service, which operates chapters around the country. Organizations in geographic locations serviced by the Christian Conciliation Service can write into their contracts with employees a commitment to utilize this service when conflicts arise. A list of Christian Conciliation Service chapters is found in Appendix B.

In addition, it is important to consider whether the process will be offered informally or more formally. If it is offered informally, management's primary task is to make sure employees are aware of the process and know how to access it. If it is a formal offer, the processes and related agencies will be included in employment agreements or personal handbooks and in giving employees notice of how unresolved conflict will be handled. Examples of contract provisions which direct conflicts to a dispute-resolution process are included in Appendix C.

## Collaborative Negotiation

The second new approach to managing conflict in the workplace is through collaborative negotiation. Described in chapter 7, the collaborative negotiation process seeks to give people involved in conflict a mechanism that addresses the issues in their dispute while being especially sensitive to their relationship. It moves from a debate on the issues to an understanding of the interests, thereby setting the stage for more creative and meaningful solutions. Its application to the workplace is based on three premises:

1. There are legitimate alternatives to the traditional chain-of-command, decision-making process.

2. People are capable of handling their own conflicts.

3. Organizations can change from competitive to collaborative methods of handling conflict if processes are available that support such a move, and if top-level management encourages such an approach.

*Legitimate Alternatives.* The 1990s opened with profound changes in the world; the most pronounced were the political and economic changes in the Soviet Union and Eastern Europe. While the changes in those countries' governments received the most attention from the world's press, a little-known but profound change began to impact their business sectors. In moving from a centrally controlled to a decentralized market economy, it suddenly was realized that those nations' business managers knew very little about negotiation—especially the kind of negotiation necessary to put business deals together. As the Soviet Union changes from an economy of dictated policies to a free marketplace, negotiation will become a more prominent and essential dimension of business management.

This change echoes American business during the 1970s, when it adapted alternative models of worker participation exemplified by "quality circles," in which labor and management participated in problem solving. Collaborative management styles, many modeled after those used in Japanese corporations, also were introduced to the workplace during this time.[11] Chrysler Corporation put a member of the United Auto Workers on its board of directors, signaling the potential for more cooperative approaches to management, as well as the resolution of conflict.[12] The Environmental Protection Agency determined that it would develop new rules through a participatory process called "negotiated rule making," rather than continue its longstanding procedure of making regulatory announcements and then facing the inevitable litigation.[13] Teachers and school districts across the country opted for relationships characterized by collaborative negotiation rather than the traditional adversarial bargaining games.[14] In short, the workplace began to recognize the value of a more participatory and cooperative approach to managing its enterprise, as well as the conflict inherent in it.

*Capable People.* A part of the rapid change taking place is a growing sense that people, if properly trained and supported, are capable of resolving most of their own disputes. As we saw in the dispute pyramid illustrated earlier in Figure 3–1, only one in ten legal disputes ever moves to the level of involving a lawyer; and in the business setting, probably far fewer ever move to the level of requiring a supervisor's or manager's intervention. People will be effective in managing and resolving their own conflicts to the same extent that they incorporate collaborative negotiation into their work skills.

It may be helpful to contrast the impacts of an autocratic decision-making process and collaborative negotiation. For a number of years in working as a consultant for a major "high-tech" firm in the Northwest, I have been amazed at the constant conflict between the production side of the company which manufactures goods to be sold and the marketing side of the company which sells those goods. Each is charged with its own responsibility and, if not closely monitored, such responsibilities clash. The production people want whatever time it takes to manufacture the highest quality product. In contrast, the marketing people want as much product as possible in the shortest time. Obviously, to the extent that marketing personnel commit the company to a particular sales schedule, the production people are limited in their production time. Similarly, marketing efforts are limited by the amount of goods that can actually be produced.

While both sides acknowledge their common interest in the company's financial success, their roles within that company obviously set the stage for conflict. When such conflict emerges, they cannot ignore it; nor can they sue each other over it. They might turn the conflict over to management for resolution; but in reality, their best hope is to communicate with each other, and recognize each other's interests. Then they can seek creative ways to satisfy those interests. Such communication places responsibility on the two sides, themselves, to negotiate compatible expectations and objectives. Those involved in the forefront of those operational areas are probably best equipped to represent the needs of their part of the organization in the negotiation. They understand the specifics, deal with the people involved, and thus have the greatest appreciation for their needs. When trained in the process of collaborative negotiation, they can reach out and directly resolve such conflicts.

*Organizations Can Change.* Just as individuals are capable of adopting more collaborative approaches to resolving conflict, entire organizations can change cultures so that such collaboration becomes the norm, both internally and externally.

Several years ago, I was invited to train members of a transit union in the art of negotiation. The union had sought this assistance because it was newly formed and inexperienced in collective bargaining. Because of my belief in more collaborative approaches, even in instances when opposite sides bargain over a working agreement, I responded that I would be pleased to train *both* union and management members *together* in the same approach to bargaining—but that I would not train either side individually. I suggested that both sides would be better off if they had a common language and a common view of how negotiations might be conducted. With a certain degree of suspicion about this rather novel approach to preparation for collective bargaining, both sides committed to the project and came together for that training.

You can imagine the tension in the room as individuals first came together outside their roles as worker and supervisor. Instead, in this setting they were co-learners thinking about the process of negotiation. During the days of training together, the participants began to see each other not just in their formal roles, but also as people who lived in the same community, had families, struggled with finances, and experienced life in much the same way. They also began to realize that there ought to be as much focus on their year-long working relationships as there was on a short period of bargaining. They helped each other understand that while one side might have the advantage in a particular bargaining session, memories were long and retaliation probably would take place for abusive tactics. All in all, they recognized the value of looking at negotiation in a broader context, seeking to include interests as well as issues, and investing time in searching for creative, mutually beneficial resolutions.

During the subsequent negotiations, which took place immediately after the training, the representatives of both labor and management dealt with forty-five different issues and disputes. In record time, they effectively addressed each one and came to terms with an overall contract.

Summarizing the novel approach to collective bargaining negotiations, one participant wrote:

A majority of the negotiations can be characterized as involving healthy and constructive discussion. They were certainly not marred with the acrimony, emotionalism, or misunderstandings that often accompany labor agreement negotiations. . . . I believe the training seminars that were held built a degree of trust, as well as understanding of the respective roles and obligations of both labor and management.[15]

Ironically, just forty miles to the north, another transit district was facing a far different outcome during its negotiation. After traditional approaches failed, workers went on strike, paralyzing that city and setting the stage for hostile relations for years to come.

It should be emphasized that just because an organization sees the benefits of a more productive and respectful approach to resolving conflict, this does not suggest that the organization should give up substantive issues that are important to it. Neither side of the transit district described above decided that the forty-five issues in dispute were unimportant. Rather, both sides agreed that by approaching the forty-five issues through collaborative negotiation, they were substantially more likely to find workable solutions and do so in the context of respecting the relationships involved.

## Mediation

Finally, mediation is the third "new" approach to be described which organizations may use in resolving conflict. As defined earlier, mediation is a process of negotiation which involves a third party who facilitates the resolution of conflict between people. Although this process has been evident in the workplace for generations, its labeling as mediation, particularly as mediation of grievances, has only recently occurred.

Mediation in the workplace need not be part of a formal process. Thousands of times each day, disputes between two or more people are resolved informally by a neutral third party who helps the disputants reach agreement. Mediation is a popular tool when people seek to break an impasse in negotiation or to avoid the use of a more formal grievance procedure.

Studies of mediation report that in more than 90 percent of the cases, the process can be successful.[16] Extremely important is the result of a study suggesting that when compared with the adjudicatory process of arbitration, disputants overwhelmingly prefer mediation.[17] This is not surprising, considering that mediation not only offers people a way to resolve the dispute themselves, it also avoids the win-lose circumstance of processes such as arbitration. When people who have resolved their own dispute in mediation go back to work on Monday morning, they go back not as winners or losers, but as individuals who have methodically and productively resolved conflict with a focus on their future relationship.

Mediation is especially effective as an alternative to litigation. And it has become most timely in light of the substantial rights provided to employees by recent legislation. Perhaps nowhere in society have rights been increased by legislative action during the last twenty years as they have been in the area of employment relations.[18] As a natural consequence of the additional rights provided by this legislation, more legal conflicts now occur in the workplace. In the past, such disputes might have been handled in a variety of ways, including costly, emotionally draining litigation. Now, many employers are using mediation instead.

A number of months ago, the Institute of Dispute Resolution was asked to attempt mediation of a wrongful-termination case involving a large employer. The man bringing the action had a good case. He had been fired after coming to the aid of a woman who was being sexually harassed. The case had been in the court system for years and, at one point, a jury had awarded the man the largest punitive damage settlement in that state's history—more than one million dollars. Unfortunately for the plaintiff, the judge had reduced the award to a thousand dollars the following day.

Under these circumstances, the two sides agreed to participate in a mediation process—but it was too late. Expectations on both sides were too high. Each could sense a "win," even though both sides had experienced a "loss." As a result, the case that might have been settled for thirty to forty thousand dollars four years previously could not be settled for ten times those amounts now. The people involved were too entrenched, too caught up in the battle, too invested in the conflict. Had such a case gone to mediation when the investments were smaller, statistics suggest it could have been settled. Once it was on the litigation track, however, settlement became more difficult—in fact, in that case it was impossible.

What will happen to it? At last report, the two sides were expecting arguments before the state's Supreme Court and were anticipating another trial and two to four more years of additional litigation—all of which might have been avoided had a mediation process been available.

Such situations explain why more and more organizations are utilizing mediation as part of their conflict-management process. They are doing so because they recognize the value of its results—which may be as simple as people being able to work together on the following Monday morning, or as complex as continuing to conduct business over a lifetime. Mediation is a process that allows the organization to address conflict in an effective way.

Conflict in the workplace is a reality. Traditionally, it has been handled in a way that is adversarial, and largely unproductive. New approaches suggest that more cooperative, creative, and respectful processes could bring to the workplace new abilities to address inevitable conflicts and do so in an effective way.

# CHAPTER SIXTEEN

---

# MANAGING CONFLICT
# IN THE COMMUNITY

"YOUR HONOR, THIS BLANKETY-BLANK dumped three tons of gravel in my yard and I want him to pay for it! It cost me two hundred bucks to hire those guys to haul it outta there, and that was after I told them they could keep the gravel. This dumb schmuck ruined my yard and caused me to miss two days' work, and now he owes me. I figure it cost me about seven hundred dollars and I want my money!"

"What's this about, Mr. Hamilton?"

"Well Judge, I ain't sayin' I did it, and I ain't sayin' I didn't; but I think what you need to be askin' her is why she keeps those junked cars out in front of her house and lets those kids of hers run crazy, and why she lets her dog bark all night and who it was that ran the hose into my basement and put two feet of water down there."

"I didn't flood your crummy ol' basement, you jerk! D'you check your pipes? And even if I did, it woulda been what you had comin' for knockin' down my fence and drivin' your car through my flower garden!"

Slowly the judge's eyes rolled toward the ceiling as charges and counter charges flew back and forth across his small-claims courtroom. Years of bickering between the two neighbors before him had finally come to this. The feud probably started with something as small as making too much noise while taking out the garbage. Over time, the neighbors' anger and outrageous behavior had grown until neither was willing to listen to reason. Other neighbors took sides, drew entertainment from the conflict, and encouraged the disputants in their vindictive creativity. But after it became old and tired, no one knew how to get it stopped. It was now another problem for the justice system, a system already overwhelmed with problems and challenges.

## A HISTORY OF FRUSTRATION

Neighborhood disputes often fall into a gray area of issues that are too bothersome to ignore, but monetarily too insufficient to take to court. They are the staple of Judge Wapner's "People's Court" television show. Anyone who has had or dealt with neighborhood disputes recognizes, however, how complex they may become. California Court of Appeals Judge Earl Johnson summarized his impression by saying, "It is somewhat ironic that 'small' claims and what many deem 'simple' disputes—rather than large cases or complex controversies—have compelled a rethinking of the prevailing model of dispute resolution."[1]

The cost and time requirements of traditional litigation make court procedures impractical for most conflicts among neighbors. The impersonalness of a judge's decision may leave neighborhood and family disputants cold. Apart from solving problems, people are concerned about maintaining relationships once a dispute is resolved. The fact that our court system provides only rigid processes for solving disputes has been a frustration of neighborhood disputants for decades. It is a problem the legal system is only now beginning to address.

In a 1906 speech titled "The Causes of Popular Dissatisfaction with the Administration of Justice," Harvard Law School Dean Roscoe Pound suggested that while discontent is inherent in any democratic legal system, much of the problem results from the way the system resolves disputes. He said America is "simply behind the times" and that much of the disgruntlement with court processes was unnecessary.[2]

## TURNING ATTENTION TO COMMUNITY DISPUTE RESOLUTION

Seventy years later, United States Supreme Court Chief Justice Warren Burger convened "The Pound Conference" to consider some of the dean's suggestions. At that conference, Professor Frank A. E. Sander, also of Harvard Law School, noted that courts were inundated with pending litigation. He suggested that many disputes could and should be resolved outside of court through processes of alternative dispute resolution. Sander proposed that by the year 2000, courthouses should no longer be arenas merely for litigation but that they should become dispute-resolution centers offering mediation, arbitration and a variety of other problem-solving methods.[3]

Also influential in the community-mediation movement was Stanford Law Professor Richard Danzig, who in a 1974 article advocated "community courts" for family, minor criminal, and other community disputes:

> The present system does not, after all, perform the job of adjudication in most of these cases. Civil proceedings are generally avoided. Many matters which may technically be criminal violations will not be prosecuted because they are viewed by the prosecuting authorities as private and trivial matters. . . . [D]ue to institutional overcrowding and established patterns of sentencing, the vast majority of people convicted of misdemeanors and some felons are not likely to be imprisoned. For these defendants, the judicial process is not a screen filtering those who are innocent from those who will be directed to the corrective parts of the process. Rather, it is the corrective process; as such it

fails to be more than a "Bleak House," profoundly alienating, rather than integrating.[4]

In the mid-1970s, criminal courts and prosecutors in some cities were already experimenting with community dispute settlement in relation to minor crimes between people who had continuing relationships. The purpose of these early programs in Philadelphia, Columbus, New York, Rochester, and Boston was to substitute negotiation and restitution for prosecution by the state.

In 1978, United States Attorney General Griffin Bell established three neighborhood justice centers in Atlanta, Kansas City, and Los Angeles. The centers were to provide citizens with a local, grassroots, decentralized forum for dispute resolution and other legal services.[5] During the 1980s, the three experimental neighborhood justice centers increased to more than four-hundred community-based dispute-resolution programs.

## One Approach: The California Experience

In 1986, the California Legislature enacted the California Dispute Resolution Programs Act to encourage "more effective and efficient dispute resolution . . . [through] greater use of alternatives to the courts, such as mediation, conciliation, and arbitration. . . ."[6] Under this act, revenues to fund local, non-court dispute-resolution programs are being collected in over one-third of California's counties, which have voluntarily decided to participate. These programs provide a wide range of dispute-resolution services, including mediation, conciliation, and arbitration.

The legislation that established these programs traces its roots at least back to the Los Angeles Neighborhood Justice Center which, in 1978, was one of the three federally funded pilot projects providing community mediation services.[7] In 1978 the first in a series of California legislative proposals promoting community alternative dispute resolution also was passed.

The 1986 Dispute Resolution Programs Act encourages courts, prosecuting authorities, law-enforcement agencies, and administrative agencies to make "greater use of alternative dispute resolution techniques whenever the administration of justice will be improved." Counties are encouraged to "consider increasing the use of alternative dispute resolution" in their "plans for court reform."

Given the early success of the act, indicated by the number of cases handled and the savings they have made for the courts in time and expense, the prospects for its continuation seem quite good. This additional legislation would be required because the original act provided funds for only a two-year trial period.

With ongoing development of programs and increased cooperation among the state, county, and local alternative dispute-resolution programs, the systematic expansion of community dispute-resolution programs throughout the state should persist. This expansion should result in a well-developed and effective system of community dispute-resolution programs in every county by the year 2000.

Many other states also have passed legislation related to dispute resolution.[8] As a result, there are now community dispute-resolution centers in at least forty-three states.[9]

## A NEW VIEW OF THE COURTHOUSE

In 1983, the American Bar Association established its Multi-Door Courthouse projects in Houston, Tulsa, and Washington, D.C. The "Multi-Door" concept is a coordinated system for referring disputants to the most appropriate dispute-resolution process for a particular problem. It may provide a referral network linking justices of the peace, small claims courts, lawyer referral, and legal aid services, district, county, and city attorney offices, community-based dispute-resolution programs, and other governmental and private agencies, including mental health services.

When efficiently implemented, the system provides intake assistance by specially trained "intake specialists" who are located throughout the county. The intake specialists try to resolve complaints initially by telephone conciliation or by giving additional information. If the case cannot be settled in one of these ways, the intake specialist refers the client to the appropriate alternative dispute-resolution mechanism and explains the policies and procedures of that service. All social services, arbitration, mediation, conciliation, and adjudication entities are incorporated into the Multi-Door system and are structured to fit most individual needs.

Multi-Door has also become identified as a community philosophy, offering ready access to the legal system, with networks that reduce frustration. The Multi-Door system usually improves community awareness about existing dispute-resolution options, enables all dispute-processing forums to obtain more appropriate case referrals, and increases the coordination among those forums. The system also develops programs which fill service gaps, making more "doors" available.

Since 1984, each of the Multi-Door programs in Houston, Tulsa, and Washington, D.C., has processed thousands of cases. Seventy-four percent of the disputants whose conflicts were processed by one of these centers said the center helped at least somewhat with the dispute, and 82 percent said they planned to use the center in the future.[10]

## WHAT HAPPENS AT A COMMUNITY DISPUTE-RESOLUTION CENTER?

Both the community-based programs and the Multi-Door Courthouse projects provide dispute-resolution services for neighbors, family members, landlords and tenants, employers and employees, and merchants and customers. The experiences of the District of Columbia Mediation Services are typical for community-based programs.[11] The center screens five times as many cases as the two hundred that are actually mediated. Many, such as serious criminal cases, are rejected as inappropriate for mediation. Only one-half of those scheduled actually go through the process, because many disputants come to agreements once third-party involvement becomes likely. Many cases handled through the center could have ended up in court, but many others would likely go unresolved without the center's involvement. Almost 80 percent of the disputes processed by the center result in written agreements, and 75 to 80 percent of the people who resolve their disputes this way indicate the agreements are maintained. Most cases take less than two hours to resolve.[12]

The agreements are respected for many reasons, not the least of which is they are the products of the disputants, rather than the ruling of a judge or arbitrator. People tend to support something they have created. Moreover, the mediation process is usually more satisfying than litigation. Participants summarize their experiences with statements such as, "I was able to say exactly what was on my mind and the mediator listened," or "We had time to explain how we felt and I think the other guy began to understand my point of view," or "We came up with a solution that works just for us. I don't think a judge could ever have done that."[13]

### MEETING A VARIETY OF NEEDS

Some community dispute settlement programs, including the Multi-Door projects, are operated by public agencies such as the courts, police, or human services agencies. Others receive their funding from private or nonprofit organizations and obtain most of their referrals from the courts and police. Finally, there are the private neighborhood-oriented centers which seek out conflicts directly from the community. Because of their often tenuous funding sources, many community centers are eventually forced to accept public money and cases. Whatever the funding and referral source, though, the center is usually staffed by volunteers, now totaling more than twenty thousand nationwide. Housing is often in a courthouse, church, or storefront, with hours of operation chosen to meet the needs of its mainly working-class clients.

Some neighborhood centers are able to serve fairly specific communities and problems using mediation grounded in an equally distinctive philosophical context. An example is the Martin Luther King Resolution Center located in the African-American, Latino, and Asian communities of south-central Los Angeles, which includes the area called Watts. Center director Dennis Westbrook believes the center's reconciliation services fulfill King's philosophy of empowering the community through nonviolence, a process which affirms justice, equality, and individual dignity. This is particularly needed in a setting of such potential violence. As Westbrook states, "When we educate people about what alternative dispute resolution offers, people can take responsibility for their own disputes and reconcile themselves. Affirming nonviolence is the only reasonable way to empower a community."[14]

## USING THE MEDIATION PROCESS
## IN THE COMMUNITY

The process most dispute-resolution centers use is mediation. As described in some detail earlier in this book, the mediator's goal is to progress from a past-centered approach to a future-centered one. Disputants often begin either with harsh denunciations, as in our example above, or they may be politely withdrawn. This is followed by venting emotions, reframing the disputants' view of the conflict from a negative experience to a more neutral challenge, problem-solving, and finally deciding.

The process is one where basic trust is built, first in the mediator, then eventually in the opponent. This trust results from the disputants' believing they are really being listened to, probably for the first time. If the mediator can convey the idea that the disputants will be respected and protected, they may begin to find solutions to small points of disagreement. Gradually, they can take some of the energy they have been putting into self-defense and transfer it to problem-solving.

In her 1986 book, *Peacemaking in Your Neighborhood*, Jennifer Beer relates a mediator's description of the moment when the mediation's energy begins to change from negative to positive:

> In every mediation I still think, "Oh this will never work," until half way through, the session reaches a peak. Emotions have been spent and people feel hopeless. At this point, a silence falls, time for absorbing and going beyond what has been said. I always hope the other mediator won't say anything. In our society we're not suppose to be silent; we have to fill the gap with music or talking. There is quiet, then suddenly it turns around. This seems to be a pattern.[15]

Once the disputants believe they can predict each other's behavior, they may be willing to risk exploring options to solve their problem.

A person enters mediation with a goal of making the opponent understand why he or she is wrong. Without taking sides, the mediator acts as an agent of reality, reflecting back to the disputants an objective view of the positions they have taken, providing a perspective they have probably lost in the emotions surrounding the conflict. This reality includes the recognition that even if the dispute were taken to court, the problem would be truly decided only when the disputants choose to abide by an agreement. Many people fail to realize the limitations a court has in enforcing its rulings, especially in minor matters which would require significant supervision. A decision which is not acceptable to both sides will likely lead only to further conflict.

## The Mediators

The number of mediators used in individual cases often reflects how close the center is linked to the community. Generally one to two mediators are assigned each case. Because the mediators are usually volunteers, they tend to be representative of the surrounding community. They also tend to be people who can afford to take time off from work. Many are professionals wanting to learn a new skill.

George Nicolau described the criteria for a community center staff member:

We didn't really care whether this person had a college degree or a high school diploma or was a drop-out because we didn't believe that education was a relevant measure of what we were looking for. We were looking for people who could postpone judgment, who did not try to impose their values on participants in the process, who were not upset by, but sensitive to and able to deal with cultural differences, people who could listen with understanding. We knew that if we could find such individuals, we could give them the skills to bring people together.[16]

What makes a good mediator depends more on training and experience in mediation than other factors such as education or job background.[17] While many states have minimum requirements for training,[18] there is a wide variance in the training actually provided volunteers.

## THE CASE FOR NEIGHBORHOOD CENTERS

At least two factors can be cited for the success of neighborhood dispute-resolution centers. First, many people are more comfortable in the neighborhood setting than they would be in the courts, because it is less formal, less expensive, and better able to address individual needs. Second, they find the process more complete and satisfying; it allows them to maintain control of both the issues addressed and possible solutions. Daniel McGillis of the U.S. Justice Department put it this way:

> Research studies support the casual impression that people like to have their cases mediated. They typically like the arrangements that are achieved. Disputants consistently report that they are satisfied with the mediation process and view outcomes as fair. . . .[19]

A Brooklyn, New York, study of mediation applied to serious criminal cases between acquaintances showed a significant preference for mediation over court proceedings. Participants found mediation more satisfying with more positive effects on the parties' relationship.[20]

The goals neighborhood mediation centers accomplish are varied. Again, McGillis has summarized them:

> Some believe that nonjudicial forums can increase access to justice because they facilitate prompt hearings, reduce or eliminate legal costs, schedule dispute settlement hearings at convenient hours and locations, and the like. Some stress improved efficiency, arguing that reliance on informal alternatives will free the courts to attend to more serious cases. Others argue that mediation provides an improved process for handling disputes because disputants are able to explore the underlying problems contributing to the dispute without the restrictions of rules and evidence, time limitations of typical lower court hearings, and the presence of attorneys as intermediaries in the discussion. Still

others point to potential community benefits deriving from mediation, arguing that such community-based programs, if developed in neighborhoods and administered locally, can increase direct citizen participation in major life decisions, reduced community tensions through effective conflict resolution, teach citizens how to solve problems collectively, and more generally improve the quality of community life. Many of the projects have sought to address varying combinations of the above goals.[21]

## COMMUNITY DISPUTE-RESOLUTION PROGRAMS OF THE CHRISTIAN CONCILIATION SERVICE

One of the most exciting developments in the last several years is the involvement of Christian Conciliation Service programs in more traditional community dispute resolution. While CCS was originally founded primarily to represent the church as a resource for dispute resolution and restricted itself to disputes involving at least one professing Christian, some CCS organizations have broadened their definitions of ministry to become a resource for conflict resolution between individuals who may not profess any particular spiritual commitment.

Through an arrangement with the court system, the Christian Conciliation Service of Los Angeles now supplies mediators to a branch of the Los Angeles Superior Court four to six hours each day. Since the expenses of this particular program are funded by public money, prayer or references to Scripture, as would be expressed in CCS sessions, would be inappropriate. Biblical concepts such as forgiveness, respect, and reconciliation, however, are readily applicable to the secular dispute-resolution process.

Hundreds of disputants each year are assisted by this service of Christian mediators, and many are touched by the spirit of Christ working through those who have accepted this ministry of helping others resolve conflict and achieve reconciliation.

The analogy for such work is to pastoral counseling. Some pastors may restrict their counseling ministry to church members or others who are professing Christians. But some may take a broader view, recognizing their opportunity for influence, example, and service, even though an overtly biblical approach may not be possible because of lack of commitment on the part of the counselee.

## RESOURCES FOR THOSE SEEKING TO BRING ABOUT RECONCILIATION

The primary purpose in describing community approaches and programs for conflict resolution is to underscore the availability of this resource. Many committed Christians find themselves involved in conflict over a diverse list of issues within their community. Christians are not removed from neighbor-to-neighbor conflict over property boundary lines. They also have problems with businesses about services rendered. And they sometimes endure conflict with community institutions such as schools or social service agencies.

If the opponent in a dispute is also a Christian, there might be agreement on bringing it under the auspices of a Church-related process. If he or she is not a Christian, the resources of a community dispute-resolution program may be attractive.

For the Christian, the efficiency of community dispute resolution reflects good stewardship of God's resources, and is responsive to Paul's caution against using the courts. Another advantage for the Christian is that the community dispute-resolution approach of mediation is respectful of relationships. Finally, the collaborative approach of a community dispute-resolution program sets the stage for God's priority of reconciliation.

Community dispute-resolution programs can be a valuable resource for the church, as well as for individual Christians. If it is not appropriate to bring a particular dispute under the auspices of the church, it becomes a resource to which the members can be referred with confidence that the benefits noted above can be achieved.

With encouragement and counseling, disputants will utilize neighborhood dispute-resolution centers as an alternative to the courts. If there is a commitment to solve the problem, the disputants will likely be successful. An honest willingness to communicate and risk exploring options can end years of stress and frustration. In her book, *Peacemaking in Your Neighborhood*, Jennifer Beer describes the power mediation has when applied to community disputes by relating the final moments of a successful mediation:

> The old woman's hands shook through the whole mediation. Her husband was angry about many things in the neighborhood. He seemed to blame thirty years of aggravation on the small children next door. It was hard to make him understand. The [person on the other side of the dispute, a] young woman started to cry. "I try so hard to respect you. I've done whatever you ask. When you had the police come, it took my heart out." [The young woman's] husband sat silent beside her, his dark eyes grave, watching. The older man talked a long time. Eventually he agreed to the usual: everyone would speak to each other politely. The mother would come over to retrieve any balls. The mediators left the room to write the final draft of the contract. We could hear them talking.
>
> "My parents were newcomers here, too," [the elderly man said.]
>
> "Raising children is a hard job; I know how it is."
>
> "I used to be an engineer at the shipyards. I can't do much but a bit of gardening now. That boy of yours, he's a good boy. And good looking, too."
>
> The mediators came back in. The young woman signed the agreement first.
>
> "If you can be nice to me just once, I can be nice to you a hundred times," she said.
>
> Everyone shook hands. The two women kissed each other. As she was leaving, the old woman took the mediator's two hands in hers, tears in her eyes. "Thank you so much," she said, still trembling. At the door, her husband turned. "I'm through fighting the neighbors' battles. From now on they'll have to fight on their own," he said, "We just want to live our last years in peace."[22]

## CONCLUSION

We began this book with former Harvard University President Derek Bok's description of the gradual change in America's dispute-resolution processes. The trend away from competitive methods, and toward the more cooperative processes, Bok said, is "the most exciting social movement of our time."

We end with another comment from Bok, a prediction of what can be achieved if this movement continues. Underscoring the timeliness of increased emphasis on collaborative dispute resolution, he declared:

> I predict society's greatest opportunities will lie in tapping human inclinations toward collaboration and compromise, rather than stirring our proclivities for competition and rivalry.[23]

His suggestion should set the focus for counselors, ministers, church leaders, and others who engage in the ministry of reconciliation.

# APPENDIX A

## CALLED TO CONCILIATE

This scriptural guide to handling conflict is used by the Christian Conciliation Service of Los Angeles* in preparing people for conflict resolution. It is divided into five lessons:

1. Understanding and Dealing with Conflict from a Christian Perspective
2. Conflict Summary—A Personal Evaluation
3. Understanding and Dealing with Diversity Within the Body of Believers
4. Scriptural Examples of Conflict-Resolution Techniques
5. Obedience—The Measure of Success

LESSON ONE: UNDERSTANDING AND DEALING WITH
CONFLICT FROM A CHRISTIAN PERSPECTIVE

## Introduction

Conflict is and has always been an inevitable part of life. Jesus experienced conflict. For example, the Pharisees charged that he was demon-possessed and attempted to stone him (John 8:12–59). They later plotted and effected his death at the hands of the Romans. At the same time, Jesus took actions that threatened others and had the effect of initiating conflict, such as healing on the Sabbath (Mark 2:1–12) and rebuking the Pharisees for hypocrisy (Matt. 23:13–36).

The first-century church also experienced conflict. See, for example, Acts 6:1–7 describing a dispute regarding food servings in the Jerusalem church, Acts 15:1–31 describing a dispute over a converted Gentile's need for circumcision, and Acts 15:36–39 describing Paul's and Barnabas's disagreement regarding Mark.

Since conflict is an inevitable part of life, we should expect to experience it occasionally, and we should study how best to handle it. Jesus summarized one aspect of our responsibilities in conflict situations in the following portion of the Sermon on the Mount.

## Text: Matthew 5:21–24 (NASB)

Verse

21 "You have heard that the ancients were told, 'YOU SHALL NOT COMMIT MURDER,' and 'Whoever commits murder shall be liable to the court.'

22 "But I say to you that everyone who is angry with his brother shall be guilty before the court; and whoever shall say to his brother, 'Raca,' shall be guilty before the supreme court; and whoever shall say, 'You fool,' shall be guilty enough to go into the fiery hell.

23 "If therefore you are presenting your offering at the altar, and there remember that your brother has something against you,

24 "leave your offering there before the altar, and go your way; first be reconciled to your brother, and then come and present your offering."

## Questions

1. What did Jesus indicate our responsibility is if we discover that another believer has something against us?

   _____

   _____

   Is the answer different if we have nothing against the other believer?

   _____

   Did Jesus provide the alternative of being reconciled to God through prayer and leaving it at that?

   _____

2. In view of our Lord's references in verses 23 and 24 to presenting one's offering at the altar, in fulfilling this responsibility may we wait for the other believer to sue us, or to hire a lawyer who sends us a "demand" letter or to personally bring his or her complaint to our attention? Or does our responsibility exist as soon as we learn of his or her complaint from any source?

   _____

   May we wait until the next time we happen to see the other believer?

   _____

3. What do Jesus' references to presenting one's offering at the altar suggest concerning his view of the importance of being reconciled to a fellow believer?

   _____

   _____

4. What did Jesus mean by the words "has something against you" in verse 23?

   _____

   _____

5. What does it mean to "be reconciled" to another person?

_____

_____

_____

List three words which describe what you believe "reconciliation" means.

_____

_____

List three words which describe the opposite of what you believe "reconciliation" means.

_____

_____

6. Notice the "therefore" near the beginning of verse 23, relating back to verse 22. How does verse 22 furnish a reason for us to be reconciled to our fellow believer?

_____

_____

For whose benefit are we to seek reconciliation?

_____

7. Are you angry with the other party in this dispute?

_____

Is the other party angry with you?

_____

In light of verse 22, are you willing to seek reconciliation—for your own spiritual health and/or the other party's?

_____

_____

_____

## Discussion

At this point in the process, you may believe that the other party is partly, primarily, or even entirely at fault in this dispute. That's acceptable. But Jesus' call to you is to be reconciled to your fellow believer. See also Galatians 6:1–2.

The premier example of reconciliation in the Scriptures was set by our Lord. His incarnation, death, and resurrection were for our sakes. Jesus did not wait for us to come to God to seek forgiveness. He initiated, and fully accomplished, reconciliation by dying for us "while we were yet sinners" (Rom. 5:8). He calls us to be initiators of reconciliation, too, both between people and God (evangelism) and among people (peacemaking).

You and the other party are to be commended. By entering into the conciliation process, you are each seeking, with the aid of CCS, to fulfill Jesus' call to be reconciled with the other.

We in CCS view the process of reconciliation as involving two components: *resolving* the dispute and *restoring* the relationship. Resolving the dispute involves issue-spotting and problem-solving. Restoring the relationship involves recognition and confession of shortcomings and mistakes, and seeking and giving forgiveness. One component involves the *principle;* the other involves the *people.*

Both components are important. In fact, each component is derived from an attribute of God. The "principle" component stems from the *justice* of God, and the "people" component stems from the love and *mercy* of God. The Bible teaches that we are to demonstrate *both* justice and mercy (see, Matthew 23:23, Micah 6:8 and Zechariah 7:9).

Accordingly, God wants our disputes to be resolved and our broken relationships to be restored in ways that are at the same time just and fair *and* loving and compassionate. Exactly how that is worked out differs in each situation. Although dealing with conflict responsibly is difficult and at times unpleasant, it also presents a valuable window of opportunity for growth and healthy change, in ourselves and in our relationships with others. We in CCS look forward to assisting you and the other party in a process which many before have found to be positive and liberating.

### LESSON TWO: CONFLICT SUMMARY—
### A PERSONAL EVALUATION

We in CCS have found it extremely helpful before conciliation begins for both parties in a conflict to put into writing their perspectives concerning the conflict. This exercise is helpful since writing out perspectives and seeing them on paper tends to clarify one's thoughts. It is invaluable for the CCS conciliators, who are better able to assist the parties in resolving their dispute and in restoring their relationship if they know each party's perspectives early in the process.

Accordingly, please complete this Conflict Summary and bring it (or a copy) with you to the first conciliation session. Feel free to use additional pages as necessary.

1. Briefly summarize the conflict as you perceive it, placing events in chronological order as much as possible.

   _____

   _____

   _____

2. Place a check by the following elements this conflict includes; cross out those it definitely does not include.

   _____ Disagreements as to facts.

   _____ Disagreements as to the "rightness" or propriety of certain actions.

   _____ Disagreements as to the requirements of the civil or criminal law.

   _____ Personal feelings of hurt, anger, loss, or guilt.

3. Write a brief comment in each space below indicating what effect this conflict is having in your life:

   On your attitudes (resentment, bitterness, etc.):

   _____

   _____

   _____

   On your emotional energies for your family and friends:

   _____

   _____

   On your personal devotional life:

   _____

   _____

   On your sense of joy and vitality:

   _____

   _____

On your outlook in life (thankfulness, hope, etc.):

_____

_____

On your finances:

_____

_____

On your reputation in the community or church:

_____

_____

4. This conflict could have been substantially avoided or minimized if:

   I had . . .

   _____

   _____

   _____

   The other party had . . .

   _____

   _____

   _____

5. How would your relationship with the other party be different if you were reconciled?

   _____

   _____

6. What is the very best conclusion you can imagine to this conflict?

   _____

   _____

   _____

7. What would be a first step you could take toward reconciliation with the other party?

_____

_____

_____

### LESSON THREE: UNDERSTANDING AND DEALING WITH DIVERSITY WITHIN THE BODY OF BELIEVERS

### Introduction

The Scriptures teach us that (1) conflict is and always has been an inevitable part of life—for Jesus, for the first-century church, and for us, and (2) Jesus calls each of us, if we discover that another believer "has something" against us, to go immediately and take the initiative in seeking to be reconciled to the other believer. By entering into the conciliation process, you and the other party are each seeking, with the aid of CCS, to fulfill this call of our Lord.

This study is intended to help establish the kind of climate needed for the upcoming conciliation session by focusing on how we regard ourselves and other believers. The portion of Scripture selected is the leading passage on the proper functioning of the "Body of Christ,"— the body of believers in Jesus Christ.

### Text: 1 Corinthians 12:12–27 (NASB)

Verse

12 For even as the body is one and yet has many members, and all the members of the body, though they are many, are one body, so also is Christ.

13 For by one Spirit we were all baptized into one body, whether Jews or Greeks, whether slaves or free, and we were all made to drink of one Spirit.

14 For the body is not one member, but many.

15 If the foot should say, "Because I am not a hand, I am not a part of the body," it is not for this reason any the less a part of the body.

16 And if the ear should say, "Because I am not an eye, I am not a part of the body," it is not for this reason any the less a part of the body.

236

17 If the whole body were an eye, where would the hearing be? If the whole were hearing, where would the sense of smell be?

18 But now God has placed the members, each one of them, in the body, just as He desired.

19 And if they were all one member, where would the body be?

20 But now there are many members, but one body.

21 And the eye cannot say to the hand, "I have no need of you"; or again the head to the feet, "I have no need of you."

22 On the contrary, it is much truer that the members of the body which seem to be weaker are necessary;

23 and those members of the body, which we deem less honorable, on these we bestow more abundant honor, and our unseemly members come to have more abundant seemliness,

24 whereas our seemly members have no need of it. But God has so composed the body, giving more abundant honor to that member which lacked.

25 that there should be no division in the body, but that the members should have the same care for one another.

26 And if one member suffers, all the members suffer with it; if one member is honored, all the members rejoice with it.

27 Now you are Christ's body, and individually members of it.

## Questions

1. What are some likely reasons why the apostle Paul selected the human body as an analogy for the proper functioning of the body of believers?

_____

_____

_____

2. What did Paul indicate all believers have in common?

_____

_____

_____

3. What differences among believers did Paul point out?

_____

_____

_____

What reasons did Paul suggest for the existence of these differences?

_____

_____

_____

4. What two attitudes harm the body of believers according to Paul? First, in verses 15–19?

_____

_____

_____

Second, in verses 21–25?

_____

_____

_____

How does God regard the various members of the body of believers (verses 22–24)?

_____

_____

_____

5. What behavior does God want his people to exhibit toward each other (verses 25–26)?

_____

_____

_____

6. Visualize your relationship with the other party as a "miniature" body of Christ. To what extent do you perceive either of

the harmful attitudes noted above in yourself, in relation to the other party?

_____

_____

_____

To what extent do you perceive either of these harmful attitudes in the other party, in relation to yourself?

_____

_____

_____

What impact have these attitudes had on your relationship with the other party generally, and on this dispute in particular?

_____

_____

_____

7. In light of this passage, as you approach the upcoming conciliation session, how do you want to perceive yourself and your importance in this dispute?

_____

_____

_____

How do you want to perceive the other party and his or her importance in this dispute?

_____

_____

_____

How do you want to perceive the differences in your perspectives on the dispute?

_____

_____

_____

8. How have others within the community of believers been affected by this dispute?

_____

_____

_____

How will the ways in which you and the other party deal with this dispute move the body of believers toward or away from the mutual support and caregiving to which God calls us in verses 25–26?

_____

_____

_____

What ideas do you have as to how you and the other party can share in each other's suffering and joy?

_____

_____

## Discussion

In his wisdom, God determined that his people would be characterized by "diversity within unity." Unity—in that every believer has and serves the same Savior and Lord, Jesus Christ, and has been baptized into the same body by the same Holy Spirit. Diversity—in that God has given every believer a different function in the body, stemming from different spiritual gifts, different abilities, different interests, and yes, different perspectives.

Just as a sprinter who seeks to run his fastest needs top performance not only from his legs, but also from his feet, his arms, and the rest of his body, so also the body of believers will achieve its intended purposes in this world only to the extent each member performs faithfully his or her particular functions.

Sometimes the diversity overshadows the unity, and the differences lead believers to erect the barriers of inferiority ("I'm not needed") or superiority ("You're not needed"). But these barriers are lies, for just as with the human body, every member is needed by the others (verses 15–19) and needs the others (verses 21–25). In fact, in God's sight those members which may seem to be weaker are indispensable and worthy of greater honor (verses 22–24).

In the context of a believer who differs from us, Paul's call to us is to see both ourselves and that believer as God does—as nothing less, and nothing more, than a gifted, needed member of the same body of believers. Then we can seek together to fulfill God's desire that, despite our differences, there be no division in that body, but rather the same care for one another marked by shared suffering and rejoicing.

We in CCS look forward to assisting you and the other party to achieve a resolution of your dispute that benefits both of you, and to do so in a manner that unifies, rather than divides, the body of believers.

Included here for your review are Guidelines for Sharing which we in CCS believe flow from this passage and are proposing for your conciliation sessions. If you have any questions or desired changes or additions, please share them with your CCS moderator at the beginning of the next session.

## Guidelines for Sharing

1. No interruptions. We will not interrupt the person who is speaking.
2. Listen actively. Let's work at understanding what each speaker is trying to communicate. Pretend you're in school and you'll be quizzed afterwards on what he or she was trying to tell us.
3. Defer judgment. Until we've concluded our discussion of an issue, try to resist the temptation to jump to a conclusion or solution and to tune out those who express different viewpoints.
4. Ask questions. If what someone else is saying is not clear to you, ask him or her a clarifying question. That says, "I want to understand what you're saying."
5. Be honest. When speaking, don't hedge the truth. Express in appropriate ways your understanding of the facts, your interpretation of events, and your feelings (including hurt or anger). We need to face the issues together, in love.
6. Communicate with "I messages," not "You messages." Examples of "I messages" are: "I felt as though you didn't respect my intelligence when . . .";  "It would make things easier for me if you would . . . .";  "I've been deeply hurt by some things you've done recently." Examples of "you messages" are: "You totally disregard my feelings and act like you think I'm a fool"; "You have got to stop . . .";  "You're obnoxious and unkind."

LESSON FOUR: SCRIPTURAL EXAMPLES
OF CONFLICT-RESOLUTION TECHNIQUES

**Introduction**

Scripture helps Christians in conflict remember that both parties are important members of a single body. Scripture also comforts Christians in conflict by recording instances when other godly men and women were involved in conflict. This study will focus on several techniques that biblical characters utilized to resolve their conflicts and will challenge you to consider which of these techniques might help resolve your conflict.

**Text: Joshua 22:9–18, 21–27, 30–31**

Verse

9 So the Reubenites, the Gadites and the half-tribe of Manasseh left the Israelites at Shiloh in Canaan to return to Gilead, their own land, which they had acquired in accordance with the command of the LORD through Moses.

10 When they came to Geliloth near the Jordan in the land of Canaan, the Reubenites, the Gadites and the half-tribe of Manasseh built an imposing altar there by the Jordan.

11 And when the Israelites heard that they had built the altar on the border of Canaan at Geliloth near the Jordan on the Israelite side,

12 the whole assembly of Israel gathered at Shiloh to go to war against them.

13 So the Israelites sent Phinehas son of Eleazar, the priest, to the land of Gilead—to Reuben, Gad and the half-tribe of Manasseh.

14 With him they sent ten of the chief men, one for each of the tribes of Israel, each the head of a family division among the Israelite clans.

15 When they went to Gilead—to Reuben, Gad and the half-tribe of Manasseh—they said to them:

16 "The whole assembly of the LORD says: 'How could you break faith with the God of Israel like this? How could you turn away from the LORD and build yourselves an altar in rebellion against him now?

242

17 "'Was not the sin of Peor enough for us? Up to this very day we have not cleansed ourselves from that sin, even though a plague fell on the community of the LORD!

18 "'And are you now turning away from the LORD?

"'If you rebel against the LORD today, tomorrow he will be angry with the whole community of Israel.'"

21 Then Reuben, Gad and the half-tribe of Manasseh replied to the heads of the clans of Israel:

22 "The Mighty One, God, the LORD! The Mighty One, God, the LORD! He knows! And let Israel know! If this has been in rebellion or disobedience to the LORD, do not spare us this day.

23 "If we have built our own altar to turn away from the LORD and to offer burnt offerings and grain offerings, or to sacrifice fellowship offerings on it, may the LORD himself call us to account.

24. "No! We did it for fear that some day your descendants might say to ours, 'What do you have to do with the LORD, the God of Israel?

25 "'The LORD has made the Jordan a boundary between us and you—you Reubenites and Gadites! You have no share in the LORD.' So your descendants might cause ours to stop fearing the LORD.

26 "That is why we said, 'Let us get ready and build an altar—but not for burnt offerings or sacrifices.'

27 "On the contrary, it is to be a witness between us and you and the generations that follow, that we will worship the LORD at his sanctuary with our burnt offerings, sacrifices and fellowship offerings. Then in the future your descendants will not be able to say to ours, 'You have no share in the LORD.'"

30 When Phinehas the priest and the leaders of the community—the heads of the clans of the Israelites—heard what Reuben, Gad and Manasseh had to say, they were pleased.

31 And Phinehas son of Eleazar, the priest, said to Reuben, Gad and Manasseh, "Today we know that the LORD is with us, because you have not acted unfaithfully toward the LORD in this matter. Now you have rescued the Israelites from the LORD's hand."

**Questions**

1. Why were most of the tribes of Israel ready to go to war with the tribes of Reuben, Gad, and half of Manasseh?

   _____

   _____

   _____

2. What meaning did the tribes of Reuben, Gad, and Manasseh intend by this action?

   _____

   _____

   _____

3. How did the other nine and a half tribes avoid unnecessary violence against their fellow countrymen?

   _____

   _____

4. How could the tribes of Reuben, Gad, and half of Manasseh have avoided this nearly catastrophic misunderstanding?

   _____

   _____

   _____

5. How might have your actions in this conflict been misinterpreted by the other party?

   _____

   _____

   _____

6. How might have you misinterpreted the other party's actions in this conflict?

   _____

   _____

   _____

7. Are you willing to inquire about the other party's intentions and to share your intentions?

_____

_____

_____

## Discussion

Often the root of conflict is some misunderstanding of statements, purposes, or expectations. Christ's exhortation to maintain unity with other Christians requires Christians in conflict, at a minimum, to make sure that both parties understand each other's intentions. This alone may resolve the dispute, as in the passage above. However, at times parties do have conflicting interests and desires which need to be addressed. Scripture also provides insight into handling those situations.

## Text: Acts 6:1–6

Verse

1 In those days when the number of disciples was increasing, the Grecian Jews among them complained against those of the Hebraic Jews because their widows were being overlooked in the daily distribution of food.

2 So the Twelve gathered all the disciples together and said, "It would not be right for us to neglect the ministry of the word of God in order to wait on tables.

3 Brothers, choose seven men from among you who are known to be full of the Spirit and wisdom. We will turn this responsibility over to them

4 and will give our attention to prayer and the ministry of the word."

5 This proposal pleased the whole group. They chose Stephen, a man full of faith and of the Holy Spirit; also Philip, Procorus, Nicanor, Timon, Parmenas, and Nicolas from Antioch, a convert to Judaism.

6 They presented these men to the apostles, who prayed and laid their hands on them.

## Questions

1. What goals did the Grecian Jews have in this conflict?

   _____

   _____

   _____

2. Were the Grecian Jews expecting the twelve disciples to be involved in the food distribution?

   _____

   _____

   _____

3. What goals did the twelve disciples have in this conflict?

   _____

   _____

   _____

4. How did the proposal by the twelve disciples satisfy both sets of goals and thus prevent a church split?

   _____

   _____

   _____

5. What goals do you have in your conflict?

   _____

   _____

   _____

6. What goals does the other party have in the conflict?

   _____

   _____

   _____

7. What creative solutions might meet both sets of goals and permit both of you to continue in your pre-conflict relationship?

_____

_____

_____

## Discussion

Sometimes it is possible to resolve conflict by working together to meet both parties' goals. Each party completely achieves his objective and thus is completely satisfied. It is often work to develop the creative solution that fully satisfies all interests. It is often easier to conclude that the other person's perspectives, feelings, and desires are not as righteous and important as yours and thus do not need to be acknowledged or fulfilled. The exhortation in Philippians 2:4 to "look not only to your own interests, but also to the interests of others" should motivate Christians in conflict to wrestle in prayer for ways to satisfy both people's goals. When we are not able to determine those solutions, Scripture still provides a guide.

### Text: Romans 14:1–6, 12–13, 19–22

Verse

1 Accept him whose faith is weak, without passing judgment on disputable matters.

2 One man's faith allows him to eat everything, but another man, whose faith is weak, eats only vegetables.

3 The man who eats everything must not look down on him who does not, and the man who does not eat everything must not condemn the man who does, for God has accepted him.

4 Who are you to judge someone else's servant? To his own master he stands or falls. And he will stand, for the Lord is able to make him stand.

5 One man considers one day more sacred than another; another man considers every day alike. Each one should be fully convinced in his own mind.

6 He who regards one day as special, does so to the Lord. He who eats meat, eats to the Lord, for he gives thanks to God; and he who abstains, does so to the Lord and gives thanks to God.

12 So then, each of us will give an account of himself to God.

13 Therefore let us stop passing judgment on one another. Instead, make up your mind not to put any stumbling block or obstacle in your brother's way.

19 Let us therefore make every effort to do what leads to peace and to mutual edification.

20 Do not destroy the work of God for the sake of food. All food is clean, but it is wrong for a man to eat anything that causes someone else to stumble.

21 It is better not to eat meat or drink wine or to do anything else that will cause your brother to fall.

22 So whatever you believe about these things keep between yourself and God. Blessed is the man who does not condemn himself by what he approves.

**Questions**

1. Does every dispute have only one true answer or solution?

   _____

2. What spiritual issues did Paul identify that were better left to each individual's conscience?

   _____

   _____

3. Do you think the people of that day considered those issues serious or inconsequential?

   _____

   _____

4. What reasons did Paul provide for not judging other believers concerning disputable matters?

   _____

   _____

   _____

5. What four actions did Paul instruct a believer in conflict to take, or to refrain from taking, in relation to the other party?

   _____

_____

_____

6. Does your conflict involve a "disputable matter" (verse 1) about which you could accept the other party without passing judgment?

_____

_____

7. If so, can you live at peace with the other party without resolving this dispute (that is, keeping your viewpoint "between yourself and God")?

_____

_____

**Discussion**

Not all conflicts need to be resolved. If you are certain that the other party's and your intentions are in conflict and you have not been able to determine a solution that satisfies the goals of both parties, then you should give serious consideration as to whether this conflict must be resolved. Remembering that the diversity within the Christian church is God-ordained and far-reaching (1 Corinthians 12), you may conclude that it is possible for you to live at peace with the other person despite this difference. If your dispute is one that must be resolved, Scripture still serves as a guide.

**Text: Joshua 18:1–7**

Verse

1 The whole assembly of the Israelites gathered at Shiloh and set up the Tent of Meeting there. The country was brought under their control,

2 but there were still seven Israelite tribes who had not yet received their inheritance.

3 So Joshua said to the Israelites: "How long will you wait before you begin to take possession of the land that the LORD, the God of your fathers, has given you?

4 Appoint three men from each tribe. I will send them out to make a survey of the land and to write a description of it, according to the inheritance of each. Then they will return to me.

5 You are to divide the land into seven parts. Judah is to remain in its territory on the south and the house of Joseph in its territory on the north.

6 After you have written descriptions of the seven parts of the land, bring them here to me and I will cast lots for you in the presence of the LORD our God.

7 The Levites, however, do not get a portion among you, because the priestly service of the LORD is their inheritance. And Gad, Reuben and the half-tribe of Manasseh have already received their inheritance on the east side of the Jordan. Moses the servant of the LORD gave it to them."

## Questions

1. When Joshua specified that Judah must keep its territory on the south, Joseph its territory on the north, and Gad, Reuben, and half of Manasseh their territories on the east, was he forcing the remaining seven tribes to divide a "fixed pie"?

   _____

   _____

2. What problems did Joshua avoid by having the seven tribes agree on the division into seven tracts—presumably equal in value—prior to agreeing on ownership of any tract?

   _____

   _____

   _____

   (Joshua may have adapted the idea from Abraham's method of having one party divide the land in half, and the other party choose which half he desired. See Genesis 13:5–9.)

3. If the tribes had created seven equally valuable tracts, why do you think Joshua chose to assign those tracts to the tribes by casting lots "in the presence of the Lord"?

   _____

   _____

4. Does your dispute involve a "fixed pie" including noncash items that need to be divided? If so, in what shares would you be

willing to see it divided prior to the assignment of ownership of those shares?

_____

_____

_____

5. What are your suggestions for a process to assign those shares (one divides and the other chooses, divide into many components and take turns making selections, casting lots, etc.)?

_____

_____

_____

## Discussion

At times conflict is best resolved by parties terminating their joint venture. This often requires the division of joint property. The Christian's call to do justice (Matt. 23:23) calls him or her to seek a fair division. Often parties who cannot agree on what constitutes a fair division can agree on a fair process to determine the division. Such an agreement generally facilitates reconciliation between the parties. If the parties cannot reach such an agreement, Scripture still serves as a guide.

**Text: 1 Samuel 24:2–15**

Verse

2 So Saul took three thousand chosen men from all Israel and set out to look for David and his men near the Crags of the Wild Goats.

3 He came to the sheep pens along the way; a cave was there, and Saul went in to relieve himself. David and his men were far back in the cave.

4 The men said, "This is the day the LORD spoke of when he said to you, 'I will give your enemy into your hands for you to deal with as you wish.'" Then David crept up unnoticed and cut off a corner of Saul's robe.

5 Afterward, David was conscience-stricken for having cut off a corner of his robe.

6 He said to his men, "The LORD forbid that I should do such a thing to my master, the LORD's anointed, or lift my hand against him; for he is the anointed of the LORD."

7 With these words David rebuked his men and did not allow them to attack Saul. And Saul left the cave and went his way.

8 Then David went out of the cave and called out to Saul, "My lord the king!" When Saul looked behind him, David bowed down and prostrated himself with his face to the ground.

9 He said to Saul, "Why do you listen when men say, 'David is bent on harming you'?

10 "This day you have seen with your own eyes how the LORD delivered you into my hands in the cave. Some urged me to kill you, but I spared you; I said, 'I will not lift my hand against my master, because he is the LORD's anointed.'

11 "See, my father, look at this piece of your robe in my hand! I cut off the corner of your robe but did not kill you. Now understand and recognize that I am not guilty of wrongdoing or rebellion. I have not wronged you, but you are hunting me down to take my life.

12 "May the LORD judge between you and me. And may the LORD avenge the wrongs you have done to me, but my hand will not touch you.

13 "As the old saying goes, 'From evildoers come evil deeds,' so my hand will not touch you.

14 "Against whom has the king of Israel come out? Whom are you pursuing? A dead dog? A flea?

15 "May the Lord be our judge and decide between us. May he consider my cause and uphold it; may he vindicate me by delivering me from your hand."

## Questions

1. Was Saul seeking to injure David?

   _____

   _____

2. What are two ways David could have justified injuring Saul?

_____

_____

_____

3. What attitude did David have toward Saul that caused David to refrain from inflicting injury?

_____

_____

_____

4. How do you think Saul felt when David promised never to injure Saul, but to let the Lord judge between them?

_____

_____

_____

5. Do you believe that the other party to your dispute is seeking to injure you physically, emotionally, or monetarily? Explain.

_____

_____

_____

6. Have you tried to injure the other party, either to protect yourself or because the Lord has delivered the other party into your hands?

_____

_____

_____

7. Do you believe that the other person is valuable to the Lord?

_____

_____

_____

8. What do you think would happen if you promised never to injure the other party, but to let the Lord judge between the two of you?

_____

_____

9.  Could you make the above promise *and* forgive the other party?

_____

_____

### Discussion

There are times when the Christian faith calls one to resolve conflict by making oneself vulnerable to injury and trusting in God for the result. Scripture teaches the value of every human life, even those considered of little value by human estimations (Matt. 25:31–46, Mark 9:33–37, and Matt. 18:10–14). If we are to be like Christ, there will be times when God asks us to conquer evil and injustice by turning the other cheek in love and forgiveness. Christ's death on the cross establishes that sometimes God uses unjust suffering and death to achieve essential purposes. Christians in conflict should consider whether God's purposes in that situation might be best promoted by using good to defeat evil and relying on God as the ultimate judge. (See Romans 12:17–21, Acts 5:1–11, and Numbers 16:1–35.) If you believe that is not appropriate in your situation, Scripture still serves as a guide.

### Text: 1 Corinthians 6:1–7

Verse

1  If any of you has a dispute with another, dare he take it before the ungodly for judgment instead of before the saints?

2  Do you not know that the saints will judge the world? And if you are to judge the world, are you not competent to judge trivial cases?

3  Do you not know that we will judge angels? How much more the things of this life!

4  Therefore, if you have disputes about such matters, appoint as judges even men of little account in the church!

5  I say this to shame you. Is it possible that there is nobody among you wise enough to judge a dispute between believers?

6 But instead, one brother goes to law against another—and this in front of unbelievers!

7 The very fact that you have lawsuits among you means you have been completely defeated already. Why not rather be cheated?

**Questions**

1. Who does Paul suggest should judge disputes between Christians?

   _____

   _____

2. What are the qualifications of the community of God's people?

   _____

   _____

3. Why do you think Paul was so strong about not taking disputes between Christians to civil law courts?

   _____

   _____

4. Would you be willing to submit this dispute to representatives of the Christian community for a legally binding arbitration decision?

   _____

   _____

5. Which Christians would you trust and respect to act as arbitrators?

   _____

   _____

**Discussion**

Scripture is very clear that if a judge/arbitrator is needed to resolve a dispute between Christians, that judge/arbitrator should be a Christian. Matthew 18:15–20 assures us that God will be present when such a process is followed. God's cause will have been promoted because the process of resolving the dispute will have been obedient to Scripture.

## Conclusion

Men and women throughout history have used a variety of approaches to resolve disputes in a manner pleasing to God. You have now studied instances where disputes were resolved by:

- clarifying intentions
- determining creative solutions meeting the goals of all parties
- leaving the dispute unresolved and accepting the other party
- dividing assets into equal shares and then determining the ownership of the shares
- resolving not to injure the other party and trusting that God will act as judge
- submitting the dispute to Christians for a judgment

One or more of these approaches may be helpful to you as you prayerfully seek God's leading as to how you should handle your conflict.

### LESSON FIVE: OBEDIENCE—THE MEASURE OF SUCCESS

## Introduction

Scripture helps us when we are in conflict by reminding us of God's emphasis on reconciliation, the high value God places on both parties, and various conflict resolution methods used by other godly men and women. Scripture also teaches that obedience is the measure of a Christian's success and that God's sovereignty assures us that he will guide and determine our future.

**Text: Acts 9:1–18**

Verse

1 Meanwhile, Saul was still breathing out murderous threats against the Lord's disciples. He went to the high priest

2 and asked him for letters to the synagogues in Damascus, so that if he found any there who belonged to the Way, whether men or women, he might take them as prisoners to Jerusalem.

3 As he neared Damascus on his journey, suddenly a light from heaven flashed around him.

4 He fell to the ground and heard a voice say to him, "Saul, Saul, why do you persecute me?"

5  "Who are you, Lord?" Saul asked.

"I am Jesus, whom you are persecuting," he replied.

6  "Now get up and go into the city, and you will be told what you must do."

7  The men traveling with Saul stood there speechless; they heard the sound but did not see anyone.

8  Saul got up from the ground, but when he opened his eyes he could see nothing. So they led him by the hand into Damascus.

9  For three days he was blind, and did not eat or drink anything.

10 In Damascus there was a disciple named Ananias. The Lord called to him in a vision, "Ananias!"

"Yes, Lord," he answered.

11 The Lord told him, "Go to the house of Judas on Straight Street and ask for a man from Tarsus named Saul, for he is praying.

12 In a vision he has seen a man named Ananias come and place his hands on him to restore his sight."

13 "Lord," Ananias answered, "I have heard many reports about this man and all the harm he has done to your saints in Jerusalem.

14 And he has come here with authority from the chief priests to arrest all who call on your name."

15 But the Lord said to Ananias, "Go! This man is my chosen instrument to carry my name before the Gentiles and their kings and before the people of Israel.

16 I will show him how much he must suffer for my name."

17 Then Ananias went to the house and entered it. Placing his hands on Saul, he said, "Brother Saul, the Lord—Jesus, who appeared to you on the road as you were coming here—has sent me so that you may see again and be filled with the Holy Spirit."

18 Immediately, something like scales fell from Saul's eyes, and he could see again. He got up and was baptized.

## Questions

1. Why was Ananias reluctant to visit Saul?

_____

_____

2. Whose understanding and plan for the future did Ananias need to rely on and trust in order to be able to visit Saul?

_____

_____

(Do you think Ananias was familiar with Proverbs 3:5–7? "Trust in the LORD with all your heart and lean not on your own understanding; in all your ways acknowledge him, and he will make your paths straight. Do not be wise in your own eyes; fear the LORD and shun evil.")

3. How did Ananias refer to Saul in his dialogue with the Lord?

_____

How did he address Saul when he visited him?

_____

What did he do for Saul?

_____

4. Did Ananias's obedience cause him to suffer?

_____

_____

See Acts 21:10–14, 27–36 for a situation in which obedience to God's will resulted in a significant cost, eventually including Paul's life.

5. Was Ananias a success or a failure in God's eyes? Why?

_____

_____

6. In what ways did God use Ananias's visit with Saul to further God's kingdom on earth?

_____

_____

7. What conflict-resolution approach do you believe God wants you to utilize in your conflict?

_____

_____

8. What risks are associated with that approach and how do you feel about trusting God with those possible losses?

 

 

9. You are already being obedient to God if you are seeking to use a scriptural process to resolve this dispute. Has God given you any blessings, such as peace or joy, because of that obedience?

 

 

10. What do you think would happen if you made a commitment to follow God's leading, regardless of how the other party acts or reacts?

 

 

11. Do you have confidence that your future—whether prosperity or hardship—is in God's hands?

 

 

See Genesis 45:1–8 for Joseph's reminder of God's using even an adversary's unjust act to bring ultimate prosperity to Joseph and to further God's kingdom.

**Discussion**

There are times when a Christian's response to a situation must be determined out of obedience to God and his word. At times this will be convenient, and at other times it will be very costly. It is that commitment to costly obedience that causes Christ to truly become "Lord" in our lives. It is obedience to Christ that determines a Christian's success. (See John 8:31.)

With regard to your dispute, God's word clearly teaches that you should forgive your opponent for any of his or her wrongs and you should seek to be reconciled. (See Matthew 18:21–35 and 5:23–24.) Have you participated in an objective process to determine which solutions are acceptable to your opponent? If any of those solutions are acceptable to you, then resolve the conflict according to those terms and resolve the internal spiritual concerns by deciding to forgive and be reconciled. If you cannot accept any of your opponent's solutions, then agree to abide by the decision of a neutral, wise Christian and forgive and be reconciled. The measure of your success in resolving this dispute must include an evaluation of the biblical command to forgive and be reconciled.

Even if the solution is not perfect from your perspective, it may be the best that can be arranged under the circumstances. Out of obedience to Christ, accept the best solution possible at this time and forgive and be reconciled. God is glorified when you make such a commitment in an effort to please and honor the Lord Jesus Christ.

# APPENDIX B

# MEDIATION AND CONFLICT-MANAGEMENT RESOURCES

The Alban Institute, Inc.
4125 Nebraska Ave., NW
Washington, DC 20016

Institute for Dispute Resolution
Pepperdine University School of Law
24255 Pacific Coast Highway
Malibu, California 90265
213-456-4655

Mennonite Conciliation Service
c/o The Mennonite Central Committee
21 South Twelfth Street, Box M
Akron, PA 17501

Some of the Christian Conciliation Service (CCS) chapters in the United States are listed below. If no chapter is listed in your area, consult your local telephone directory, or contact the Association of Christian Conciliation Services, Inc., 1537 Avenue D, Suite 352, Billings, Montana 59102; telephone: 406-256-1583.

### California

Bay Area CCS
P.O. Box 617
Novato, California 94948
415-382-9162

CCS of Los Angeles
1800 N. Highland, Suite 507
Hollywood, California 90028
213-467-3331

CCS of Orange County
3855 E. LaPalma Ave., Suite 125
Anaheim, California 92807
714-630-2622

### Colorado

Shepherds for Peace
746 C.R. 514
Ignacio, Colorado 81137
303-884-2360

CCS of Denver
1545 S. Kline Ct.
Lakewood, Colorado 80226
303-988-3230

### Florida

CCS of Central Florida
P.O. Box 1649
Orlando, Florida 32802
407-849-0020

CCS of Brevard
427 Timberlake Dr.
Melbourne, Florida 32940
407-242-1421

## Illinois

CCS of Northern Illinois
P.O. Box 54
Elmhurst, Illinois 60126
312-834-4740

## Kansas

CCS of Kansas City
6405 Metcalf, Suite 307
Overland Park, Kansas 66202
913-362-2102

## Kentucky

CCM of Louisville
1270 Starks Building
Louisville, Kentucky 40202
502-585-4673

## Michigan

CCS of Central Michigan
1710 E. Michigan Ave.
Lansing, Michigan 48912
517-485-2270

CCS of Northern Michigan
P.O. Box 458
Boyne City, Michigan 49712
616-582-6940

CCS of Southeastern Michigan
(Detroit area)
27350 W. Chicago
Redford, Michigan 48239
313-937-3939

CCS of the Upper Peninsula
   and Northeastern Wisconsin
115 E. Ayer St.
Ironwood, Michigan 49938
906-932-5202

**Minnesota**

CCS of Minnesota
P.O. Box 24772
Edina, Minnesota 55424
612-949-2336

**Mississippi**

CCS of Central Mississippi
P.O. Box 55552
Jackson, Mississippi 39296
601-366-5497

**Missouri**

CCS of Kansas City
6405 Metcalf, Suite 307
Overland Park, Kansas 66202
913-362-2102

**Montana**

CCS of Montana
1537 Avenue D, Suite 352
Billings, Montana 59102
406-256-1583

**New York**

CCS of Western New York
(Buffalo area)
8226 Main St.
Williamsville, New York 14221
716-631-5661

**North Carolina**

Trinity CCS
415 Creekview Dr.
Trinity, North Carolina 27370
919-434-5449

**North Dakota**

Professional Christian Resource Center
1501 N. Twelfth St.
Bismarck, North Dakota 58501
701-255-3325

## Ohio

CCS of Greater Toledo
127 North Erie St.
Toledo, Ohio 43606
419-244-3817

## Oklahoma

CCS of Oklahoma City
c/o 1813 Running Branch Rd.
Edmond, Oklahoma 73013
405-341-2253

## Oregon

CCS of Portland/Vancouver
P.O. Box 9070
Portland, Oregon 97207
503-231-1624

## Pennsylvania

CCS of Western Pennsylvania
P.O. Box 1805
Butler, Pennsylvania 16003
412-285-5102

Delaware Valley CCS
(Philadelphia area)
212 Cricket Ave.
Ardmore, Pennsylvania 19003
215-649-2852

## Rhode Island

CCS of Rhode Island
P.O. Box 793
Newport, Rhode Island 02840
401-624-6259

## South Carolina

CCS of Spartanburg
364 S. Pine St.
Spartanburg, South Carolina 29302
803-582-3740

## Tennessee

CCS of Eastern Tennessee
1304 Knightsbridge Dr. SW
Knoxville, Tennessee 37922
615-694-8906

## Texas

CCS of Dallas/Fort Worth
P.O. Box 331142
Fort Worth, Texas 76163
817-568-2000

CCS of Greater Houston
P.O. Box 218945
Houston, Texas 77218
713-578-8787

CCS of San Antonio
P.O. Box 15717
San Antonio, Texas 78212
512-227-0638

Christian Reconciliation Center
P.O. Box 50057
Austin, Texas 78763
512-474-9663

## Washington

CCS of Puget Sound
424 N. 130th St.
Seattle, Washington 98133
206-367-2245

## Wisconsin

CCS of the Upper Peninsula
  and Northeastern Wisconsin
115 E. Ayer St.
Ironwood, Michigan 49938
916-932-5202

# APPENDIX C

# CONCILIATION PROVISIONS FOR CONTRACTS AND WILLS

To encourage people to resolve their disputes out of court, the Association of Christian Conciliation Services recommends that the following mediation/arbitration clauses be inserted in contracts and wills.

**For Contracts**

*Any claim or dispute arising out of or relating to this agreement shall be settled by mediation and, if necessary, arbitration in accordance with the Rules of Procedure for Christian Conciliation of the Association of Christian Conciliation Services, and judgment upon an arbitration award may be entered in any court of competent jurisdiction.*

This clause will be legally enforceable in most states. It may be used in employment, construction, commercial, and any other agreements that could someday give rise to a lawsuit. By using it when contract relationships are still new and positive, individuals may avoid a great deal of unnecessary stress and expense should unforeseen problems arise in the future. The legal requirements of mediation/arbitration clauses vary from state to state. For example, somes states require that notice of arbitration provisions be printed on the front page of the contract in underlined capital letters. So it is wise to get advice from an attorney when first using such clauses in agreements.

**For Wills**

A similar clause may be inserted in a will. Though it is not legally enforceable in most states, this clause will often encourage people who have disagreements over a will to settle their differences in a conciliatory manner rather than through litigation.

*I ask that any questions or disputes that may arise during the administration of my estate be settled by mediation and, if necessary, arbitration in accordance with the Rules of Procedure for Christian Conciliation of the Association of Christian Conciliation Services.*

This request may carry more weight if it is accompanied by an explanation of the writer's intentions and desires. For example, it could be preceded by these words:

*I believe that God wants Christians to make every effort to live at peace and to resolve disputes with one another in private or within the church (see Matt. 18:15–20; 1 Cor. 6:1–8; Eph. 4:1–3). I believe that obedience to these principles honors and pleases God, leads others to believe in Christ, and benefits those involved. With these thoughts in mind, and trusting that those who will receive my property will honor my beliefs, . . .*

# BIBLIOGRAPHY

Auerbach, J. *Justice Without Law?* New York: Oxford University Press, 1983.

Beavers, W. (F. Walsh, ed.) *Healthy, Midrange, and Severely Dysfunctional Families, in Normal Family Processes.* New York: New Guilford Press, 1982.

Beer, J. *Peacemaking in Your Neighborhood.* Philadelphia: New Society Resources, 1988.

Blake, R., and J. Mouton. *Solving Costly Organizational Conflicts.* San Francisco: Jossey-Bass, 1985.

Blayre, A. *The Heart of the Dragon.* Boston: Houghton Mifflin, 1985.

Bolton, Robert. *People Skills.* Englewood Cliffs, N.J.: Prentice-Hall, 1979.

Bossart, D. *Creative Conflict in Religious Education and Church Administration.* Birmingham: Religious Education Press, 1980.

Bostrom, R. N., ed. *Competence in Communication: A Multidisciplinary Approach.* Beverly Hills: Sage, 1984.

Brazil, W. *Effective Approaches to Settlement.* Clifton, N.J.: Prentice-Hall, 1988.

Burton, John. *Conflict Resolution and Prevention.* New York: St. Martin's Press, 1990.

Buzzard, Lynn, and Laurence Ek. *Tell It to the Church.* Wheaton, Ill.: Tyndale House Publishers, 1985.

Campolo, Anthony. *We Have Met the Enemy, and They Are Partly Right*. Waco, Texas: Jarrell, a division of Word, 1985.

Carter, Jimmy. *The Blood of Abraham*. Boston: Houghton Mifflin, 1985.

Cunningham, Will. *How to Enjoy a Family Fight*. Phoenix: Questar Publishers, 1988.

Curle, A. *Making Peace*. London: Tavistock, 1971.

Dana, D. *Managing Differences*. Wolcott, Conn.: MTI Publications, 1989.

Deutsch, M. *The Resolution of Conflict: Constructive and Destructive Processes*. New Haven: Yale University Press, 1973.

Dobson, James C. *Parenting Isn't for Cowards*. Waco, Texas: Word, 1987.

Fenton, Horace L., Jr. *When Christians Clash*. Downers Grove, Ill.: Inter-Varsity, 1987.

Filley, Alan C. *Interpersonal Conflict Resolution*. Glenview, Ill.: Scott, Foresman and Company, 1974.

Fine, E., ed. *Containing Legal Costs*. New York: Center for Public Resources, 1988.

Fisher, R., and Scott Brown. *Getting Together—Building a Relationship that Gets to Yes*. Boston: Houghton Mifflin Co., 1988.

Fisher, R., and W. Ury. *Getting to Yes*. New York: Viking Penguin 1981.

Flynn, Leslie B. *When the Saints Come Storming In*. Wheaton, Ill.: Victor Books, 1988.

Folberg, J., and A. Milne, eds. *Divorce Mediation*. New York: The Guilford Press, 1988.

Folberg, J., and Alison Taylor. *Mediation*. San Francisco: Jossey-Bass, 1986.

Frascogna, Xavier M., Jr., and H. Lee Hetherton. *Negotiation Strategy for Lawyers*. Englewood Cliffs, N. J.: Prentice-Hall, 1984.

Friedmann, I. M. *Helping Resolve Conflict: True Experiences of a Christian Anthropologist*. Scottsdale, Pa. and Waterloo, Ontario: Herald Press, 1990.

George, R. *Counseling: Theory and Practice*. Englewood Cliffs, N.J.: Prentice-Hall, 1990.

Goldberg, S., E. Green, and F. Sander. *Dispute Resolution*. Boston: Little, Brown, 1985.

Haley, J. *Problem Solving Therapy*. San Francisco: Jossey-Bass, 1976.

Hanson, Freya Ottem, and Terje C. Hausken. *Mediation for Troubled Marriages*. Minneapolis: Augsburg, 1989.

Henry, J., and J. Lieberman. *The Manager's Guide to Resolving Legal Disputes: Better Results Without Litigation.* New York: Harper and Row, 1985.

Hicks, H. *Preaching Through a Storm.* Grand Rapids: Zondervan, 1987.

Hinkle, J., and T. Woodroof. *Among Friends.* Colorado Springs: Navpress, 1989.

Jandt, F. *Win-Win Negotiating—Turning Conflict into Agreement.* New York: John Wiley & Sons, 1985.

Jaspers, K. *The Way to Wisdom.* New Haven: Yale University Press, 1951.

Kakalik, J., and R. Ross. *Costs of the Civil Justice System: Court Expenditures for Various Types of Civil Cases.* Santa Monica: C.A. Rand Corporation, 1983.

Kohn, Alfe. *No Contest.* Boston: Houghton Mifflin Co., 1986.

Kreider, Robert S., and Rachel Waltner Goosen. *When Good People Quarrel: Studies of Conflict Resolution.* Scottsdale, Pa. and Kitchener, Ontario: Herald Press, 1989.

Kressel, Kenneth, Dean G. Pruitt, and Associates, eds. *Mediation Research: The Process and Effectiveness of Third-Party Intervention.* San Francisco: Jossey-Bass, 1989.

Laney, J. *A Guide to Church Discipline.* Minneapolis: Bethany House Publisher, 1985.

Lax, David A., and James K. Sebenius. *The Manager as Negotiator.* New York: The Free Press, 1986.

Leas, Speed. *Leadership and Conflict.* Nashville: Abingdon Press, 1982.

Leas, Speed, and P. Kittlaus. *Church Fights: Managing Conflict in the Local Church.* Philadelphia: The Westminster Press, 1973.

Lewis, G. Douglass. *Resolving Church Conflicts.* San Francisco: Harper and Row, 1981.

Lieberman, Jethro. *The Litigious Society.* New York: Basic Books, 1983.

Likert, Rensis, and Jane Gibson Likert. *New Ways of Managing Conflict.* New York: McGraw-Hill, 1976.

Lincoln, William. *Collaborative Negotiation.* A training book published by the Center for Dispute Resolution, Willamette University College of Law, 1986.

Mallory, James, and S. Baldwin. *The Kink and I.* Wheaton, Ill.: Victor Books, 1973.

McCollough, Charles R. *Resolving Conflict with Justice and Peace.* New York: Pilgrim Press, 1991.

McGillis, D. *Community Dispute Resolution—Programs and Public Policy.* U.S. Department of Justice, 1986.

McSwain, Larry L., and William C. Treadwell, Jr. *Conflict Ministry in the Church.* Nashville: Broadman Press, 1981.

Moore, Christopher. *The Mediation Process.* San Francisco: Jossey-Bass, 1987.

Nierenberg, Gerard I. *The Complete Negotiator.* New York: Nierenberg and Zeif, 1986.

Pritzker, D., and D. Dalton. *Negotiated Rulemaking Sourcebook.* Washington, D.C.: United States Printing Office, 1990.

Raiffa, Howard. *The Art and Science of Negotiation.* Cambridge, Mass.: Belknap Press, 1982.

Sande, Ken. *The Peacemaker: A Biblical Guide to Resolving Personal Conflict.* Grand Rapids, Mich.: Baker, 1991.

Schaller, Lyle. *The Pastor and the People: Building a New Partnership for Effective Ministry.* Nashville: Abingdon, 1973.

Singer, L. *Settling Disputes.* Boulder, Colo.: Westview Press, 1990.

Stulberg, Joseph. *Taking Charge, Managing Conflict.* Lexington, Mass.: D. C. Heath and Co., 1987.

Swindoll, Charles. *Strengthening Your Grip.* Waco, Texas: Word, 1982.

Vale, John, and Robert Hughes. *Getting Even.* Grand Rapids: Zondervan, 1987.

Wallerstein, Judith S., and Sandra Blakeslee. *Second Chances: Men, Women and Children a Decade after Divorce.* New York: Ticknor and Fields, 1989.

# NOTES

## Chapter 1  Discovering the Ministry of Reconciliation

1. Derek Bok, "A Flawed System (Part I)," reprinted in *New York State Bar Journal* 55 (October 1983), 8. "A Flawed System (Part II)," was reprinted in *New York State Bar Journal* 55 (November 1983), 31, 32.

2. See Jay Folberg, "Mediation of Child Custody Disputes," *Columbia Journal of Law and Social Problems* 19 (1985), 413–449.

3. The American Arbitration Association, the nation's largest nonprofit dispute-resolution organization, reported 55,520 case filings for mediation and arbitration in 1989 involving disputes totaling just under $2.5 billion (*1990 Annual Report*, American Arbitration Association, 7).

4. M. Deutsch, *The Resolution of Conflict: Constructive and Destructive Processes* (New Haven: Yale University Press, 1973), 360.

5. See S. Goldberg, "The Rise in Grievance Mediation," *Proceedings, New York University Annual National Conference on Labor* 37 (1983), chapter 13, page 1.

6. See D. Pritzker and D. Dalton, *Negotiated Rulemaking Sourcebook* (Washington, D.C.: United States Printing Office, 1990), 1–10.

7. For a listing of Christian Conciliation Service chapters, see Appendix B.

8. See L. Singer, *Settling Disputes* (Boulder, Colo.: Westview Press, 1990), 111.

9. See S. Goldberg, E. Green, and F. Sander, *Dispute Resolution* (Boston: Little, Brown, 1985), 512–15.

10. A. J. Salius, ed., *Program Description: Services Provided in Minor Criminal Cases in Geographical Area Courts*, unpublished training manual, Family Division, Connecticut Superior Court, 1983.

11. T. Arendell, *Mothers and Divorce: Legal, Economic, and Social Dilemmas* (Berkeley: University of California Press, 1986), 1.

12. See Judith Wallerstein and Sandra Blakeslee, *Second Chances: Men, Women and Children a Decade after Divorce* (New York: Ticknor and Fields, 1989).

13. See Kenneth W. Thomas and W. H. Schmidt, "A Survey of Managerial Interests with Respect to Conflict," *Academy of Management Journal*, June 1976.

14. "Who's Liable for Stress on the Job?" *Harvard Business Review*, March/April 1985, 60.

15. Horace L. Fenton, Jr., *When Christians Clash* (Downers Grove, Ill.: Press, 1987), 10.

16. "Finding God on Flight 232," *Life* magazine, September 1989, 28.

17. "John F. Kennedy's Legacy," *Newsday*, 20 November 1988, 2.

18. Address by United States Supreme Court Chief Justice Warren E. Burger, Annual Meeting of the American Law Institute, 14 May 1985.

## Chapter 2 Conflict: Danger and Opportunity

1. "Scars from the Eighties, Hope for the Nineties," *Financial Times*, 8 June 1990, I-22.

2. *Oxford English Dictionary* (1970), 809.

3. See Speed Leas, *Leadership and Conflict* (Nashville: Abingdon Press, 1982), 49–54.

4. D. Bossart, *Creative Conflict in Religious Education and Church Administration* (Birmingham: Religious Education Press, 1980), 11.

5. "Neutral Clergy Feel Pressure in Rift Among Southern Baptists," *Los Angeles Times*, 18 August 1990, F-14.

6. John Burton, *Conflict Resolution and Prevention* (New York: St. Martin's Press, 1990), 37.

7. Lawrence H. Tribe, *Abortion: The Clash of Absolutes* (New York: W. W. Norton, 1990), jacket notes.

8. H. Hicks, *Preaching Through a Storm* (Grand Rapids: Zondervan, 1987), 74.

9. Ibid.

10. Speed Leas and P. Kittlaus, *Church Fights: Managing Conflict in the Local Church* (Philadelphia: Westminster Press, 1973), 29–35.

11. "Experts on the Environment Are Legal Field's Hottest Stars," *The Business Journal,* 17 December 1990, 18.

12. James Mallory and S. Baldwin, *The Kink and I* (Wheaton, Ill.: Victor Books, 1973).

## Chapter 3 Responding to Conflict

1. Bruce Regier, "Dealing with Conflict: A Survey of Orange County Ministers," unpublished research completed by the Christian Conciliation Service of Orange County, 1989.

2. Lyle Schaller, *The Pastor and the People: Building a New Partnership for Effective Ministry* (Nashville: Abingdon, 1973).

3. Thomas and Schmidt, "A Survey of Managerial Interests with Respect to Conflict."

4. Regier, "Dealing with Conflict."

5. Interview with Loren Vickery, church-building program consultant, at Western Baptist College, Salem, Oregon, January 1990.

6. Interview with Dr. Rodger Bufford, chair, George Fox Graduate School of Psychology, Newberg, Oregon, April 1989 at Western Conservative Baptist Seminary, Portland, Oregon.

7. Interview with Peter Robinson, associate director, Institute for Dispute Resolution, Pepperdine University School of Law, Malibu, California, 27 September 1990.

8. Telephone survey completed by the Institute for Dispute Resolution, Pepperdine University School of Law. The survey, which involved interviews with ministers of nineteen churches in Ventura County, California, was completed in October 1988.

9. See Richard E. Miller and Austin Sarat, "Grievances, Claims, and Disputes: Assessing the Adversary Culture," *Law and Society Review* 15 (1980-1981), 525, reprinted in J. Murray, A. Rau, and E. Sherman, eds., *Process of Dispute Resolution: The Role of Lawyers* (Westbury, N.Y.: Foundation Press, 1989), 2.

10. Ibid., 4–10.

11. Speed Leas, *Leadership and Conflict* (Nashville: Abingdon, 1982), 96–106. In this book, Leas, a nationally recognized consultant to churches, recommends strategies for "curbing conflict" through

de-escalation by establishing boundaries, structuring the process, searching for common goals, responding to threats with position statements, and utilizing a third party.

12. See J. Hinkle and T. Woodroof, *Among Friends* (Colorado Springs: Navpress, 1989), 125–46.

13. Alfe Kohn, *No Contest* (Boston: Houghton Mifflin, 1986).

## Chapter 4  Biblical Principles for Reconciliation

1. H. Liddell and R. Scott, *A Greek-English Lexicon* (Oxford: Clarendon Press, 1968), 899.

2. Ron Kraybill, "From Head to Heart: The Cycle of Reconciliation," *Conciliation Quarterly*, Fall 1988, 2.

3. Ibid.

4. Ibid.

5. See Lynn Buzzard and Laurence Ek, *Tell It to the Church* (Wheaton, Ill.: Tyndale House Publishers, 1985).

6. J. Laney, *A Guide to Church Discipline* (Minneapolis: Bethany House, 1985), 79.

7. John Vale and Robert Hughes, *Getting Even* (Grand Rapids, Zondervan, 1987), 46.

8. See Christopher Moore's *The Mediation Process* for an excellent description of the difficult work involved in entering a dispute (San Francisco: Jossey-Bass, 1987), 44–60.

9. William Barclay, *The Gospel of Matthew* (Philadelphia: Westminster Press, 1958), 140.

10. Leslie B. Flynn, *When the Saints Come Storming In* (Wheaton, Ill.: Victor Books, 1988), 90.

11. M. Augsburger, *Matthew,* in *The Communicator's Commentary* (Waco, Texas: Word, 1986).

12. Matthew 5:14 "You are the light of the world. A city on a hill cannot be hidden." See also Acts 13:47, "I have made you a light for the Gentiles, that you may bring salvation to the ends of the earth."

13. A. Lincoln, notes for law lecture (July 1, 1850), in J. Nicolay and J. Hays, eds., *Complete Works of Abraham Lincoln,* vol. 2 (New York: Frances D. Tandy, 1905), 140, 142.

14. Judge Learned Hand, quoted in J. Frank, *Courts on Trial: Myth and Reality in American Justice* (Princeton, N.J.: Princeton University Press, 1949), 40.

15. "Backyard Liabilities," *Business Week,* 10 July 1978, 102.

16. J. Kakalik and R. Ross, *Costs of the Civil Justice System: Court Expenditures for Various Types of Civil Cases* (Santa Monica: C.A. Rand, 1983).

17. Buzzard and Ek, *Tell It to the Church*, 25.

18. H. Fenton, *When Christians Clash*, 19.

## Chapter 5  Christians' Alternatives to Litigation

1. Goldberg, Green, and Sander, *Dispute Resolution*, 8–9.

2. Jethro Lieberman, *The Litigious Society* (New York: Basic Books, 1983), 18.

3. Warren Burger, "The State of Justice," *American Bar Association Journal* 70 (April 1984), 66.

4. See, for example, Mark 6:30–32.

5. "Put your sword back in its place," Jesus said to him, "for all who draw the sword will die by the sword," Matt. 26:52.

6. For example, see Mark 10:32.

7. "Then he entered the temple area and began driving out those who were selling. 'It is written,' he said to them, '"My house will be a house of prayer"; but you have made it "a den of robbers,"'" Luke 19:45.

8. See Acts 15:1–11.

9. See Acts 15:36–40.

10. "[Negotiation] is back-and-forth communication designed to reach an agreement when you and the other side have some interests that are shared and others that are opposed," according to R. Fisher and W. Ury in *Getting to Yes* (New York: Viking Penguin, 1981), xi.

11. See Goldberg, Green, and Sander, *Dispute Resolution*, 19. Even in disputes that are taken to the court system, 90–95 percent are resolved through some form of negotiation. See also B. Paulson, *Alternative Dispute Resolution* (Washington, D. C.: American Bar Association, undated), 1.

12. "Conflict in the Church: A Survey of Southern California Ministers," unpublished study by the Institute for Dispute Resolution, 5 December 1988.

13. Christopher Moore, *The Mediation Process*, 11.

14. J. Folberg and Alison Taylor, *Mediation: A Comprehensive Guide to Resolving Conflicts Without Litigation* (San Francisco: Jossey-Bass, 1986).

15. J. Auerbach, *Justice Without Law?* (New York: Oxford University Press, 1983), 20. "Expulsion and criminal prosecution aside, the

only alternative consistent with group harmony was mediation, which turns disputants toward each other in reconciliation, not away from each other in acrimonious pursuit of self-interest."

16. A. Blayre, *The Heart of the Dragon* (Boston: Houghton Mifflin, 1985), 104–108. Facilitated dispute resolution has also been found to be preferable to local courts by villagers in Turkey, Lebanon, Bavaria, Sardinia, and Scandinavia.

17. Bruce Monroe, "California's Institutionalization of Alternative Dispute Resolution," *Pepperdine Law Review* 14 (1987), 943, 951. In January 1981, California became the first state to legislatively mandate mediation for contested child custody and visitation rights. Under the Child Custody Mediation Statute each superior court must provide a qualified mediator for these cases. Mediation is also required when a stepparent or grandparent has applied for visitation rights. Mediators may make recommendations to the court regarding disputed custody or visitation. California's mediation requirement has achieved substantial success in these cases. Courts in San Francisco and Los Angeles Counties report dramatic reductions in court custody hearings. A survey conducted by the Los Angeles Superior Court indicated that results similar to those produced by traditional court hearings occurred when the parties reached agreement through mediation, but at a fraction of the cost, and with the benefit of a less hostile environment.

It appears additional benefits are to be gained by expanding the scope of mandatory mediation to include other divorce-related matters, such as child and/or spousal support, alimony, and property division. These matters could naturally and reasonably be mediated concurrently with child custody and visitation since they arise out of the same relationship.

Delaware has provided for pre-trial mediation of all such issues by court rule. The California Civil Code permits courts to submit the division of community property to arbitration "any time it believes the parties are unable to come to agreement. . . ."

18. J. Beer, *Peacemaking in Your Neighborhood* (Philadelphia: New Society Resources, 1988), iv.

19. E. Fine, ed., *Containing Legal Costs* (New York: Center for Public Resources, 1988), 1.

20. See, for example, *Report on Effectiveness of Judicial Arbitration,* Judicial Council of California, 1984, 11.

21. Le Sourd, "Striving to be Peacemakers," *Christian Legal Society Quarterly,* Summer 1990, 13.

22. Ibid.

23. Ibid.
24. Ibid.


## Chapter 6  Capturing the Value of Relationships

1. For a divorce lawyer's view of the importance of a relationship in reconciliation, see R. Supancic, *When All Else Fails* (Old Tappan, N.J.: Fleming H. Revell, 1986), 15–26.

2. Jimmy Carter, *The Blood of Abraham* (Boston: Houghton Mifflin, 1985), 196.

3. Luke 19:1–10.

4. John 4:7–26.

5. See K. Jaspers, *The Way to Wisdom* (New Haven: Yale University Press, 1951), 147, which says, "Man's supreme achievement in the world is communication from personality to personality."

6. See L. Singer, *Settling Disputes*, 118.

7. For a short discussion of who should be involved in a commercial mediation and the participants' relationship, see Randall W. Wulff, "A Mediation Primer," in Donovan, Leisure, Newton, and Irvine, *ADR Practice Book*, J. Wilkinson, ed. (New York: John Wiley and Sons, 1990), 122.

8. *Washington Post*, 3 August 1983, Maryland Weekly Section, 10.

9. Jennifer Beer describes this as "uninterrupted time," in *Peacemaking in Your Neighborhood*, 13–14.

10. Roger Fisher and Scott Brown, *Getting Together—Building a Relationship That Gets to Yes* (Boston: Houghton Mifflin, 1988), 11.

11. Ibid., 7–9, 14, 25–30.

12. "Two Air Disasters, Two Cultures, Two Remedies," *U.S. News and World Report*, 26 August 1985, 25.

13. Ibid.

14. Anthony Campolo, *We Have Met the Enemy, and They Are Partly Right* (Waco, Texas: Jarrell, a division of Word, 1985).


## Chapter 7  Negotiating Agreements

1. For a discussion of focusing on substance and stemming emotion, see Chester L. Karrass's chapter, "Emotions: The Penalty for Losing Your Cool," in *Give and Take: The Complete Guide to Negotiating*

*Strategy and Tactics* (New York: Thomas Y. Crowell, 1974), 56–7. See also Roger Fisher and Scott Brown's chapter, "Rationality: Balance Emotions With Reason," in *Getting Together.*

2. Bryan Johnston is professor of law and former director of the Center for Dispute Resolution, Willamette University College of Law in Salem, Oregon. Professor Johnston is a leader in the dispute-resolution field and co-author of *Ending It, Dispute Resolution in America* (Anderson, 1988).

3. See Luke 19:1–10.

4. For more information on the importance of relationships in negotiation, see Leonard Greenbalgh, "Relationships in Negotiation," *Negotiation Journal* 2 (1986), 235–43. See also Fisher and Brown, *Getting Together,* 16–23.

5. A scenario of a typical situation involving a personal attack and a brief analysis of the appropriate method for effectively dealing with it is outlined in Robert Bolton's chapter, "Handling Hostile Response," in *People Skills* (Englewood Cliffs, N.J.: Prentice-Hall, 1979), 169–71. See also Roger Fisher and Wayne H. Davis, "Remaining Rational in the Face of Strong Feelings, Six Basic Interpersonal Skills for a Negotiator's Repertoire," *Negotiation Journal* 3 (1987), 117–22.

6. See Xavier M. Frascogna, Jr., and H. Lee Hetherton, "Two Subtle Techniques to Help You Control Focus," in *Negotiation Strategy for Lawyers* (Englewood Cliffs, N. J.: Prentice-Hall, 1984), 98–100.

7. See Fisher and Ury, *Getting to Yes,* 17–40.

8. Fisher and Ury, *Getting to Yes,* 58–83.

9. William Lincoln, *Collaborative Negotiation,* a training book published by the Center for Dispute Resolution, Willamette University College of Law, 1986.

10. On the separation of interests, issues, and positions, see David A. Lax and James K. Sebenius, *The Manager as Negotiator* (New York: The Free Press, 1986), 63–87. Reported with variations in "Interests: The Measure of Negotiation," *Negotiation Journal* 2 (1986), 73–92.

11. The Institute for Dispute Resolution was established in 1986 at Pepperdine University School of Law. Under the auspices of its Continuing Education and Training Program, the institute offers specific training programs throughout the country emphasizing interest-based negotiation.

12. On the importance of understanding the situation before taking a stand, see Donald Strauss, "Collaborating to Understand Without Being a Wimp," *Negotiation Journal* 2 (1986), 155–65.

13. See Fisher and Brown, *Getting Together,* 70–73.

14. For an overview of the use of questions in negotiation, see the following: Jay Folberg and Alison Taylor, "Types of Questions," in *Mediation: A Comprehensive Guide to Resolving Conflicts without Litigation*, 109–13, and Christopher Moore, "Interviewing: Appropriate Questions and the Listening Process," *Mediation Process: Practical Strategies for Resolving Conflict* (San Francisco: Jossey-Bass, 1986), 90–95.

15. Fisher and Ury, *Getting to Yes,* 42–43.

16. For a firsthand account of the Sadat-Begin negotiations completed at Camp David, see Jimmy Carter, *The Blood of Abraham,* 43–50, 204.

17. See Exodus 2:1–10.

18.

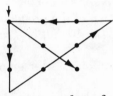

19. For an analysis of various modes of solutions, see Edward Levin, "How to Wrap Up a Deal and Bring Home the Bacon," in *Negotiation Tactics: Bargaining Your Way to Winning* (New York: Fawcett Columbine, 1980), 176–89.

20. See David A. Lax and James K. Sebenius, "Alternatives to Agreement: The Limits of Negotiation," *The Manager as Negotiator,* 46-62. Also reported with variations in "The Power of Alternatives or the Limits to Negotiation," *Negotiation Journal* 1 (1985), 163–79.

21. For a specific example of developing creative alternatives in order to reach a solution, see Gerard I. Nierenberg, "An Operational Example of Creative Alternatives and Strategies and Tactics," in *The Complete Negotiator* (New York: Nierenberg and Zeif, 1986), 184–86.

22. See "First Batch of Traveling Trash Goes into Brooklyn Incinerator," *Los Angeles Times,* 2 September 1987, A-17.

## Chapter 8  The Power of Alternatives

1. "Only Luke is with me. Take [John] Mark, and bring him with thee: for he is profitable to me for the ministry," 2 Tim. 4:11.

## Chapter 9 The Value of Mediation

1. A short description of the mediator's role may be found in C. Moore, *The Mediation Process*, 18.

2. "Making Peace; Children Learn to Mediate Arguments," *Newsday*, 10 March 1991, 1. See also "Reacting to Rising Violence, Schools Introduce 'Fourth R': Reconciliation," *New York Times*, 26 December 1990, B-15.

3. Jeanne B. Brett and Stephen B. Goldberg, "Grievance Mediation in the Coal Industry," *Industrial and Labor Relations Review* 37, no. 1 (1983), 49–69, cited in Roberts, et al., "Grievance Mediation: A Management Perspective," *Arbitration Journal* 25 (September 1990), 15–16.

4. Carter, *The Blood of Abraham*.

5. A good description of the process of beginning the mediation session is in C. Moore, *The Mediation Process* (San Francisco: Jossey-Bass, 1986), 153–71.

6. Sample mediation clauses for employment contracts are provided in Appendix C.

7. Jay Folberg and Alison Taylor, *Mediation*, 47, 49. In their book, Folberg and Taylor state, "The mediator must help the participants fully understand their areas of agreement and conflict. This stage comes to a close when the mediator knows where the disagreements and conflicts lie, what the underlying conflicts are, and what each participant wants and will not under any circumstances accept. . . . At this point the mediator, along with the participants, must determine a case-specific set of goals, objectives and strategies that incorporate the participants' values and intentions."

8. David Lax and James Sebenius make some useful distinctions between interests, issues, and positions in their article, "Interests: The Measure of Negotiation," *Negotiation Journal* 2 (January 1986), 73, 76–8.

9. Margaret Shaw and Patrick Phear, "New Perspectives on the Options Generation Process," *Mediation Quarterly*, Summer 1987, 65–73.

10. For a discussion of closure and settlement in the context of divorce mediation, see Alison Taylor, "A General Theory of Divorce Mediation," in J. Folberg and A. Milne, eds., *Divorce Mediation* (New York: Guilford Press, 1988), 75–6. For a lively illustration of this part of the mediation process, see also F. Knebel and G. Clay, *Before You Sue* (New York: William Morrow, 1987), 126–33.

11. Carlton J. Snow, professor of law and founder of the Center for Dispute Resolution, Willamette University College of Law, is a nationally recognized arbitrator and an early visionary in the dispute-resolution movement.

## Chapter 10 Skills of the Mediator

1. A detailed description of the mediator's role can be found in Joseph Stulberg, *Taking Charge, Managing Conflict* (Lexington, Mass.: D. C. Heath, 1987), 31–41.

2. Howard Raiffa, *The Art and Science of Negotiation* (Cambridge, Mass.: Belknap Press, 1982), 11–19.

3. See Folberg and Taylor, *Mediation,* 38–47.

4. L. Singer, *Settling Disputes* (Boulder, Colo.: Westview Press, 1990), 119.

5. For a short discussion of the role of mediator in settling corporate disputes, including the role of facilitating communication, see Joseph Stulberg, "Tactics of the Mediator," in Donovan, Leisure, Newton, and Irvine, *ADR Practice Book,* 138–39.

6. Joseph Stulberg, "The Theory and Practice of Mediation: A Replay to Professor Susskind," *Vermont Law Review* 6 (1981), 85, 97. In this article, Stulberg describes this reality testing by stating, "The mediator is an agent of reality. Persons frequently become committed to advocating one and only one solution to a problem. . . . The mediator is in the best position to inform a party, as directly and as candidly as possible, that its objective is simply not obtainable. . . ."

7. W. Brazil, *Effective Approaches to Settlement* (Clifton, N.J.: Prentice-Hall Law and Business, 1988), 18.

8. See Haynes, "Power Balancing in Divorce Mediation," in J. Folberg and A. Milne, eds, *Divorce Mediation* (New York: Guilford Press, 1988), 277–296.

9. Beer, *Peacemaking in Your Neighborhood,* 27.

## Chapter 11 Achieving Agreements that Last

1. William F. Lincoln, et al., *The Course in Collaborative Negotiation* (Tacoma, Wash.: National Center Associates, Inc., and Salem, Ore.: Willamette University College of Law, 1986).

2. For an outline of the state of California's approach to this difficult situation, see Michelle Desi, "California's Answer: Mandatory Mediation of Child Custody and Visitation Disputes," *Journal on Dispute Resolution* 1 (1985), 149–79.

3. For a discussion on the use of mediation in determining child custody and support and an example of a mediated custody and child support plan, see Jay Folberg and Alison Taylor, *Mediation: A Comprehensive Guide to Resolving Conflicts without Litigation* (San Francisco: Jossey-Bass, 1986), 169–84, 343–47.

4. See Robert R. Blake and Jane Srygley Mouton, *Solving Costly Organizational Conflicts: Achieving Intergroup Trust, Cooperation, and Teamwork* (San Francisco: Jossey-Bass, 1985). See also Samuel B. Bacharach and Edmund J. Lawler, *Power and Politics in Organizations: The Social Psychology of Conflict, Coalitions and Bargaining* (San Francisco: Jossey-Bass, 1982).

5. For an in-depth look at the art of dealing with people in conflict situations in order to achieve greater psychological satisfaction, see Robert Bolton, *People Skills: How to Assert Yourself, Listen to Others, and Resolve Conflicts* (Englewood Cliffs, N.J.: Prentice-Hall, 1979).

6. "From [verse] 24, [in the apostolic letter to Antioch at the conclusion of the Conference, the Jerusalem church states 'some went out without our authorization'] it appears that Judaea means Jerusalem and that the Judaisers claimed the authority of James and the elders. The dispute was sharp [and] the word rendered 'dissension' [in 15:2] suggests a state of strife and disunity," (G. W. H. Lampe, "Acts," in *Peake's Commentary on the Bible,* Matthew Black, ed. [Nairobi, Kenya: Thomas Nelson and Sons, 1962], 908).

7. The return to Antioch by Paul and Barnabas and preparation for the Council is reported in Acts 14:21–28 and 15:1–4.

8. "To the Jews the rite of circumcision is a sign of the covenant relationship which they have with God, so it is only natural that they should think the same act would be required of Gentile Christians. But the more serious misconception lies in their belief that circumcision is required as part of keeping the Law of Moses. They are not only urging Gentiles to be circumcised, but demanding that they keep the entire law, just as the Jewish Christians are continuing to do," (F. LaGard Smith, *The Narrated Bible* [Eugene, Ore.: Harvest House, 1984], 1510).

9. "You are to abstain from food sacrificed to idols, from blood, from meat of strangled animals and from sexual immorality," Acts 15:29.

10. "After reviewing the work of the Holy Spirit in leading the way to Gentile evangelism, and after consulting Scripture for prophesy concerning the Gentiles, they all agree that circumcision (and by implication the law itself) is not binding on the Gentiles. This message is sent to Gentile Christians, along with a warning that they avoid certain idolatrous practices common among pagan Gentiles. As a result of this agreement, unity will finally prevail, at least temporarily," (F. LaGard Smith, *The Narrated Bible*, 1511).

11. This was vital to the Jerusalem church because "the conversion of a large enough number of Pharisees to be influential in the Church represents a remarkable advance . . . and shows how promising the mission of the Jews must have seemed and correspondingly how much might be lost by supporting the Pauline mission," (G. W. H. Lampe, "Acts," in *Peake's Commentary on the Bible*, 908).

12. Paul's confrontation with Peter over the issue of circumcision is reported in Galatians 2:11–21. There is a lack of consensus regarding the dating of Paul's letter to the Galatians. Scholars disagree whether it was written just before leaving for the Jerusalem Conference, during his journey to Jerusalem, or shortly after the Conference while he was in Antioch or in Ephesus. All raise certain historical problems; however, the later dating seems to be most logical and supports the seeming tensions of the agreement even though there was great support at the Conference. However, whatever the case "the problem posed by these so-called 'Judaizing teachers' continue[d] to divide the church in the ensuing years, and . . . [was] a subject of discussion in several of Paul's letters," (F. LaGard Smith, *The Narrated Bible*, 1511).

## Chapter 12 Counselors and Mediators: Comparing Perspectives

1. Joan B. Kelly, "Mediation and Psychotherapy: Distinguishing the Differences," in Leonard L. Riskin, ed., *Divorce Mediation: Readings* (American Bar Association, 1985); also in J. A. Lemmon, ed., "Dimensions and Practice of Divorce Mediation," *Mediation Quarterly* 1 (September 1983), 33.

2. Lois Gold, "Reflections on the Transition from Therapist to Mediator," in J. A. Lemmon, ed., "Legal and Family Perspectives in Divorce Mediation," *Mediation Quarterly* 9 (September 1985), 15–26.

3. For a general overview of counseling processes, see R. George, *Counseling: Theory and Practice* (Englewood Cliffs, N.J.: Prentice-Hall, 1990).

4. Kelly, "Mediation and Psychotherapy."

5. For a different view of the role of therapy in mediation, see H. Irving and M. Benjamin, *Family Mediation* (Toronto: Carswell, 1987).

6. The mediator must control the level of tension through communication "competence," or "the knowledge of appropriate communication patterns in a given situation and the ability to use the knowledge." See R. E. Cooley and D. A. Roach, "A Conceptual Framework," in R. N. Bostrom, ed., *Competence in Communication: A Multidisciplinary Approach* (Beverly Hills: Sage, 1984), 25.

7. Most critical is keeping the conflict from growing to the point that the disputants harden their positions such that negotiation is not possible. See W. A. Donohue and D. Weider-Hatfield, "Communication Strategies," in Jay Folberg and Ann Milne, eds., *Divorce Mediation: Theory and Practice*, 297–318.

8. D. Saposnek, "Strategies in Child Custody Mediation: A Family Systems Approach," in J. A. Lemmon, ed., "Successful Techniques for Mediating Family Breakup," *Mediation Quarterly*, 1 (1983); and J. A. Wall, Jr., "Mediation: An Analysis, Review, and Proposed Research," *Journal of Conflict Resolution* 25, no. 1 (1981), 157–180.

9. A. Curle, *Making Peace* (London: Tavistock, 1971), 177.

10. Christopher W. Moore, *The Mediation Process*, 124.

11. William A. Donohue, "Communicative Competence in Mediators," in Kenneth Kressel, Dean G. Pruitt, and Associates, eds. *Mediation Research: The Process and Effectiveness of Third-Party Intervention* (San Francisco: Jossey-Bass, 1989), 322–43.

12. A. L. Milne, *Divorce Mediation: The State of the Art*, cited in J. A. Lemmon, ed., "Dimensions and Practice of Divorce Mediation," *Mediation Quarterly*, 1 (1983).

13. David J. Hellesgrave, "Beyond Pragmatism: Brief Therapy and Christian Counseling," *Journal of Psychology and Theology*, 16, no. 3 (1988), 246–253. See also Paul Watzlawick, John Weakland, and Richard Frisch, *Change: Principles of Problem Formation and Problem Resolution* (New York: Norton, 1974).

14. Other examples of Jesus' reframing issues are in Luke 12:24: "Consider the ravens: They do not sow or reap, they have no store-room or bar; yet God feeds them. And how much more you are than birds!" and in Matthew 10:39: "Whoever finds his life shall lose it, and whoever loses his life for my sake will find it."

## Chapter 13  Managing Conflict in Families

1. *The Family, Preserving America's Future: A Report to the President from the White House Working Group on the Family*, 2 December 1986, p. 2. Cited in Charles R. Swindoll, *Growing Wise in Family Life* (Portland, Ore.: Multnomah Press, 1988), 19–20.

2. Zig Ziglar, *Raising Positive Kids in a Negative World* (Nashville: Oliver-Nelson, 1985), 36–37.

3. Swindoll, *Growing Wise in Family Life* (Portland, Ore.: Multnomah, 1988), 21.

4. Karen Springer and Barbara Kantrowitz, "The Long Goodbye: When Parents Give a Disabled Child Up for Adoption, the Pain Often Lingers," *Newsweek*, 22 October 1990, 77.

5. Robert Coles, *Harvard Diary: Reflections on the Sacred and the Secular* (New York: Crossroads Publishing, 1990), 67.

6. Charles Swindoll, *Strengthening Your Grip* (Waco, Texas: Word, 1982), 265.

7. "Esau held a grudge against Jacob because of the blessing his father had given him. He said to himself, 'The days of mourning for my father are near; then I will kill my brother Jacob,'" Gen. 27:41. "His brothers were jealous of him, but his father kept the matter in mind," Gen. 37:11.

8. "A greedy man brings trouble to his family, but he who hates bribes will live," Prov. 15:27.

9. "If a man has a stubborn and rebellious son who does not obey his father and mother and will not listen to them when they discipline him, his father and mother shall take hold of him and bring him to the elders at the gate of his town. They shall say to the elders, 'This son of ours is stubborn and rebellious. He will not obey us. He is a profligate and a drunkard.' Then all the men of his town shall stone him to death. You must purge the evil from among you. All Israel will hear of it and be afraid," Deut. 21:18–21.

10. "With eyes full of adultery, they never stop sinning; they seduce the unstable; they are experts in greed—an accursed brood!" 2 Pet. 2:14.

11. James C. Dobson, *Parenting Isn't for Cowards* (Waco, Texas: Word, 1987), 51.

12. Will Cunningham, *How to Enjoy a Family Fight* (Phoenix: Questar Publishers, 1988), 9–10.

13. For example, see J. Meyrowitz, *No Sense of Place* (New York: Oxford University Press, 1985).

14. "New Minority Mom," *Los Angeles Times*, 3 December 1989, E-1.

15. Four basic patterns of behavior have been identified in dysfunctional families and couples: enmeshed, autistic, direct-conflict and disengaged-conflict. See Kressel, et al., "A Typology of Divorcing Couples: Implications for Mediation and the Divorce Process," *Family Process* 191 (1980), 101–116. These categories are based on the family's degree of ambivalence, communication style, and level of overt conflict. Enmeshed and autistic patterns are opposites as far as communication and overt conflict, enmeshed showing high levels of each while autistic is characterized by physical and emotional avoidance.

The counselor or mediator dealing with an enmeshed family or couple must control the communication and continually identify the destructive and conflicted interchanges. Enmeshed families may need family therapy as well as mediation. The mediator's role with an enmeshed family is very similar to a referee. He or she will seek to focus the attention on the process of the family's communication and away from the content. The family will need to learn more about the way it communicates than about the issues dividing them. Once a more constructive communication process is developed, family members may begin to address their more specific concerns.

Autistic families or couples, on the other hand, have likely sought to hide their conflicts behind noncommunication and conflict avoidance behaviors. There is little negotiation or problem-solving; family members who act out are given a wide berth so as to escape direct confrontations. Individual therapy may be necessary in severe cases. The mediator dealing with an autistic family must explain that there is little likelihood of any positive change when communication is so limited. It may be useful to ask family members to describe the kind of circumstances they would prefer in their family relationships. The purpose is to make real the dissatisfaction that exists with present patterns of communication. It is likely the depth of this dissatisfaction is unrealized out of a desire to avoid conflict.

Families and couples in a direct-conflict pattern also manifest their conflict but with less intensity than enmeshed families. Such families are more open to mediator intervention since they may be searching for their own solutions to the poor communication. The mediator's role will be to facilitate this process by objectively presenting options and encouraging the family to continue through the painful change process.

Disengaged-conflict families and couples, like autistic families, have little emotion, interest, or communication, but they are different from autistic families in that there is no underlying rage or pain that they are seeking to avoid. They are not suppressing their conflict; they are truly disinterested. Such a family may welcome mediation, not to bring them closer together, but rather to facilitate their completing the disengagment. They may already be fairly adept at negotiating problems; if so, the work of the mediator may be only to help move this process along.

16. See Folberg and Taylor, *Mediation: A Comprehensive Guide to Resolving Conflicts Without Litigation,* 147–89. Much of the remainder of this chapter is based on Folberg and Taylor's discussion of families in divorce.

17. See Salvador Minuchin, *Families and Family Therapy* (Cambridge, Mass.: Harvard University Press, 1974).

18. J. Haley, *Problem Solving Therapy* (San Francisco: Jossey-Bass, 1976).

19. Along with identifying codependent behavior, the mediator must acknowledge feelings. See W. Beavers, *Healthy, Midrange, and Severely Dysfunctional Families, in Normal Family Processes,* F. Walsh, ed. (New York: New Guilford Press, 1982). In any group conflict, causes and results can become interchangable. In a divorce, for example, a court ruling on custody often fails to settle issues between the parents. Such a ruling may actually *increase* the conflict rather than reduce it. One result simply becomes another cause in an ongoing battle. The mediator must acknowledge and process feelings in order to break the patterns which operate within the family and, hopefully, to allow some issues to be resolved.

20. It may be necessary to address serious individual problems in therapy concurrent with mediation rather than in the mediation process itself. Factors which may make mediation inappropriate include severe psychological problems or antisocial behavior, child abuse or neglect, erratic or violent behavior, substance abuse, longstanding or bitter conflicts, extreme inequality of bargaining power, a high level of mistrust, or an unwillingness to bargain in good faith.

Mediation focuses on resolving fairly immediate issues, not on providing psychotherapy for individual family members. The average healing time for a divorce, for example, is two years (or longer, if there is unresolved anger), well beyond the average time for a family/divorce mediation. Mediation may be able to shorten the time needed for healing, but it cannot substitute for the deeper emotional work which may be necessary to put a family back together.

21. H. Norman Wright, *Communication, the Key to Your Marriage* (Ventura, Calif.: Regal, 1979).

22. David Augsburger, *Caring Enough to Confront* (Ventura, Calif.: Regal, 1980).

23. Cunningham, *How to Enjoy a Family Fight*, 137–138.

24. Judith S. Wallerstein and Sandra Blakeslee, *Second Chances* (New York: Ticknor and Fields, 1990), 16.

25. Freya Ottem Hanson and Terje C. Hausken, *Mediation for Troubled Marriages* (Minneapolis: Augsburg, 1989), 34.

26. Ibid., 33.

27. Folberg, "Mediation of Child Custody Disputes," 413–449.

28. Lynn Simruss, "Consumers: Tempering Custody Trials, Tributions," *Los Angeles Times*, 18 April 1990.

29. Jessica Pearson, Ph.D., director of Denver's Divorce Mediation Research Project, quoted in "Divorce American Style," *Newsweek*, 10 January 1983, 42.

30. "Mediation to Replace Adversary Divorce," *P.R. Newswire*, 15 August 1983.

31. Hanson and Hausken, *Mediation for Troubled Marriages*, 34.

## Chapter 14: Managing Conflict in the Church

1. Horace Fenton, Jr., *When Christians Clash*, 19.

2. Speed Leas and Paul Kittlaus, *Church Fights*, 125–32.

3. Alan C. Filley, *Interpersonal Conflict Resolution* (Glenview, Ill.: Scott, Foresman and Company, 1974), 4–5.

4. Larry L. McSwain and William C. Treadwell, Jr., *Conflict Ministry in the Church* (Nashville: Broadman Press, 1981), 133.

5. Ronald Kraybill, *Leadership Journal*, Fall Quarter, 1986, 32.

6. McSwain and Treadwell, *Conflict Ministry in the Church*, 36.

7. Leas and Kittlaus, *Church Fights*, 158.

8. McSwain and Treadwell, *Conflict Ministry in the Church*, 134.

9. In a study of court-annexed arbitration—a process of informal adjudication—it was found that there was not a significant difference in satisfaction with the process between those who won and those who lost.

10. G. Douglass Lewis, *Resolving Church Conflicts* (San Francisco: Harper and Row, 1981), 68–73.

11. A. W. Tozer, *The Pursuit of God*, cited in Leslie B. Flynn, *When the Saints Come Storming In*, 147.

## Chapter 15 Managing Conflict in the Workplace

1. See R. Blake and J. Mouton, *Solving Costly Organizational Conflicts* (San Francisco: Jossey-Bass, 1985), 5.

2. K. Cloke, *Mediation of Workplace Disputes.*

3. See F. Jandt, *Win-Win Negotiating—Turning Conflict into Agreement* (New York: John Wiley & Sons, 1985), 29–61, which says, in part, "Subgroups within an organization tend to think of themselves as primary, and the members of each subgroup tend to apply their own standards to the other subgroups—with the result that conflict is inescapable."

4. D. Dana, *Managing Differences* (Wolcott, Conn.: MTI Publications, 1989), 4.

5. *Washington Post,* 10 May 1986, A-12.

6. D. Dana, *Managing Differences,* 15–16.

7. Kenneth Thomas and W. H. Schmidt, "A Survey of Managerial Interest with Respect to Conflict," *Academy of Management Journal,* June 1976.

8. Andrew Jaffe, "Firing: There's (Almost) Always a Better Way," *Psychology Today,* July-August 1989, 68–9.

9. J. Henry and J. Lieberman, *The Manager's Guide to Resolving Legal Disputes: Better Results Without Litigation* (New York: Harper & Row, 1985), 103–112. Henry and Lieberman assert, "Disputes that never arise need never be settled. In the long run, learning to head off disputes by avoiding the accidents, disruptions, and actions that cause them is the most effective form of dispute resolution."

10. See *Alternative Dispute Resolution Report,* Bureau of National Affairs, 19 January 1989, 30.

11. See T. Deal and A. Kennedy, *Corporate Cultures: The Rites and Rituals of Corporate Life* (Reading, Mass.: Addison-Wesley, 1982); and W. Ouchi, *Theory Z: How American Business Can Meet the Japanese Challenge* (Reading, Mass.: Addison-Wesley, 1981).

12. "The Union Moves In," *Business Week,* 12 November 1979, 148.

13. See D. Pritzker and D. Dalton, *Negotiating Rulemaking Sourcebook* (Washington, D.C.: Government Printing Office, 1990).

14. See Sylvia Skratek "Grievance Mediation: Does It Really Work?" *Negotiations Journal* 6 (1990), 269.

15. Letter to L. Randolph Lowry (name withheld at writer's request).

16. "Grievance Mediation Cheaper, Quicker than Arbitration, Seminar Speakers Agree," Bureau of National Affairs, *Daily Labor Report*, 5 June 1990, A-11.

17. Skratek, "Grievance Mediation," 276.

18. For example, see section 703(a) (1) Title VII, 42 United States Code section 1000e-2(a): "It shall be an unlawful employment practice for an employer . . . to fail to refuse to hire or discharge any individual with respect to his compensation, terms, conditions, or privileges of employment, because of such individual's race, color, religion, sex, or national origin."

### Chapter 16: Managing Conflict in the Community

1. Quoted in D. McGillis, *Community Dispute Resolution — Programs and Public Policy* (U.S. Department of Justice, 1986).

2. *American Bar Association Report* 29 (1906), 395; see also *Federal Rules Decision* 35 (1964), 273 (full text), and *American Bar Association Journal* 57 (1971, abridged version).

3. *Federal Rules Decisions* 35 (1964), 290.

4. "Towards the Creation of a Complementary, Decentralized System of Criminal Justice," *Stanford Law Review* 26 (1974), 1.

5. Griffin Bell, "The Pound Conference Follow-Up: A Response from the United States Department of Justice," *Federal Rules Decisions* 76 (1977), 320. Former Attorney General Bell served as chair of the Pound Conference Follow-Up Task Force.

6. See M. Coleman, "Implementation of California's Dispute Resolution Programs Act: A State-Local Government Partnership," *Pepperdine Law Review* 16 (1989), 75.

7. L. Kanowitz, *Alternative Dispute Resolution Cases and Materials* (St. Paul, Minn.: West Publishing, 1985), 29.

8. American Bar Association Standing Committee on Dispute Resolution.

9. L. Singer, *Settling Disputes: Conflict Resolution in Business, Families, and the Legal System* (Boulder, Colo.: Westview Press, 1990), 111.

10. See "The Multi-door Courthouse," *National Institute of Justice Reports*, U.S. Department of Justice, July 1986. The five stages of the intake interview are: (1) Introduction: the intake specialist makes the client comfortable and establishes rapport; (2) Narration by the client: the intake specialist maintains an open, sensitive attitude while gathering information; (3) Identification of the problem:

the intake specialist frames the complaint in the form of a concrete, addressable problem; (4) Review of the options and consequences: the intake specialist considers the client's resources and possible outcomes; (5) Selection of options: the intake specialist constructs a plan and encourages the client to implement the plan.

11. Singer, *Settling Disputes*, 118–119.

12. Beer, *Peacemaking in Your Neighborhood*, 26.

13. As noted by the U.S. Department of Justice's Daniel McGillis, "Complainants very often withdrew their complaints as trial neared because their opponent was a neighbor, relative, or acquaintance. The complainants were not seeking incarceration for the adversary or a fine (to be paid to the state); they wanted changed behavior, an apology, or money paid to them for restitution for the harm done," *Community Dispute Resolution—Programs and Public Policy* (U.S. Department of Justice, 1986), quoted in Singer, *Settling Disputes*.

14. In "Ethnic Neighborhoods," *Christian Legal Society Quarterly* 9 (Summer 1990), 11.

15. Beer, *Peacemaking in Your Neighborhood*.

16. G. Nicolau, *Community Mediation: Progress and Problems* (1986), quoted in Singer, *Settling Disputes*.

17. J. Pearson, N. Thoennes, and L. Vander Kooi, "Mediation of Contested Custody Disputes," *Colorado Lawyer* 11 (1982), 336.

18. New York requires twenty-five hours while Massachusetts requires thirty. This should probably not, however, be taken as an endorsement that such levels of training are sufficient.

19. McGillis, *Community Dispute Resolution—Programs and Public Policy*.

20. R. Davis, "Mediation: The Brooklyn Experiment," in R. Tomasic and M. Feeley, eds., *Neighborhood Justice: Assessment of an Emerging Idea* ( New York: Longman, 1982), 154.

21. Daniel McGillis, "Minor Dispute Processing: A Review of Recent Developments," in Tomasic and Feeley, eds., *Neighborhood Justice: Assessment of an Emerging Idea*.

22. Beer, *Peacemaking in Your Neighborhood*, 233.

23. Derek Bok, "A Flawed System," *Harvard Magazine*, May-June 1985, 45.

# INDEX

## L. Randolph Lowry

## Richard W. Meyers

L. Randolph (Randy) Lowry is director of the Institute for Dispute Resolution at Pepperdine University School of Law in Malibu, California, where he also serves on the full-time law faculty. His leadership in the field of conflict management began in 1984 when he assisted in establishing one of the first dispute resolution programs in the nation at Willamette University School of Law in Salem, Oregon.

Professor Lowry holds a bachelor's degree in political science and a master's degree in public administration from Pepperdine, and a juris doctor degree from Hamline University in Minnesota. He lives with his wife, Rhonda, and their three children, John, Janet, and Melinda, in Westlake Village, California.

Richard W. Meyers is chairman of the department of psychology at Western Baptist College in Salem, Oregon. He also serves as a consultant and counselor in private practice with the Mid-Valley Center for Clinical and Consulting Services in Salem. His involvement in conflict management includes extensive experience in the pastoral, military, and public service fields.

Mr. Meyers holds a B.S. degree in social science from Western Baptist College, and a B.A. degree in psychology from California State University in Hayward. He also has M.A. degrees from Trinity Evangelical Divinity School and from Western Conservative Baptist Seminary. He is a Psy.D. candidate in the George Fox Graduate School of Psychology, and serves as a chaplain in the Oregon Army National Guard, holding the rank of major.

He and his wife, Dianne, live in Salem with their sons Jonathan and Daniel.